BUILDERS OF
BRITISH COLUMBIA
An Industrial History

BUILDERS OF
BRITISH COLUMBIA

An Industrial History

G. W. TAYLOR

1982

MORRISS PUBLISHING

VICTORIA, BRITISH COLUMBIA

Canadian Cataloguing in Publication Data

Taylor, G. W. (Geoffrey Wilson), 1905-
    Builders of British Columbia

    Includes index.
    ISBN 0-919203-22-1

    1. British Columbia — Industries — History.
2. British Columbia — Economic conditions.
I. Title.
HC117.B8T39   338.09711   C82-091179-8

First Printing July 1982
Second Printing February 1983

This book has been published with the assistance of the Canada Council Block
Grant Program and with the help of a grant from the British Columbia Heritage
Trust.

Published by
MORRISS PUBLISHING LTD.
1745 Blanshard Street
Victoria, British Columbia v8w 2J8

Designed and printed in Canada by
MORRISS PRINTING COMPANY LTD.
Victoria, British Columbia

*to the men of vision
through whose investment
this province grew*

CONTENTS

Photographs following pages 68 and 152

INTRODUCTION

Every public figure in British Columbia since the Union has emphasized the special character of the province. The geography, climate, and resources are directly responsible for a most unusual economic and social profile.

B.C. is bordered by Alaska and the Yukon to the north, Washington State to the south, and Alberta to the east. Four hundred miles wide, eight hundred miles long, it is the third largest Canadian province, and could easily accommodate California, Oregon, and Washington within its borders.

Beyond its inlet-carved coastline on the Pacific Ocean lie many islands, principally Vancouver Island to the south, and the Queen Charlotte Islands to the north.

The Rockies, which straddle the Alberta border, once rendered B.C. almost inaccessible from the east. Twelve major passes were discovered through this range—from 2,000 feet in altitude in the Peace River Valley, to over 7,000 in the Kootenays.

Progressively west from the Rockies are the Rocky Mountain Trench, a valley which stretches 700 miles to the north; the interior mountain ranges collectively known as the Selkirks; the great upland plateau which supported the large cattle ranches in pioneer days; and finally the Coast Range which descends to the sea.

Ninety-seven percent of B.C.'s surface area is mountainous. Out of approximately 234 million acres of land, 133 million are productive — the rest is water, swamp, and barren rock. Of this productive land, only 2-3 percent, or 1/40 of the land surface is suitable for agriculture or human habitation. The rest is forested and supports B.C.'s primary industry — lumbering, pulp, and paper.

Mineral deposits are found throughout the province from the American boundary to the B.C.-Yukon border. Mines and mining settlements have been established everywhere from the coal-mining towns on Vancouver Island to the lead-zinc mine at Kimberley; from the copper mine at Britannia Beach on Howe Sound to stripping a mountain top for asbestos at Cassiar.

B.C. also possesses immense resources and ideal conditions for hydroelectric power — large volume, swift flowing rivers, and an extensive system of lakes with steep drops in altitude.

The climate of the province is unique in the sense that nowhere else in the world can there be found so many variations in such a short distance.

Mild temperatures and heavy rainfall create ideal conditions for lush forest growth on Vancouver Island and along the Pacific coast. Here, the magnificent stands of timber such as fir, spruce, and hemlock support the coast's large sawmilling, newsprint, and pulp industries. Mild winters and cool summers provide fair year-round conditions for construction and other outdoor activities, and keep ports for shipping and fishing ice-free.

In central and southeastern B.C., the winters are more severe and the summers drier. Thirty percent of this precipitation is snow, which melts in the late spring, providing water which turns the turbines and large electric generators.

Long, cold winters, and short, hot summers in the northern interior create conditions which demand different building techniques, and a shorter building season.

The Peace region east of the Rocky Mountains enjoys the same type of continental weather as northern Alberta — lengthy, severe winters, and short, warm summers which are well adapted for such types of agriculture as wheat-growing.

The habits and life cycles of fish in lake, river, and ocean are also greatly affected by climatic variations.

The methods of utilization and perpetuation of the provincial forest resources are influenced by climatic conditions; reforestation can be carried out year round in coastal regions; but in the interior it cannot because the ground is frozen. The industry also suffers when hot, dry spells create hazardous conditions conducive to fire.

Transportation networks are always affected by climatic conditions — snow, mudslides, and washed-out bridges plague railways and roads.

It is this great diversity of climate and terrain which forms the basis for another one of B.C.'s most important industries — tourism. The forest and mountains provide spectacular scenery. While the mild year-round conditions of southwestern B.C. attract those who don't like harsh winters, the snow conditions in the mountains and other parts of the province are perfect for skiing and draw visitors from around the world.

New Caledonia, as it was known 125 years ago, was a wilderness; a vast game preserve administered for the profit and by the pleasure of the Hudson's Bay Company.

"The largest portion of the entire territory is an inhospitable wilderness . . . it wants fine land, it wants climate, it wants prairies, it wants everything except snow, sleet, and rain," wrote D. G. F. McDonald in *British Columbia and Vancouver Island* (1862).

Mining, more than any other industry, has contributed to the building of the towns and cities, the communications networks, the school systems, and the laying of the foundation of a modern society. It has built more communities, encouraged the opening of more local businesses, and contributed more to the knowledge of geography and natural resources of B.C. than any community group, or business and professional organization.

The discovery of gold made the founding of the Colony of B.C. possible. The attention of London merchants and financiers was drawn to the economic potential in this part of the world; and they were the first to aid the Colonial government and new enterprising businessmen.

The precious metal was discovered along the Fraser and up into the Cariboo, creating a need for trails, wagon roads, and service industries like packers, express companies, horse dealers, restaurants, and retail merchants such as butchers and bakers. If it hadn't been for the establishment of the London-financed Bank of British Columbia which provided aid, much of this early expansion would have never been possible.

As the gold fever subsided, many a goldseeker stayed behind to start businesses of a more stable nature, but thousands of those who had poured into the colony during the gold rush left again. There were only 9,000 whites in B.C. at the time of Confederation in 1871, 1,000 of whom lived in the Cariboo.

A few hundred dedicated prospectors still roamed the province in search of more gold. There were a series of minor rushes that followed — Wild Horse Creek (1863-64); the Big Bend (1865-66); the Omineca (1869-70); and the Cassiar (1873-74). There was little actual growth in B.C. over the next 25 years, but mines still operated, machinery was bought, supplies purchased, and prospectors outfitted.

The second big mining boom came when silver-lead ore was discovered in the Kootenays. Investment money was plentiful, coming from Spokane, which financed most of the early Kootenay mines, and soon, from Toronto, London, and New York. The new towns of Kaslo, Sandon, New Denver, and Nelson grew up almost overnight, bringing an immense surge of building activity to the region.

Further south, back of Rossland, the famous Red Mountain became dotted with mine shafts. With the consequent building of Trail and Rossland, the West Kootenay Light and Power project was developed at Bonnington Falls, financed by English capital.

Soon, new mines in nearby Boundary country opened, producing high-volume, low-grade copper; smelters were built and fired by coal from the Crow's Nest Pass. Thousands of new workers streamed into the area, doubling its population within a decade. Along with the new arrivals came the retail merchants, the banks, the lawyers, the doctors, and the civil service.

Within a space of 20 years (1892-1912) the silver, lead, and coal mines of the Kootenays had peopled southeastern B.C. with a group of small mining and smelter towns tied together by a communication network of steamers, wagon roads, railways, and telegraph lines. Brick business blocks, post offices, courthouses, hotels, stores, schools, churches, and many finely built residential homes sprang up in a dozen new communities almost overnight.

New technology in the smelters of Grand Forks, Greenwood, and Boundary Falls made it possible to produce copper at the lowest price in the world.

Coal mining on Vancouver Island showed a slow but unspectacular growth up to 1912. Nanaimo grew, and new coal towns such as Ladysmith and Union Bay were built. A network of colliery railways gradually grew around Nanaimo; new technology brought electric traction and electric light to the New Vancouver Coal Company's mine in the heart of that city. But the growth of the Vancouver Island communities in this period was never as rapid as it was in the Kootenays and on the lower mainland.

The inter-war years (1919-1939) were times of consolidation, not expansion. Some new mines opened, such as Copper Mountain in Princeton, but many closed, especially in Boundary country. The spectacular growth at Grand Forks, Phoenix, and other smelter towns came to an abrupt halt when the price of copper collapsed in 1919. The Boundary mines and smelters closed down; stores, hotels, restaurants, and homes were abandoned. The low prices of other metals offered no encouragement for further development. With two years' supply of unsaleable copper on hand, Granby Consolidated closed Anyox — once the hallmark of what an industrial town should be.

The only mineral with any future seemed to be gold, so practically all mining activities in the Depression were in search of it or in the development of gold mines.

After the end of World War II, the mining industry of B.C. had a third resurgence in response to foreign demand. The booming Japanese post-war economy required enormous amounts of the base metals — iron ore, copper, and coal. Coastal iron ore mines opened up for this Japanese market; copper mines were developed in the Highland Valley and the northern interior (Granisle). Vast new developments took place in the Kootenay coal fields and necessitated the building of a new port on the lower mainland. Once again, "instant towns" sprang up in isolated areas.

Three periods of startling expansion and growth in B.C.'s history were directly sparked by these mining booms. The decade following 1858 brought the infrastructure to build a mid-Victorian British capitalistic society in an unknown wilderness. These structures continued to function until the 1890-1912 mining boom when even further growth was stimulated, which brought thousands of new arrivals to find homes, jobs, and schooling.

The post-war expansion after 1945 provided additional jobs and the means by which all British Columbians could upgrade their standard of living. During this period, more and better hospitals, educational institutions, new libraries, community centres, and other buildings were constructed.

Forestry also contributed vastly to the growth of the province. Lumbering was practiced in B.C. long before the days of the first gold rush; it started when the Spaniards built a fort in 1789 at Friendly Cove, Nootka Sound, and constructed it from logs cut in the surrounding forest. In the next seventy years, every fort built by fur traders used locally sawn lumber.

The pioneer mining settlements were all constructed of wood; the erection of a sawmill came almost simultaneously with the creation of any settlement or village. Lumber was essential in the erection of houses, town buildings, and in the making of roads and bridges.

It was not long before entrepreneurs both in B.C. and London saw the value of lumber as an export commodity; thus came into being the great pioneer export mills — Anderson's of Alberni, Moodyville, and Hastings Mill. Around these mills grew communities which needed roads and service industries, banks, and schools. In the ten lean years after Confederation, lumbering on Burrard Inlet and coal at Nanaimo provided jobs and the money to keep the economy going. When Onderdonk finished his railway building in 1886, his workmen tried to find jobs in the Burrard Inlet sawmills.

The growth of international trade after 1890, the availability of investment capital, and the mining boom, stirred the sawmilling industry out of its rut. New sawmills were built (Chemainus, Fraser Mills), and new communities were founded. Changes in logging techniques, which included a new reliance on the railroad, brought in men with capital who set up railway logging operations like Bloedel, Stewart & Welch's outfit at Myrtle Point.

Up the coast and in the interior, more railways and logging communities were being built in isolated spots. The expanding prairie market prompted the building of sawmills and communities in the East Kootenays, creating a demand for housing, service industries, and roads.

The forest industry has always created new products and industries which have done much to broaden the base of economy. Newsprint is a case in point — it was not a Canadian manufactured commodity in the nineteenth century. It. was only after 1911 when it acquired free entry into the United States that it was possible for it to be manufactured in B.C. Two newsprint mills and several pulp mills were built around this time; they entailed not only large amounts of capital, but much complicated machinery, and the building of large machine rooms, warehouses, and towns to house the workers.

They were built in the forested wilderness many miles from any settled area. At Powell River, an electric generating plant, the mill, and a town housing over a thousand workers with all modern urban services was built within a period of three years in an area which had only known the Indian and the logger. It was the same at Swanson Bay, Ocean Falls, and Port Alice.

Sawmilling, pulp, and paper became big business and spawned many secondary industries. Machine shops, sash and door factories, paper conversion plants, manufacturers' agents for sawmilling and logging equipment were set up mostly concentrated in the cities. These industries attracted workers who had to be housed, fed, and their children provided with schools, so there was a continual need for building.

Pulp and paper are international commodities, and with the expansion of world trade after World War II, more mills were required. New newsprint mills were built at Crofton and Campbell River; pulp mills at Port Alberni and at Harmac near Nanaimo. In the sixties, the north became important as pulp mills were built at Quesnel, Prince George, Mackenzie, Prince Rupert, and Kitimat. This not only involved the construction of the mill buildings and equipping them with the necessary machinery, but the housing of the work people. This meant expansion of the towns, the building of new municipal services such as water and sewerage, and in cases such as Mackenzie and Kitimat, the creation of a new town from scratch.

The third great natural resource industry that has contributed greatly to the growth of B.C. is hydroelectric power. In this province, it is purely a twentieth-century phenomenon, and like other resource industries had to wait until there was a demand. It was not practical in the early days to build large hydroelectric plants if there was no large industrial user to buy the power; and so expansion of the industry in the first 50 years was determined by the demand.

When the provincial government took over in the sixties the situation changed. Because it had large resources not available to private industry, it was able to plan ahead of demand and build generating plants.

The big users of electrical power are mining corporations for their smelters and concentrators, newsprint manufacturers, pulp mills, and cement works. Many of these operations have been established in remote areas to be near inexpensive power, like Powell River and Kitimat.

The availability of cheap hydroelectric power is an important determinant in the location of industry and the establishment of new communities. The pulp mill explosion of the sixties owes its origins to the building of the dams on the Peace and the Columbia.

In 1900, the electric energy industry began humbly in the West Kootenays to serve the smelter at Trail and the mines around Rossland. In its early stage, it only developed about 9,500 horsepower.

The early newsprint mills (Powell River, Ocean Falls), and pulp mills (Swanson Bay, Port Alice) all installed at their own expense their electrical plants. The Consolidated Mining and Smelting Company took over West Kootenay Power, which now not only supplies the industrial requirements of Cominco but also serves the towns and villages as far west as the Okanagan Valley.

British Columbia is rich in water resources. In the natural state the water flow of the rivers varies considerably. In the spring, there is too much; in the winter there is too little. In order to generate firm power (a constant supply of electricity at uniform levels), expensive dams must be built for the storage of water. This makes the capital cost of installing a system more expensive and almost compels the builder to have a buyer for his energy before construction starts. But once the project is underway, millions of dollars flow into the economy, a boom is experienced in the towns in the vicinity, and thousands of jobs are created for a period of several years.

The series of dams built by the provincial government on the Peace and Columbia Rivers have had a tremendous impact on the economy of B.C. The contracts were worth millions; jobs soared into the thousands; big international construction companies came in to do the job. For the first time since the building of the railways, B.C. entered the big-time construction field. The third mining boom, and the pulp mill explosion were happening at the same time; the spin-off effect was felt in every home and community in the province.

The seasonal fishing industry takes place mostly on the coast and in coastal waters. The work period of salmon canning, which makes up the greatest segment of the industry, lasts only three to four months and hires large numbers of people.

In the past, canning took place in remote spots up the coast. Anyone with capital could build a cannery — all that was required was a wharf, and a frame building capable of housing the canning machinery. Much of the help were Chinese or native Indians.

No permanent towns like Powell River or Anyox were ever established around a cannery. From six to eight months of the year, these sites were uninhabited except for a watchman. As the industry became more centralized, packing in these canneries was abandoned and the buildings were allowed to fall into decay.

From the peak of 94 canneries in 1917, it has dropped to less than a dozen in 1980, situated in urban areas such as Vancouver, Victoria, and Prince Rupert. There were a few that became more permanent and supported small communities, like those in Namu and Butedale along the steamer route to Prince Rupert.

The fishing industry has built no roads, attracted no railways, established no major towns (with the possible exception of Steveston), and has not opened any new districts for exploration or settlement. It isn't a large user of industrial power, and played no part like the pulp and paper industry did in the great hydroelectrical generating programs.

Tourism, however, is now B.C.'s third largest industry. Not only has it pumped billions of dollars into the province's economy, but has been responsible for the continuing construction of roads, hotels, and motels, and the development of parks, ski, and vacation resorts.

From colonial days, the province always attracted visitors who came not just for work but pleasure. In the 1860's, Captain C. E. Barrett-Lennard, a yachtsman, ventured out west to become the first man to circumnavigate Vancouver Island.

Artist, writer, and mountaineer Frederick Whymper came out seeking adventure. He travelled to the Cariboo while sketching for the *Illustrated London News*; then accompanied Waddington's party who were trying to build a wagon road from the head of Bute Inlet to Quesnel.

In 1865, two partners, Oliver Hocking and Fred Houston, built a hotel on Burrard Inlet just west of the Second Narrows Bridge and called it "Brighton," "soon to be a favourite resort for pleasure seekers," according to the *British Columbian* in that year. George Black erected a second hotel in 1880 called "New Brighton House." Brighton, the location of these two fine hotels, became known as the most fashionable watering place in B.C.

The real start of the tourist trade was in the last quarter of the nineteenth century, when rising living standards enabled people of the middle classes both in Europe and America to travel for pleasure for the first time. Sir William Van Horne, fully aware of this trend, made enormous efforts to attract visitors to Western Canada and build up traffic on his railway.

"Artists, editors, men of science, churchmen, politicians, and manufacturers were sent through to the Pacific," wrote Walter Vaughan in his biography of Horne. "They were treated royally and returned to their homes to talk, or write, or lecture on the opportunities offered by the newly opened lands."

He provided private cars and free transportation to prominent public figures like Winston Churchill's father, Sir Randolph, so

17

they could visit the West Coast and intervening points. He made arrangements for wealthy Americans like Dr. William Seward Webb to charter special trains to run independent of any timetable. It was company policy to provide free passes to journalists and writers so they would write books and articles about B.C. and Western Canada. Van Horne personally commissioned author Douglas Sladen to write a book on his experience travelling on the C.P.R.

Van Horne was not only a great salesman but also a great builder. To provide tourists with suitable accommodation, he built a series of picturesque and famous hotels in the mountains and on the West Coast — Banff, Lake Louise, Glacier House, the Hotel Vancouver, and Victoria's Empress.

Private entrepreneurs were not far behind. The first hotel at Harrison Hot Springs was built for J. P. Brown in 1885-86. Named the St. Alice, it was a three-storey wooden structure with 40 rooms accommodating 160 guests. It served the tourist trade well until 1920 when it was destroyed by fire.

The present hotel and convention centre, the Harrison Hot Springs Hotel, opened May 24, 1926. It is a substantial structure accommodating up to 600 guests.

Vancouver, as the terminus of the "Empresses to the Orient" and the royal mail steamers to Australia and New Zealand, was the stopping-off place for many visitors. Leaders of Asiatic countries, diplomatic personnel coming from or going to their posts, politicians, lecturers, or writers going to the Orient or Australia, would check into the Hotel Vancouver for a week or so to wait for their ships. These ocean liners brought a steady flow of visitors who helped to spread the word about B.C.

The coming of the car and improved roads provided Americans with the opportunity to visit B.C. At first, accommodation was in camping grounds in the public parks; one of the most popular was in Central Park on Kingsway. Gradually, motels were built to cater to the automobile trade. Now there is not a town or village in the province without one. Prior to 1919, there were only 13 hotels on Vancouver Island. In 1979, hotels and motor hotels numbered 76; and countless motels have sprung up.

The full impact of tourism was not felt in B.C. until after World War II. The growing prosperity of both Canada and the U.S. brought more and more visitors to the province; it witnessed a spectacular increase in the number of hotels and motels. The provincial park system, which was originally developed for residents of B.C., was stimulated and expanded by the demands of the tourist trade. From one park in 1911, it has grown to a total of 342 in 1977. Over the years, this has meant a considerable building program of park lodges, roads, and trails.

Skiing has attracted hundreds of thousands to the province over the last 30 years. Twelve major resorts have been developed, including Whistler, which is a self-contained skiing village. The convention business resulted in the building of the first convention centre in B.C. — the Peach Bowl in Penticton. Museums have been built, historical sites restored, and cultural centres created.

Worthy of its own ministry, the industry now brings in over one and one-half billion dollars a year.

The building of B.C. was never easy. The areas suitable for settlement are often small in size, isolated, and difficult to reach; hence, the cost of roads, railways, and other means of communication were excessively high. The cost of bringing supplies for the settlements and towns, machinery for the mines, building materials for the pulp and paper mills and even supplying the population with food, was greater than in other parts of Canada. For the five years 1899-1904, the province and municipalities of B.C. spent $4.49 per person per year on the making and upkeep of their roads. Between the years 1867 and 1888 2,333 miles of roads were built in northern Ontario at a cost of $294 per mile. In 1904, the average cost per mile to build a road in B.C. was $2,000; they were always inadequate even for the needs of the settled districts up until recent times.

The province's development has always been hindered by the high cost of living. This is reflected in the high cost of labour, transportation, and materials necessary for its growth, including machinery for mine and mill. This has also been reflected in the high rate of provincial taxation. For thirty-two years (1871-1903) the provincial government spent more annually than it took in. With the exception of one or two years in this period, there was always a provincial deficit. At times, government credit became exhausted and the bank would refuse to advance any more money.

Up to 1914, B.C. had only three things to sell, either to other provinces or the outside world — minerals, lumber, and fish. When there was no demand, as shown in the 1860's, for silver or lead, there was no development. When the gold mines in the Cariboo became unworkable, and all the gold was washed from the creeks, the economy faltered. The building of B.C. came to a halt. When the prices slumped as had happened many times in the lumber and salmon canning markets, the mills and canneries closed down, or the proprietors cut wages below subsistence levels, as did Dunsmuir in his coal mines in the 1870's. Workers either left the province or lived in poverty.

Growth depended mainly on outside influences, such as foreign demand, and the availability of foreign capital. During the Cariboo gold boom, money was plentiful in the city of London, and looking for investment. The Colonial government, with the help of the Bank of British Columbia, was able to dispose of its debentures without undue trouble. They were able to pay for their ambitious road-building schemes.

On the other hand, the commoner metals more extensively distributed through the province like lead, silver, and copper could find no buyers. George Hearst, the great American mining engineer and father of Randolph Hearst, the newspaper publisher, made a special trip to the Bluebell Mine in the Kootenays in the 1860's, but was unable to interest any of the great capitalists of that day in investing.

It was only in the 1890's when new technologies based on electricity and oil required huge amounts of iron, lead, and copper that the base metal mines of B.C. started to be developed.

The telegraph was the major means of communication throughout the world at that time. In the thousands of miles of telegraph wires and submarine cables, great amounts of copper were required and created a demand which far exceeded the supply. In the field of electrical energy, the 1890's saw the start of electric traction (tramways and railways) and its use in the industrial workshops of America and Europe. All these created huge demands for the industrial metals — copper, lead, and zinc.

This surge in international demand coincided with a market expansion in trade both in Europe and America, as well as the building up of capital surpluses in London and New York. Between 1890 and 1912, vast amounts of foreign money poured into B.C.; not only to develop the mines, the forests, and transportation, but into community projects such as streetcar lines, waterworks, electric light systems, and sewerage. During this period, Vancouver attained metropolitan status; Victoria became known as the "City of Beautiful Homes"; Nelson acquired its street railway. This was one of the greatest growth periods in B.C. history.

World War I showed no slackening of demand. Metals were in short supply; lumber was needed for housing, boatbuilding, ties for

Canadian and U.K. railways; engineering trades were extended to the limit. War orders came not only to supply the Canadian war effort, but also from Great Britain, France, and Russia.

When the slump came after the war's end, the great resource industries languished. As copper prices collapsed, the Boundary country smelters closed, never to reopen. The copper mines shut down — some permanently; others like Granby's Phoenix mine to reopen years later on the surge of the next great world copper boom. The shipyards on Burrard Inlet and in Victoria were reduced to skeletons; the machine shops vanished. The repair shops in the pulp and newsprint plants returned to the routine of maintaining the plant machinery. In the twenty inter-war years of 1919-39, there was little progress or growth in B.C.

The next period of spectacular growth after World War II came once more in response to a foreign demand. Revitalized by the Americans, the Japanese economy demanded B.C.'s industrial metals, and caused the third great mining boom. Simultaneously, twelve new major pulp mills were built, and the provincial government decided to harness the Peace and Columbia Rivers for hydro-electrical generation.

For the first time, central B.C., which for a century had been starved for power, was able to attract large-scale industry; nine of the twelve new pulp mills were built there.

This new growth (which compares favourably to the period 1890-1912) sparked innumerable new construction projects. For the first time, the province acquired a network of first-class highways connecting the chief centres. Small towns like Prince George or Kamloops — railway towns of the older period — now blossomed into manufacturing centres. The airplane became prominent in the transportation picture. Kelowna, which in the 30's could only be reached from Vancouver by an overnight train trip, could now be reached in 45 minutes by air. Quesnel, which in 1864 took four days of hard coaching from the coast on the Cariboo Road, can now be reached via air by regular passenger service in four hours.

In the past, the province was isolated from all main commercial centres and trade routes, and could only be reached by sea. The mountain ranges made access from the eastern U.S. and Canada almost impossible. But the people of the world wanted gold so they carved their way in.

This period of isolation persisted up to the coming of the railways in 1886. From 1871 to 1890, few people were interested in this out-of-the-way, isolated part of Canada. There was a small foreign demand for lumber, especially ship's spars cut on the coast; and for coal for the San Francisco market; but in terms of trade, it did not amount to much.

It was the great trade expansion in the nineties, sparked to some extent by the new discoveries in electricity and metallurgy, that drew the attention of the outside world to the mineral riches of southeastern B.C. This ushered in the greatest period of growth and expansion in the province's history. The population in a period of 25 years increased fivefold. Cities and towns were built in the southern interior. The majority of these changes came about because of outside or foreign demands for our natural resources. If the demands had been lacking, it is highly probable that the growth would not have taken place as rapidly as it did.

Over the years between 1912 and 1946, there have been minor demands from outside the country. The Americans wanted newsprint, and the British in the 30's wanted lumber, plywood, and doors. But these were not powerful enough to spark another major period of expansion until 1946.

British Columbia is not isolated any more, but is now in the full stream of the North American economy. But the fact remains that most of its products are shipped outside the provincial boundaries. It cannot be emphasized strongly enough that the growth of the province is still subject to outside influences beyond provincial control. When foreign demand slackens, all aspects of the B.C. economy decline.

CHAPTER ONE

TRANSPORTATION

Roads

The gold rushes of 1858-65 presented some unique transportation problems to the authorities of the newly formed Crown colony of British Columbia. When supplies were available, it was relatively easy to provide the necessities for the thousands of gold seekers working on the sandbanks of the Lower Fraser: the natural avenue was the waterway from Victoria to Hope and Yale.

Once they ascended into the upper country, however, the problems multiplied. In the winter of 1860-61, it was impossible to pack enough food into the interior on the existing trails. To save themselves from privation or worse fates, all but a handful of miners wintered on the coast or in California.

To prepare for the expected rush in 1862, more roads were needed; Sir James Douglas and his colonial officials were fully aware of this and made plans accordingly. At least four options were available.

The most logical and least difficult choice for the construction of a wagon road was the route that Alexander Caulfield Anderson had surveyed on behalf of the Hudson's Bay Company in 1846. It started at the head of steamboat navigation at the northern end of Harrison Lake, and continued via a series of lakes and portages to Lillooet on the Fraser. The main problem with this route was that it lay between the series of lakes — Lillooet, Anderson, and Seton — making it necessary that wagons would have to be loaded and unloaded four times.

The second alternative was to go through the Fraser Canyon, which, in the words of Judge Begbie, was "utterly impassable for any animal but a man, a dog, or a goat."

The third choice was the trail which explorer Alexander Caulfield Anderson had taken over the Coquihalla Pass from Hope in 1846.

It had proven so dangerous that the Hudson's Bay Company fur brigades had abandoned it years ago.

The easiest route was that which the fur traders had used for over half a century. Starting at Portland, Oregon, the Columbia River was ascended by canoe to Fort Okanogan, in what is now north-central Washington State. Horses were then used to traverse the Okanagan Valley to Kamloops. From there, it was a short step to the Cariboo. There were no formidable natural obstacles — either mountains or the bridging of great rivers. Fully half the distance could be travelled by water, and the land was park-like; well-adapted for horse travel.

Sir James Douglas and other Hudson's Bay Company officials knew its advantages well, as did some American miners. In the summer of 1858, Joel Palmer had driven seven wagons loaded with tools, goods, and food from Walla Walla along this route to Kamloops, where he sold his merchandise at a handsome profit. Along the way, he reported passing companies of 400-500 men.

To the Hudson's Bay Company officials, however, this route presented two great obstacles — it originated in American territory, and the Indians south of the border were extremely hostile. These two factors ran counter to two long established company policies — there could be no American entanglements, and peaceful relations must be kept with the Indians.

It is not surprising that Sir James Douglas opted for the Harrison-Lillooet route. It was easy from the point of building, but most expensive from the point of freighting. This wagon road was completed in 1861. Along with the Lillooet-Soda Creek Road which G. B. Wright completed the following year, Douglas' new route provided the first access for wheeled traffic from the coast to the interior.

The cost of freighting continued to be excessive, until the Cariboo Wagon Road was built through the Fraser Canyon when the cost of shipping to Williams Creek and Barkerville dropped from 90¢ to between 18¢ and 21¢ per pound.

Other roads and trails were being built at the same time. In response to the Big Bend gold rush of 1866, the wagon road was extended eastward from Cache Creek to Savona. It was a step "towards the consummation of the much desired line of road communications through British Territory between the Sea Coast to British Columbia and Canada," according to the Chief Commissioner of Lands and Works, J. W. Trutch. The Dewdney Trail brought the Kootenays under colonial control. A road was built east of Hope for 23 miles in the vicinity of the Hudson's Bay Trail that had been pioneered by Anderson in 1846. In the words of engineer Walter Moberly, it was "valuable as a frontier road for military purposes." In more settled areas, a telegraph road was partially opened from New Westminster to Yale; in and around New Westminster, several strategic roads were built, like the North Road and the Pitt River Road.

What resources did the colony have to embark on such an ambitious road-building program? Firstly, there were some extremely capable officials in the employment of the Colonial government, one of whom was the respected and feared governor, Sir James Douglas. He was a man of autocratic traits, accustomed to exercising absolute power in the affairs of the Hudson's Bay Company's Pacific department. With 45 years of experience in the ways of western frontiersmen, he was determined, dominating, clear-sighted both in business and government, and fit the job as a glove fits the hand. He knew the development of the mining frontier depended upon adequate means of transportation, and he set out to provide it.

Other important figures in government included Colonel Richard Clement Moody, R.E., the Chief Commissioner of Lands and Works — a trained engineer and experienced colonial administrator, who had been governor of the Falkland Islands. The administration of justice was in the hands of Judge Matthew Baillie Begbie and Chartres Brew, inspector of police. In the field was a small group of government officials known as the Gold Commissioners. They were stationed in the mining communities, often the only link between the government and the miners. Selected for their background, education, and ability, they were expected to be able to act on their own initiative and to respond to adventurous situations in unorthodox ways.

To provide the technical services required in developing a new country, the British government supplied a detachment of the Royal Engineers. This corps came out from England in three parties — the first two in 1858 and the third, the main group, arriving in Esquimalt on April 19, 1859. There were 165 volunteers in the contingent altogether, carefully selected. The officers were chosen for their professional qualifications — Captain J. M. Grant for his knowledge of contracting and construction, Captain R. M. Parsons as a highly competent surveyor, and Captain H. R. Luard for his technical knowledge of military engineering. The non-commissioned

25

officers and men embraced practically every trade known at that time — surveyors, architects, draughtsmen, artists, printers, carpenters, blacksmiths, painters, and miners.

In his instructions, Secretary of the Colonies, Sir E. Bulwar Lytton, told Colonel Moody "to give immediate attention to the improvement of the means of communication by land and water." How well the Royal Engineers accomplished this order is seen in the number of trails and roads built in the colony during this period — their assistance was invaluable in location and construction. They also helped to explore and survey unknown parts of the country, lay out townsites, erect public buildings, report on the resources of the country, prepare and make maps, and gave aid in advising and reporting on work done by civilian contractors. Even non-commissioned officers were given individual assignments and expected to submit competent technical reports on the locations of possible roads or the sites for major bridges; such work today would be entrusted to teams of high-salaried experts.

There was also a small group of civil engineers who had come out to B.C. in the hope of finding professional employment. The most prominent and best known of the group was Sir Joseph Trutch. Born in England, he had apprenticed in the Great Western Railway shops at Swindon under the railway engineer, Sir Daniel Gooch. He arrived in Victoria in the early days of the gold rush, surveyed some townsites, with the assistance of his brother, John Trutch, and became involved in road-building on the Harrison-Lillooet route into the interior.

When plans for the Cariboo Wagon Road were announced, he put in a tender and became the leading contractor on that project. Trutch also planned and built the first Alexandria bridge at Spuzzum — a major engineering achievement. Eventually, he succeeded Colonel R. C. Moody as Chief Commissioner of Lands and Works and later became the first Lieutenant-Governor of British Columbia. His engineering ability contributed much in the construction of some of the most difficult stretches of the Cariboo Road.

Walter Moberly made the first survey done by a professional engineer on the mainland of British Columbia in 1858, when he studied the Harrison-Lillooet route to the interior. He was born in England, but had travelled to Ontario with his family as a child. Later, he articled in the office of Cumberland & Storm, leading architects and engineers of the day, who designed such public buildings as the University of Toronto and St. James Cathedral.

He arrived in Victoria late in 1858, surveyed the Harrison-Lillooet Road, and two years later, went into the construction business on the wagon road east of Hope, which was thought would cross the mountains into the interior through the Coquihalla Pass. When the time came, he contracted to build a section of the Cariboo Wagon Road, but fell into difficulties, went bankrupt, and ended up as superintendent of construction on the very road that he had contracted to build. As Assistant Surveyor of B.C. in the Colonial Government Service in 1866, he explored eastward from Shuswap Lake with a view towards the construction of a trans-provincial coaching road. This was to join up with a road built westward from the Red River and provide a link with eastern Canada.

Edgar Dewdney, creator of the famous Dewdney Trail, was born in England, and educated and trained there as a civil engineer. He came to B.C. in 1859 and found employment under Governor James Douglas and Colonel R. C. Moody, laying out townsites. He became one of the great trail builders, contracted for the route over the Cascades to the southern interior which was to bear his name for decades. Dewdney was also a great financial backer of pioneer mining claims and mining properties. During his later political career, he became a federal cabinet minister, Lieutenant-Governor of the Northwest Territories and, in 1892, Lieutenant-Governor of B.C. He was a prominent figure in the development of the west.

There was also a small group of entrepreneurs who were adventurous in spirit, and had a faith in the country that only westerners possessed. They had no engineering knowledge and varied educational backgrounds, but were willing to take chances, so they bid on the trail and road contracts published in the newspapers. Among them were Gustavus Blin Wright, considered by some to be the greatest road builder of them all, Thomas Spence of Spence's Bridge, and Charles Oppenheimer of Yale and Lytton.

Not to be forgotten are the workers who wielded picks and shovels. They lived for months at a time in isolated camps under the most primitive conditions, and often suffered death or injury when blasts went off prematurely. Most of these workers were discouraged miners who reached the creeks and could not find a strike. Broke, they were unable to stay in the upper country where the prices were high, so they went to work on the roads. In the boom days of the Cariboo, the numbers of workers ran into the thousands; the

27

contractors could never find enough. Many were Chinese or Indians. Whenever rumours circulated about the discovery of a new gold-bearing creek, workers often just dropped their tools and took off.

In October of 1861, under pressure from the miners and merchants, Governor Douglas decided to build a wagon road through the Fraser Canyon to Cook's Ferry on the Thompson. It was the most ambitious scheme ever launched in B.C. until the coming of the railway in the eighties. For a small colony with scant resources and very little revenue, it seemed a dubious venture.

The distance of seven miles from Yale to Sailor's Bar was built by Captain Grant and a party of 53 sappers in six months. In the words of the *British Columbian*, it was "an enduring monument of skill and patient toil." Thomas Spence contracted to do the section from Sailor's Bar to the suspension bridge, a job which entailed much heavy blasting, side-cutting, and timbering.

The suspension bridge was the first of its kind in British Columbia, and probably the first suspension bridge in the west. A purely speculative private venture by Joseph Trutch, this engineering wonder was built by the San Francisco firm of Halliday and Co. in the summer of 1863 at a cost of $45,000.

The distance from the suspension bridge to Boston Bar was also Joseph Trutch's responsibility; a distance of 11 miles, of which seven involved work of the heaviest kind — high wall building, immense amounts of blasting, heavy side cutting, and timbering. The 32 miles from Boston Bar to Lytton built by Thomas Spence also required much bridging, timbering, and blasting.

Northward from Lytton to Spence's Bridge was contracted to Moberly and Oppenheimer. They also worked north of Spence's Bridge, but ran into difficulties in the summer of 1862 when the Cariboo creeks were just beginning to acquire their fame as the richest pieces of real estate in North America. Their work force suddenly disappeared in that direction; the Indians in the area were decimated by smallpox; and the few Chinese that could be recruited were not sufficient to keep the work going. The Colonial government then stepped in, took over all the contractors' tools, and sent in the Royal Engineers to complete the job.

The bankrupt Moberly accepted a job as engineer under the government and, as a paid employee, completed the project that he had originally planned to finish as an independent contractor. In the process, he had piled up a huge personal debt which took him years to pay off. To make matters worse, his partner Charles Oppenheimer left the country. Such was one of the many hazards faced by the pioneer contractors.

The gap between Spence's Bridge and Clinton was finally bridged in summer of 1863 by William Hood of Cache Creek. Many considered Hood's road to be the best made in the country, in spite of the fact that he received no cash for his endeavours. He was paid in bonds of the colony, bearing 6 percent interest and redeemable in four annual installments.

Earlier, G. B. Wright had built from Lillooet to the steamboat landing at Soda Creek. Then, from Quesnel, wagon roads were built successively to Cottonwood (1864), Williams Creek, and Barkerville (1865). The last stretch from Soda Creek to Quesnel was built by Robert Smith in 1866.

The Cariboo Wagon Road must rank as one of the greatest road-building achievements of the nineteenth century. It was a wonder to all travellers and an object of pride for British Columbians. Eighteen feet in width, the road surface was covered by broken stones and gravel, with drainage ditches on one or both sides as required, and bridges and culverts substantially built of timber. Loads up to seven or eight tons were hauled over it by teams of mules or oxen harnessed to wagons. The express company ran stagecoaches with two, four, or six horses on regular schedules at a rate of nine miles per hour. The famous pioneer, Charles Major, is credited with driving the first four-horse stage on the new road in March 1864.

Not only was the Cariboo Road a great engineering achievement successfully accomplished, but it opened up the interior of British Columbia to commercial development. The Honourable H. L. Langevin, Federal Minister of Public Works, described the situation in 1872:

This small population [of B.C.] however, did not hesitate to submit to great sacrifices to open the great highways from Yale to Cariboo which gave, and still gives, comparatively easy access to the rich mines of the District of Cariboo and which, for boldness of enterprise and solidity of construction, is worthy of a great people.

This road was built for animal-drawn traffic, and it is surprising to discover how many different beasts and forms of locomotion were tried. The most common was the mule team, consisting of 16 to 48 animals winding their way single file. Each mule knew its place and would follow the leader, usually a white mare, for hours. The freight weighed from 250 to 400 pounds and was strapped on the backs of the mules on top of straw-stuffed leather sacks and secured by diamond hitches. The crew consisted of the mule train boss, the cook, and one man to every eight mules. Later, wagons, drawn by 8 to 16 heads of mules or oxen, traversed the road carrying 7 or 8 tons per load.

The individual traveller could either walk or ride horseback with stops at strategically located roadhouses. Lady travellers and those with money usually rode in the six-horse mail coaches driven on regular schedules by local whips. It took a packer about two months to make the journey from Yale to Barkerville and return. For the season, it was a matter of only three round trips. By stage, however, the journey could be done in little over a week.

One of the most bizarre experiments tried was to pack by camel. Calbreath, a Cariboo entrepreneur (acting for packer Frank Laumeister) and two Americans, went down to San Francisco in the spring of 1862 to find out whether camels could do the job better than mules or horses. He came back to Victoria with a string of over 20 beasts purchased from a San Francisco merchant, Otto Esche, who, in turn, had imported them from Manchuria via Siberia. In the summer of 1862, the camels were put on the Harrison-Lillooet Road and seemed to perform satisfactorily. As freight declined on this route because of the opening of the Cariboo Road through the Fraser Canyon, the camels were moved to Quesnel to work the 60-mile stretch into Barkerville. Their splay feet were expected to prevent them from sinking into the holes made in the road by the iron hooves of passing pack-train mules and horses.

As it turned out, the camels' feet sank into the water-filled holes. Burdened with heavy loads, they became strung out along the road and obstructed more mobile traffic. Much time and effort was spent in freeing them. One of the biggest misfortunes turned out to be their peculiar odour, for all the other animals on the road would react by panicking and rushing off in all directions, scattering their loads. Several packers took the matter to court and, by court injunction, the animals were ordered off the road. They were then turned loose to forage for themselves, frightening many future travellers by their ungainly size.

It is not surprising that, in the "Age of the Steam Engine," efforts were directed towards using steam traction. It seemed obvious to some far-sighted people in the colony that the more heavy machinery like pumps and steam engines weighing over 7 or 8 tons could only be carried on animal-drawn wagons with difficulty.

The solution seemed to be in the use of road traction engines hauling trains of cars carrying 6 to 7 tons at seven miles per hour. The challenge was accepted by John Fowler and Co. of Leeds, England. They had developed a steam traction engine drawing a train which could carry up to 12 tons. Both Colonel R. C. Moody and Joseph Trutch enthusiastically witnessed a demonstration put on by the manufacturer at Leeds. On the strength of this demonstration, a company was formed, British Columbia Steam Traction Co., and 23 of the machines with their drivers and mechanics were ordered to run on the wagon roads of the province. The promoters, in their petition to the Colonial government, said they were convinced "that these machines are exactly adapted to perform the services which would be required of them in British Columbia and that, by employing them, the cost of transporting the freight into the interior would be materially reduced." Permission was granted on March 10, 1864.

By the time the machines could be delivered in the spring and summer of 1865, conditions had changed. People were now leaving the Cariboo and freight was on the decline. The machines were never shipped; it will never be known how successful this venture might have been. Someone must have had a second thought and found out that the bridges on the Cariboo Road were not made for weights of 12 tons.

If this was the first proposal to put steam on the roads of B.C., Francis Jones Barnard became the first to put it into practice. Barnard had an Express that carried mail, passengers, and gold from Barkerville to Yale. He used excellent Concord stages made in California, the best of the locally-bred horses, and took advantage of the numerous roadhouses where frequent changes could be made. He was also fully aware of the harsh climatic conditions — snow in winter and mud in spring — which might make it difficult for steam traction.

An Edinburgh engineer, R. W. Thomson, had perfected a more suitable traction engine that was lighter by four tons than Fowler's. It had also a novel feature, solid India rubber tires attached to the wheels. It was now in production at Tennant & Co.'s foundry in Leith, Scotland. Barnard made arrangements for several of these machines to be sent to B.C., two of which were to be custom-made for the Cariboo passenger traffic.

The rubber tires were the most important feature. It was claimed they acted as excellent springs, easing wear and tear on the engine, and enabling the machine to run at reasonable speed. They were also noiseless and would do little damage to the roads, a great selling point with government officials.

In April of 1871, the first train from Yale got stuck a third of the way to its destination; another stalled on Jackass Mountain, a victim of the spring thaw. This was the end of the steam traction engines, except for the one which ended up as a logging locomotive on Jeremiah Roger's logging operations on English Bay. The rest were sent back to Scotland, where some of the same Tennant-built Thomson steamers were still hauling heavy loads on the streets of Glasgow in 1919.

This was not the end of their use in B.C. for, at the turn of the century, a road traction engine was hauling ore from a mine in the vicinity of Kamloops along the road to the C.P.R. tracks. A five-ton steam wagon for hauling gravel was supplied to the District of North Vancouver by Bayfield and Archibald, a manufacturer's agent of heavy engineering equipment in Vancouver. The District of Point Grey, and the Municipality of Oak Bay also expressed their interest in acquiring similar wagons. Up in the Yukon, in 1910, Hornsby of Lincoln had supplied a steam caterpillar traction engine to haul coal from a mine 40 miles away to Dawson City. But the days of steam traction were numbered. After the end of World War I, it was the automobile that took over and brought the roads of B.C. back into general use.

It is interesting to note that the planning of trunk roads in colonial days did not stop with the Cariboo Wagon Road. Governor Douglas also had it in mind to build a coaching road to Kamloops, then north up the Thompson through the Yellowhead Pass to connect with the one to be built westward from the Red River. It was suggested in one of his last reports to the Duke of Newcastle in 1863. "I had everything ready to make a beginning," he wrote to a friend in 1868. "A large force of engineers, tools, labourers, the means of transport, and other appliances requisite for the new enterprise."

It might have been one last attempt to try and persuade the Imperial government to keep the Royal Engineers in B.C. It is surprising how the concept persisted. Joseph Trutch was asked to report on the progress made in establishing an Overland Coaching Road. In a report submitted on February 19, 1868, he wrote, "But although the work of building a road over the Rocky Mountains has yet to be commenced, much has already been effected by this colony." He goes on to state that one of the most difficult sections "traversing the great barrier of the Cascade Range of Mountains has been pierced — which presented a far more difficult engineering obstacle and one more expensive to overcome than the Rocky Mountains themselves." The agitation for an overland road finally reached its peak in the proposals taken by the British Columbia delegates to Ottawa for the terms of entry into Confederation. In the field of communications, British Columbia proposed:

Inasmuch as no real Union can subsist between this Colony and Canada without the speedy establishment of communications across the Rocky Mountains by Coach Road or Railway, the Dominion shall, within three years from date of Union, construct and open for traffic such Coach Road, from some point on the line of the Main Trunk Road of this Colony to Fort Garry.

In the final Terms of Union, no mention is made of a coach road, but the Dominion government, in its generosity, agreed to "connect the seaboard of British Columbia (by a railway) with the railway system of Canada." Thus ended the first great road-building era in the history of this province.

For the next 50 years, B.C. roads were neglected, but not unused. The maintenance of roads and road-building activity became a source of important patronage to successive provincial governments, though there was no systematic work or general policy. On completion of the C.P.R. to Vancouver, a considerable number were built locally around New Westminster, Vancouver, and in the Fraser Valley. Many were short — two or three miles in length, and built by settlers with government money for their own needs. In 1899, the roads were measured by men on bicycles who were equipped with cycle-meters. By this means, the government was able to estimate the road mileage in the province in 1900 as 5,615. A notable engineering achievement in this period (1902-04) was a combined road and railway bridge over the Fraser River at New Westminster which Armstrong, Morrison & Co. built for the provincial government at a cost of one million dollars.

The coming of the automobile changed road building from a haphazard, politically-oriented activity to one of planning and organization. Roads now required smoother and tougher surfaces, better grades and curvatures. A system of trunk roads and connecting highways also had to be planned and executed. As far back as 1909, the western provinces had discussed the building of a trunk road from Winnipeg to the Pacific coast. Pressure groups like the Good

Roads Association were major factors in the struggles for better, improved roads. But it was not until 1924, on completion of the reconstruction of the Fraser Canyon Road, that motorists were able to reach the coast from the interior. By 1929, the province could boast of 18,200 miles of road, but in no way were they up to Trans-Canada standards.

In the Depression, road building slumped. A gravel road, called the Big Bend Highway, was built as a relief project during this time, and provided the first road link between Golden and Revelstoke, bypassing Rogers Pass. Another engineering landmark, built during the Depression years, was the Pattullo Bridge spanning the Fraser River at New Westminster. It opened in 1937.

Long the dream of Americans, the Alaska Highway was finally finished in 1942-43. It was a defence project built after Pearl Harbor, and extended from Dawson Creek on the B.C.-Alberta border to Fairbanks, Alaska. Purely an American venture, it was built under the supervision of the U.S. government. The B.C. portion stretched northwest from Dawson Creek to Watson Lake in the Yukon, which is 125 miles north of the Cassiar country which had witnessed a gold rush in 1872. Within weeks, the population of Dawson Creek rose from 500 to 4,500. Up until then, the town had been tied into the Alberta economy. Construction started in the spring of 1942, and the road was in place and passable by autumn.

With the opening of the Hope-Princeton Highway in 1951, the regional road network became knit into the provincial system. The John Hart Highway from Prince George to Dawson Creek brought the B.C. section of the Peace River country into the B.C. economy for the first time. The spectacular engineering feats in connection with the reconstruction of the Fraser Canyon section of the Trans-Canada Highway excited interest far beyond the borders of B.C. One of the most expensive sections of the road ever built was the 1.18 miles through the China Bar bluff at a cost of $2¼ million.

Much work has been accomplished in the building of bridges and tunnels. All major rivers in B.C. have now been bridged. The Lions Gate Bridge in 1939, the new Granville bridge in Vancouver, the Oak Street and Knight Road bridges to Lulu Island, the Second Narrows, and Port Mann freeway bridges, the Overlander at Kamloops, and the one at Kelowna spanning Lake Okanagan, and some 600 others have aroused interest in the North American construction industry. The George Massey Tunnel, the first underwater vehicular tunnel in B.C., employed new techniques of construction. It was built in concrete sections poured into a landlocked drydock, and then floated into position and sunk in the site in a prepared trench. One of the prime contractors was Peter Kiewit & Sons of Oklahoma, internationally known for their work in the construction field.

British Columbia now has a network of highways equal, if not superior, to any in North America, serving all the settled communities. Built at an enormous outlay of labour, skill, and money, the system enables commerce to flow from section to section. It has assisted in the promotion and establishment of great industries such as logging, sawmilling, pulp and paper, and mining; and has brought millions of tourists annually to the province.

Railways

British Columbia went into the Confederation negotiations asking for a coaching road and came out with the promise of a railroad to link it with the rest of Canada. Exploration and surveying began almost immediately; these activities lasted over a period of nine years and became B.C.'s fourth largest industry. Over $1,300,000 was spent in the hiring of packers, the purchase of supplies and payment in wages of the survey crews. As the surveys progressed, definite decisions could then be made on the choice of possible routes. By Order-in-Council of October 4, 1879, Burrard Inlet was designated as the western terminus for a route using the Yellowhead Pass. The line was to come via the Thompson and Fraser rivers to Port Moody at the head of Burrard Inlet.

The Mackenzie government had decided to build sections of the line under government contracts. They had prepared for this by buying large quantities of rails in England in 1874, and having them shipped out to Esquimalt and Nanaimo. They now shipped these rails to Emory, four miles west to Yale. This is why when tenders were called the starting point was Emory's Bar, not Yale. Tenders were invited to bid for construction of the railway from Emory to Savona, which was to be in four sections. There was no lack in response — some dozen or more firms submitted bids for each of the four contracts, the majority of whom were eastern Canadian firms stationed in either Ontario or Quebec. Only two had American backing. Originally, the contracts were given to the lowest bidder. For various reasons, including the inability of the parties to raise the guarantee money, the lowest bidders requested Onderdonk to take over their contracts.

Onderdonk was an American accustomed to moving in the highest financial circles in New York. His original offers had not been low, but in the middle range. What Onderdonk had which no Canadian firm did, was the backing of some of the biggest capitalists in America, including S. G. Reed of the Oregon Railway and Navigation Co.; and Darius O. Mills, the San Francisco banker and president of the Pacific Rolling Mills; Levi P. Morton of Morton, Rose & Co. of London, England, fiscal agent of the Canadian government in many financial transactions. In a year's time, Morton, Bliss & Co. was to become a member of the Canadian Pacific Syndicate, a group of private entrepreneurs who were to build the Canadian Pacific Railway.

Because the firms awarded the original contracts were unable to meet their commitments, these contracts were liable to be turned back to the government. Sir Charles Tupper, Minister of Railways, was placed in a difficult position, so he asked the advice of Joseph Trutch, the man who had contracted for and successfully built the most difficult sections of the Cariboo Wagon Road 18 years before.

"I decidedly think," wrote Trutch, "it would be of advantage to the public interests that the whole of these four sections of railway construction should be undertaken by one contractor or one firm of contractors." Sir Charles took Trutch's advice and transferred all four contracts to Andrew Onderdonk.

It is of interest to note that David Oppenheimer of Yale (later of Vancouver) submitted an offer to F. Braun, the secretary of the Department of Railways and Canals, in his letter of November 17, 1879. He offered to build and fully equip a railway from Emory to Savona with locomotives, freight and passenger cars, and all other necessary things for the sum of $12 million. Who his backers were remain a mystery. The offer was politely declined with a return of the $5,000 deposit by a letter signed, not by the Minister of Railways, but by his secretary.

The difficulties were immense, but the contracts gave to Onderdonk and his syndicate great flexibility. There were very definite limitations on how much they would have to spend, and the amount of work that was to be performed. The expenditures were limited to the amounts tendered and, if it appeared that the maximum amount should be exceeded, "the contractor then will be required to complete only such portions of the works — as will be indicated by the [government] engineer with a view to limit the total expenture under this contract to the maximum amount as stated and, as soon as the said maximum amount will be expended, this contract will then be considered as ended."

This was the rationale that enabled Onderdonk to construct "the cheapest possible line with workable curves and grades" as described in a telegram received by H. J. Cambie while on the job in April 1880. The government engineers continually urged the contractor to cut costs. Consequently, much substandard work was approved. This was a very great source of controversy when the line was turned over to the C.P.R. Unlike Van Horne, Onderdonk was building a railway that he would not have to run.

One of the greatest difficulties was the shortage of labour. In a province with a white population under 35,000, from eight to nine thousand jobs were created. It was obvious that few workers could be recruited locally. Because of the railway boom in the western States, there was a shortage of construction workers. Moreover, Onderdonk was offering less in wages than that paid south of the border. The employment agents in San Francisco sent up men who had never done a hard day's work in their lives — hangers-on in the city saloons, broken-down bartenders, down-and-outers who had not made it. The turnover was heavy, production poor. Onderdonk experimented with bringing in Chinese who had been working on the railways in Oregon or Washington. Desperate for men, he worked through Chinese labour contractors and brought them in by the shipload from Hong Kong in 1880-81. They were brought by steamer to Yale, given a little rice, and told to make their way on foot to the construction camps, which could be 30 or 50 miles up the Cariboo Road. Steady streams of them could be seen on the road every day. If one got sick or fell by the wayside, the others would leave him on the road to starve or die. Many were brought back to Yale by the engineers or their wives to be given a meal or sent to hospital, as the situation warranted. There were constant accidents on the job, sickness, or just plain inability to cope with strange situations. At peak of construction, the Chinese work force was estimated at 6,500, but over 15,000 were brought in by the agents representing the Chinese labour contractors.

37

Onderdonk had been working on his contracts for 16 months before the first grade west of Portage la Prairie had been levelled by the syndicate that was to build the Canadian Pacific Railway. It took 18 months before the first four tunnels east of Yale had been blasted. To the travellers on the Cariboo Road, tunnelling was a constant source of danger, as the wife of Bishop A. W. Sillitoe (first Anglican bishop of New Westminster) found in 1881. She wrote:

Another source of danger is to be found in the fact that blasting is perpetually going on, a loud report, a shower of stones being sometimes the first and only notice you receive of the discharge. I was told the other day by a gentleman in Yale — that nobody who can avoid it now drives over the first thirteen miles of the road. "If you are riding," he said, "you can dodge the rocks flying about, but if you are driving, you are powerless."

So many tons of dynamite had to be used, that Onderdonk found it cheaper to build a factory at Yale than buy it from the explosive companies. Constant use dimmed its dangers, and accidents occurred almost daily. When it got wet in rainy weather, the construction crews would dry it out in an oven and hope for the best. In the early days, before the Rand air compressed drills were introduced, all boring had to be done by hand. It was a case of hammers and chisels, picks and shovels, and blasting day and night. In the camps, they ran two shifts per day — one from 7 a.m. to 7 p.m., the other from 7 p.m. to 7 a.m. Inside the tunnels, as Mrs. Sillitoe wrote, "the noise was deafening, the drills being worked by machinery and, shouting our loudest, we could hardly hear one another speak." There was no recreation, no time or place to relax. It was work, sleep, and work again. The contractor was under obligation, according to the contract, "not to permit, allow, or encourage the sale of any spiriterous liquors on or near the works." He tried to keep liquor outside of the camps, with varying success.

In Yale, it was a different story. Reverend H. H. Gowen writes in his biography of Bishop A. W. Sillitoe:

Yale, at this time (1881), bore a most unenviable reputation. Pay day was signalized by the most fearful riots — drunkenness and disorder filled the place day and night — tattered dirt-bespattered drunkards rolled about the streets, wallowing in the mud, cursing and fighting, driving all respectable people into the recesses of their homes.

The conditions in the settlements and towns along Onderdonk's contracts were no better or worse than those in the railway construction communities south of the border, along the way of the Northern Pacific, or its branches. In both cases, authority was weak, law and order was constantly violated, and the saloons and gambling dens operated day and night. There was a slight difference between conditions existing along the government contracts and those under the Canadian Pacific Railway. The administration of law and order in the zones embracing government contracts were in the hands of the B.C. provincial police and the civil magistrates. In the C.P.R. zones, administration was the responsibility of the North West Mounted Police and the police officers usually functioned as the magistrates. There was nobody from Yale to Savona with the prestige and ability to exercise authority like Superintendent Sam Steele did in the mountain camps of the Rockies and the Selkirks. By sheer force of character and influence (he got Ottawa to increase the railway belt from 20 to 40 miles), he made it impossible for the workers to walk the 20 miles over the mountains to get a drink.

The policy of the Mackenzie government, in locating the line, had been to use water communication as much as possible. When Sir John A. Macdonald regained power, he continued this policy until he was able to find a group of entrepreneurs in the private sector (the C.P.R. Syndicate) willing to assume the responsibility of building a line without any water breaks. The government contracts for building through the Fraser Canyon had been advertised under the old government, but actually signed by Sir Charles Tupper, Minister of Railways and Canals, in the new administration. The railway was to start at Emory's Bar, four miles below the head of navigation at Yale, for reasons already mentioned. There was no provision to extend the line westward to Burrard Inlet. Under the new policy, this became necessary and, in 1882, the government advertised for tenders for the 85 miles from Emory to Port Moody. Nine Canadian and four American tenders submitted bids. Due to an unfortunate error made by the Bank of Montreal, the cheque submitted by the firm with the lowest tender was marked "Good for 2 days only." The government refused to acknowledge the validity of this cheque and the contract was awarded to Onderdonk on the advice of the chief government engineer, Collingwood Schreiber.

It is interesting to note the omissions in all five of these government contracts. The steel rails, a major factor, were to be purchased and supplied by the government. The major bridge spanning the

39

Fraser at Cisco was subjected to a separate arrangement made with Onderdonk and his syndicate at a price of $259,000. This was to be a substantial structure of steel, all other bridges and trestles could be made of wood. No provision was made for equipping the line, supplying it with locomotives, freight, and passengers cars, a major expense. As previously noted, the contractor was given guarantees as to the amount he was obliged to spend, and provision for stoppage of work under certain conditions without liability.

There was no communication between the work being done in the Fraser Canyon and that undertaken westward of Calgary into the Rockies. Construction through the Rockies and the Selkirks was the responsibility of the Canadian Pacific Railway. It was contracted out to men who would become famous in Canadian financial and business affairs — William Mackenzie, Donald Mann, Herbert Holt, and James Ross. No men of national or international status emerged from those who worked under Onderdonk. The task was as difficult as that found in the Fraser Canyon. In none of his contracts did Onderdonk build a tunnel which, shortly after construction, had to be abandoned through danger of collapse. This happened in an earlier contract in Kicking Horse Canyon when the timbers in a 600-foot tunnel squeezed, and a new track had to be located over the obstacle. This was not corrected until 1905-06 when a new concrete-lined tunnel was driven through.

The momentous decision to change the routing of the C.P.R. was taken in the spring of 1881 at a meeting in St. Paul, Minnesota. Three of the four members of the executive committee were there — J. J. Hill, George Stephen, and H. B. Angus. This was when the northern route by way of the Carlton Trail and the Yellowhead Pass was dropped for a more southerly one. The southern route led directly to the Kicking Horse Pass, some 1,500 feet higher in altitude, then through the Yellowhead and over the Selkirks which were, at that time, unexplored with no known passes. This presented the railway engineers with one of their most persistent problems. The surveyors found it impossible to find acceptable grades, both in the Rockies and the Selkirks. Under the contract with the government, the C.P.R. had agreed to build a line with a maximum gradient of 2.2 percent. The descent on the western slope of the Rockies from Hector to Field showed a drop of 1,100 feet in three and one half miles. On this section, known to a generation of railroaders as the Big Hill, the grade was 4.4 percent, the steepest ever operated by a standard gauge railway on regular service. Van Horne had to get special permission from the Minister of Railways to build on the Big Hill what he called a "temporary" line; it lasted 25 years and was one of the greatest problems to the operating staff. It was replaced in 1909 by the famous Spiral Tunnels built by the Canadian contracting firm of Macdonell, Gzowaki & Co. There are two of these tunnels with a combined length of 1¼ miles; each makes a complete circle under the mountain and reduces the grade to 2.2 percent.

It took four 54-ton engines to take a 700-ton train up the Big Hill, of 14 to 20 freight, or up to 11 passenger, cars. The big worry was getting down. Air brakes and sanding equipment were inspected and tested, speed being restricted to eight miles per hour. Brakemen would drop off at intervals to make sure the wheels were not sliding or the brake boxes heating unduly. Safety spurs were constructed about 9/10 of a mile apart and were attended day and night by switch tenders who turned the switches on to the main line only long enough for a train to pass. Over the years, there have been spectacular runaways even to the point where engines have slid up the safety spurs! As their wheels were spinning in reverse, they came down again in a mass of sparks and smoke. It is recorded that a snowplow was once lost on the Big Hill, unknown to the engineer on the locomotive pushing it; it just went off the track and plunged some hundreds of feet down the mountainside.

The most troublesome spot in the Selkirks was the Rogers Pass. It is one of the most spectacular parts of the line for the traveller, but from an operating standpoint, it is a nightmare. The snowfall is phenomenal; in the early days, snowslides would block the line for weeks. A partial solution was the construction of snowsheds which were originally timber and now are concrete. Put in one continuous line, they would extend over six miles. The greatest engineering achievement on this part of the line is the Connaught Tunnel, one of the longest in North America. Completed in 1916, it was built by Foley, Welch & Stewart as a double-tracked tunnel. Today (1982), due to heavier and wider equipment, the second track has been taken out. It is now used only as a single-tracked tunnel.

In November 1885, Onderdonk (who had received a contract from the C.P.R. to build eastward from Savona) met those working westward at Graigellachie in the valley of the Illecillewaet where the last spike was driven by Donald A. Smith, Lord Strathcona.

41

"All that I have to say," declared Van Horne, "is that the work was well done in every way."

It was another two years before the railway reached Coal Harbour, marking the beginnings of the city of Vancouver.

In many important ways, the building of the Esquimalt & Nanaimo Railway on Vancouver Island was tied in with the construction of the C.P.R. As far back as 1873, the Mackenzie government, by order-in-council, had designated Esquimalt as the terminus of the Canadian Pacific Railway. Then, in July 1878, the terminus was changed to Burrard Inlet. This upset Vancouver Island residents. The B.C. government had already deeded to Ottawa a strip of land on the island, not to exceed 20 miles on each side, so they could build the proposed railway. In the words of Judge Howay, "the islanders were determined to have their railway." So this land, which comprised the famous E. & N. land grant, was offered to Robert Dunsmuir, the Vancouver Island coal baron, if he would build a line between Esquimalt and Nanaimo. Dunsmuir turned to his friends in San Francisco — Charles Crocker, Collis P. Huntington, and Leland Stanford, for money and advice. He could not have sought aid from a better group. They had built the western section of the first American transcontinental railway and had the reputation of being the best railway promotional team of their time. This syndicate supplied the capital and the knowledge, and the Dunsmuirs, father and son, reaped the benefits. It was opened in 1886 and, in later years, played a large part in the development of the coal mining industry on Vancouver Island. Not everybody was satisfied with the deal. The land grant which went along with its construction was criticized by three generations of British Columbians. In the session of the House of Commons in 1891, John Charlton, M.P., had this to say:

Here was a little line of railway — along the sea coast from Victoria to Nanaimo — a distance of 70 miles, the construction of which was necessary. To promote the construction of that railway, nearly all the coal lands of the island of Vancouver were granted to a syndicate, the greater proportion of the capital being held in San Francisco by the Southern Pacific Railway magnates.

The coming of the C.P.R. into British Columbia and the favourable railway charters offered almost gratis by the provincial legislature, focussed the attention of many businessmen and investors to this part of the country. Speculators and railway contractors rushed in to procure charters to build local lines. The Columbia &

Kootenay joined Nelson and Robson. The Kaslo & Slocan, with the financial backing of J. J. Hill, tapped the silver mines of the Slocan. The Shuswap & Okanagan gave rail access to the Okanagan, and Heinze's Red Mountain Railway from Rossland to Trail foreshadowed the British Columbia and Southern charter and its purchase by the C.P.R. All these eventually, through the lack of funds or traffic, passed into the hands of the two great western railway monopolies — the Canadian Pacific, or James J. Hill and the Great Northern.

The American railways were coming into the Kootenays and capturing the rich mining traffic. To offset this and to funnel the Kootenay trade into the Canadian economy, the C.P.R. built the Crow's Nest Line. Connecting in the east with the main line at Medicine Hat, Alberta, it eventually was built right across southern British Columbia, joining the main line in the west at Hope, 90 miles east of Vancouver. It served the coal mining towns of the Crow's Nest, the silver-lead mines of the Kootenays, the smelter at Trail and the copper mines and smelter towns of the Boundary country. It moved the coal and ore to the smelters and materially influenced the growth of the communities in southern B.C.

On July 30, 1903, the Liberal government of Sir Wilfred Laurier presented to the House of Commons in Ottawa a bill to incorporate the Grand Trunk Pacific Railway. The proposed railway was to run west from Winnipeg through the Yellowhead Pass across central British Columbia to the Pacific Ocean somewhere in the vicinity of the Skeena River mouth. It is astonishing how little was known of these parts of B.C. at the time. Apart from the few trading posts of the Hudson's Bay Company and the Indians, the country lay unoccupied. Few realized what changes would be brought about by its construction. Thousands of construction workers would pour in and millions of dollars would be spent in supplies and transportation. Industry would be attracted, sawmills and logging would boom. Construction would be started at both ends — on the Pacific side from Prince Rupert which was in the process of being built on an island just north of the mouth of the Skeena River; on the eastern side from Winnipeg via Edmonton through the Yellowhead Pass.

The general contractor for the West was Foley, Welch & Stewart of whom J. W. Stewart was the leading figure. J. W. Stewart was intimately connected, both socially and professionally, to Peter Larson, a great western entrepreneur and builder of many railways in the Western States. Through intermediates, Peter Larson purchased

43

the land on Kaien Island now occupied by Prince Rupert. He sold it a few years later to the Grand Trunk Pacific for their western terminal for what was reported to be a reasonable profit. It might have had considerable influence in channelling the huge construction contract given to Foley, Welch & Stewart by the Grand Trunk directors in London.

The contract was rather unusual for that period, as it called for the building of the lowest grade of any transcontinental railway in North America. In contrast to the building of the C.P.R., all bridges were to be of concrete and steel instead of the more economical wood. In the words of D. B. Hanna, "The Grand Trunk Pacific was built at unprecedented expenses per mile for a pioneer railway."

Unlike Onderdonk in the Fraser Canyon, they were not limited in expenditures, and bought the latest in mechanical equipment such as steam shovels, earth-moving machinery, locomotives, gravel trains, and even sternwheelers on the Skeena and Upper Fraser. The work was subcontracted in small sections, usually shorter than five miles each. Thus, they relieved themselves of much work like preparing the right-of-way, levelling the grades, drainage, and so on.

Building eastward from Prince Rupert, the railway followed the bank of the river through almost 60 miles of solid rock. In the first 211 miles, there were 13 tunnels measuring over 1½ miles in total. The terrain was so rough that, in the first 186 miles eastward, almost 12,000 miles of surveys and location studies had to be made. Angus Stewart, younger brother of J. W. Stewart, was the engineer in charge. Under great hardship, he had surveyed the Skeena country to a point near Terrace in 1907 and was reported to be the first white man to visit Kitimat. The logistic problems proved almost insurmountable, for there were neither trails nor roads up the Skeena. All supplies had to be shipped from Vancouver, 550 miles away. The first sod was turned at Prince Rupert on May 7, 1908.

It was similar in central B.C. Fort George became the distributing centre for the construction camps creeping westward from the Alberta border. There were 3,500 men in these camps to be housed, fed, supplied with tools, and looked after when disabled or sick. Once again, the Cariboo Road became a hive of activity. Freighters, hearing of the boom, came up with their horses and wagons from Washington State; salesmen and prospective merchants wishing to establish in the newly opened towns along the railway's projected right-of-way; lumbermen looking for possible sawmilling sites; prospectors and thousands looking for work all clamoured for seats on the Cariboo Road stages and riverboats. Eleven new stern-wheelers were built to handle the traffic from Soda Creek to Fort George.

But what was new was the automobile. The first auto ever seen in the Cariboo was a four-cylinder Peerless owned by an official of the Guggenheim Bros., an American mining corporation. In June 1907, he used it to make a trip up the Cariboo Road to their placer mining operation at Bullion. Three years later, practically every make of Canadian and American cars could be found on the Cariboo Road. In July 1910, the B.C. Express Co. put two Winton six-cylinder passenger cars into regular schedule from Ashcroft to Soda Creek. By 1913, the fleet had risen to eight Wintons, taking in $70,570 for the season. It dropped off dramatically when the last spike of the railway was driven at Fort Fraser in the presence of Edson J. Chamberlin, president of the Grand Trunk Railway on April 5, 1914. What traffic there was now flowed south from Prince George, augmented by Foley, Welch & Stewart's activity on the Pacific Great Eastern. This railway had been started in 1912 to connect Vancouver with Prince George via Quesnel, the only time which Foley, Welch & Stewart ever built their own railway. It is now the provincially-owned British Columbia Railway. On February 4, 1915, J. W. Stewart announced that grading had been completed on the entire line from Squamish to Prince George. Due to the necessities of war, the contractors were unable to complete the contract and the property was turned over to the provincial government. They laid the steel to Quesnel (opened August 1921) and there it stayed until 1952, when it was finally completed to Prince George.

At one time, Foley, Welch & Stewart were the biggest railway contractors in the west, with 2,000 miles of railway under construction and directing a work force of 50,000.

Another of their major contracts was the building of the Canadian Northern through the Fraser Canyon from Kamloops to Port Mann, which lies a few miles east of New Westminster. The Canadian Northern in British Columbia was built under different terms than the other two transcontinentals. The money for its construction was raised in the private sector mainly in England, but guaranteed by the province of British Columbia. There were other concessions. The government agreed to give free right-of-way over Crown lands and gave the company free lands required for stations and divisional townsites. On the prairies, Mackenzie and Mann had built most of their lines with the help of their own construction company, Mackenzie, Mann & Co., and its reputation as a railway builder was not of the highest. But the main line through British Columbia was to be built in a more substantial manner. The first construction contract was signed on June 23, 1910, for the section from Hope to Port Mann. The contract for the remaining mileage was given out in 1911. Building through the Fraser Canyon cost more than estimated and the railway soon ran into financial trouble. Great difficulty was experienced in the rock work throughout the canyon, and a huge rock slide came down at Hells Gate on February 23, 1914, completely blocking the narrow passage and doing untold damage to salmon spawning. Contrary to popular belief, this was not caused by blasting of the Canadian Northern right-of-way, for in this area the work had been done a year previously. The last spike was driven at a spot near Basque, 59 miles west of Kamloops Junction, on January 15, 1915.

Outside of the business created by construction, the railway had little impact on the economy of B.C. The main interest lay in its grand expansion plans, particularly in the city of Vancouver. The promise of the railway company to build a 250-room hotel in the city long remained a point of contention to its citizens. Outside of railway construction, the investments made by Mackenzie and Mann in B.C. industries in the hope of creating traffic for the railway were of major importance. The sawmill of the Canadian Western Lumber Co. at Fraser Mills became the largest in the Empire. The Comox Logging & Railway Co. on Vancouver Island ran the largest logging railway in the west. Canadian Colleries (Dunsmuir) Ltd. dominated the Vancouver Island coal mining industry. All were run by money raised to a large degree in London by Mackenzie and Mann.

A unique and highly successful project undertaken by Foley, Welch & Stewart was the building of the Connaught Tunnel at Glacier, B.C., on the main line of the C.P.R. in Rogers Pass. Bids were asked of the trade in early 1913 and they got the contract, not because they were the lowest bidder, but because they undertook to do the work in faster time. Their method of construction, devised by J. W. Stewart and approved by John C. Sullivan, chief engineer of C.P.R. Western lines, entailed the boring of a working tunnel or "pioneer heading" outside of the location where the regular tunnel was to be bored. It was thus possible to keep progress going in the pioneer tunnel, make enlargements of the main one, blast and take

46

away the fallen rock continuously. The project was finished 11 months ahead of contract time, at a substantial saving on the contract price.

J. W. Stewart was a remarkable man, outstanding among contractors. In the words of Sir Richard McBride, he "had an unchallenging standing as a railway builder." Born in the Highlands of Scotland in 1862, he came to Canada as a youth. He was an axeman on the original survey party that laid out the C.P.R. grant, now the city of Vancouver. In 1890, he was division engineer on the Seattle-Montana Railway Co., a division of the J. J. Hill line, which was to link New Westminster with Seattle via Bellingham Bay.

He married one of the Moran sisters, a family of seven girls, of whom six married contractors. Peter Larson, John W. Stewart, Patrick Welch, and Jim Foley, all husbands of Moran girls, were partners in the contracting firms of Foley, Welch & Stewart or Foley Bros., Welch & Stewart.

As civilian work tapered off in the war years, Stewart, as Lieutenant-Colonel, recruited and took the first battalion of Canadian Railway troops overseas. They were a hand-picked lot, chosen from the ablest subcontractors and stationmen in the company's service.

The achievements of the Canadian Railway troops under Brigadier-General Stewart, astonished senior British and French military officers. In 1916, a light railway was built within a week on the Somme, a task which British engineers estimated would take six. They built a bridge in the Ypres area in three days which British officers said would take weeks.

As the war progressed, he became one of Sir Douglas Haig's official family at General Headquarters. Lloyd George gave him the job of organizing, supervising, and constructing all the British railways in France.

On September 12, 1918, Stewart was made director-general of construction for the British Army with the rank of Major-General.

On the Vancouver scene, he was one of the backers of the *Vancouver Sun* and, when it got into difficulties, he sent in his private secretary, R. J. Cromie, who did such a great job that he became publisher. Along with other Vancouver businessmen, he underwrote the establishment of a Scottish militia unit, the 72nd Seaforth Highlanders. Backed by many prominent Vancouverites, this unit became the social and military centre for Scottish activities in the city.

47

After the war he came back to Vancouver as one of its leading citizens. At his home on Angus Drive in Shaughnessy, he entertained dozens of leading British and Commonwealth leaders. The Prince of Wales, on his official tour in 1919, stayed with General Stewart at his home while in Vancouver.

It is hard to estimate the contributions which he, and firms with which he was associated, made to the development of B.C., but it is very extensive.

The years 1913-14 really ended the great period of railway building in B.C. Outside of the 80-mile P.G.E. extension to Prince George in 1949-53, no major railway project was undertaken until the W. A. C. Bennett government decided to open up the north. The P.G.E. was extended 250 miles northward to Fort St. John in 1958, and the 240 miles northeast to Dawson Creek. A spur was built to the new pulp and sawmilling town of Mackenzie in 1966. The extension to Fort St. John just 150 miles south of the B.C.-Yukon border came in 1971. A line is projected from Prince George 500 miles northwest to Dease Lake; some work has been done on this project, but at the present (1982), activity on this extension has been indefinitely discontinued.

The P.G.E. has done much to develop north-central B.C. The pulp mills and sawmills in this region depend extensively on the railway to get their products to market. It has stimulated much growth in Williams Lake, Quesnel, Prince George, and the towns further north. Its activities in Prince George, where it has established an industrial park, have been impressive. The machine shops of Prince George now make and export logging and sawmilling machinery to many countries on the Pacific Rim.

Railways as conveyors of bulk materials such as coal, wheat, sulphur, and potash, are once again coming into their own. The introduction of the unit train by C.P. Rail in 1970 was, and still is, a major factor in the ability to sell B.C. coal overseas. This created hundreds of jobs with supporting facilities in the East Kootenays. The necessity of upgrading the rail lines in B.C. came with the increased traffic in bulk materials. Major improvements, such as continuous welded rails in quarter mile lengths, have been made on the tracks of the main line of C.P. Rail between Vancouver and Calgary. In the field of motive power, the coming of the big-powered diesel has made possible longer trains carrying greater tonnage. In the Rogers Pass, every train carrying bulk commodities is now powered by 12 diesels generating 36,000 h.p. with loads of

11,000 or 12,000 tons. Constantly sections of the line are being double tracked or relocated to reduce the grade. Traffic on the mountain section has now reached the saturation point as the annual volume has doubled since 1970. To correct the situation five major projects are planned or underway. The cost will be over $250 million which will provide over 100 miles of double tracking through the mountains on the Calgary to Vancouver section. The biggest project yet to start is the 8.9-mile tunnel through Mount MacDonald 250 feet under the existing Connaught Tunnel. This is a necessity because due to the larger equipment now used the old Connaught Tunnel can only accommodate a single track although originally built for two. The completion of these projects will enable C.P. Rail to increase its capacity by four trains per day or an estimated 18 million more tons annually, a figure which is in excess of that carried at the present day by some United States main lines.

On the main line of the Canadian National in B.C. the grades are so slight that remote mid-train power units are not required. In spite of this advantage many improvements have been made to upgrade the track, such as concrete ties, continuous welded rails, reballasting, etc. It is hoped the main line will be entirely double tracked from Edmonton to Vancouver by 1990.

Developments in the northeastern coal fields will generate much railway construction work in the eighties. $200 million will be spent by the Canadian National in upgrading the line between Prince George and Prince Rupert, within the next two years (1982-83) to carry the coal trains expected from Tumbler Ridge. B.C. Rail is building a branch from Anzac, 75 miles northeast of Prince George, to the coal fields. It will entail some major construction including two tunnels at an estimated cost of $170 million. Successful Canadian bidders on these projects were Emil Anderson Construction Co. of Hope, in partnership with the Foundation Co. of Canada, and the Commonwealth Construction Co. of Vancouver, with Guy E. Atkins of San Francisco. Employment in new construction on B.C. Rail for at least two years is bright. It is estimated 1,000 jobs will be required to bring the projects to completion in 1983.

In the last decade, the railways, with the ability to deliver quantities of bulk materials to the coast, have stimulated much building, particularly in harbour improvements in the Vancouver metropolitan area.

For 100 years, the railways have, and still are, playing a vital role in the building of British Columbia's economy. With the early railways came the eastern lumbermen from both Canada and the U.S. — James Maclaren of the Ottawa Valley; Aird Flavelle and Robert F. Thurston of southern Ontario; J. S. Emerson and J. H. Bloedel of Bellingham; and J. S. Bowman of St. Louis, to name a few. They built up great logging and sawmilling enterprises to cater, not only to the prairie market and the eastern seaboard, but offshore to Great Britain, China, and the Pacific Rim countries. It was the railways that made possible the development of the mines of the Kootenays and the Boundary country. They also supplied the raw materials to the smelters of Trail and Grand Forks. It was the railways, helped by the steamship companies, that raised Vancouver to metropolitan status. They opened up the north and materially assisted in building such cities as Prince George and Prince Rupert. The economy of north-central B.C. could stagnate without the railways as the pulp mills and sawmills depend so greatly on their services to ship their products to market. It is the grain, the coal, the potash, and the lumber brought by the railways that has enabled Vancouver to ship more bulk tonnage than any other port in North America.

CHAPTER TWO

TRANSPORTATION

River, Lake, and Coastal Steamers

In gold rush days, the prosperity of British Columbia depended largely upon the men, supplies, and gold bullion that flowed to and from the Cariboo mines. A vital link in this chain of communications between the coast and the interior were the Fraser River sternwheelers. This type of boat also played significant roles in the other gold rushes that took place within the province later in the century. The rush to the Stikine River in 1862 was by boat. The excitement caused by gold discoveries in the Omineca country in 1870 prompted the greatest feat in steamboating ever seen in B.C.'s inland waterways. G. B. Wright's sternwheeler, *Enterprise,* was taken off the Soda Creek-Quesnel run to go to the Omineca mines. She navigated the canyons below Fort George with the assistance of her passengers and ascended the Nechako River, finally arriving on Takla Lake — a feat which no other riverboat had ever accomplished, before or since. When the miners struck it rich in the Cassiar, the steamboat operators on the Fraser left with their boats for the Stikine, leaving just one to carry the whole river trade from Ladner to Yale.

The contributions these boats made to the B.C. economy at the time were of great significance but of very little lasting value. When trade on the Harrison-Lillooet route to the Cariboo declined, the once flourishing river port of Douglas became a ghost town. Hope, once the head of navigation on the Lower Fraser in the 70's, declined to the point where only a couple of cabins were occupied. Once the gold fever had subsided, Yale became a small village and, even today, is of little commercial importance. The first generation of sternwheelers, though possessed of glamour and excitement, cut no trails, built no roads, and established no industries or communities of major size.

It fell to the second generation of river and lake boats (those which acted as feeders to railway lines) to make their mark as builders of B.C. In the early 1890's, the economy of B.C. started to boom. Developments in the Kootenays brought the rich silver-lead mines of that region into production. The Kootenay mines were different from those earlier worked on the banks of the Fraser and in the Cariboo. The metals were found in hard rock and were difficult to recover. This required large amounts of capital and costly underground workings. Major industrial plants had to be set up to crush and process the ore. To extract the metal from the ore, smelters, equipped with complicated machinery and staffed by many people, had to be built. Machinery for the mines had to be shipped in and the ore taken out to the smelters. This entailed the building of settled communities to serve as smelter towns and distribution points for supplies to the mines. It required a system of communications where people and goods could be transported in safety and speed at reasonable costs. Thus, the development of the mineral wealth of the Kootenays had to wait upon the coming of an adequate transportation system. Construction of railways, in such a mountainous country, required huge amounts of capital and a vast army of workers — far more than would be required to build a fleet of boats to run on the lakes and rivers which traversed the region. The railways competing for the trade of the Kootenays were the Canadian Pacific in the north and the Great Northern in the south. From Revelstoke, on the main line of the C.P.R. in the north, a line of sternwheelers was established connecting that point with Robson and Trail via the Arrow Lakes. From Bonners Ferry on the south, which connected with the Great Northern, other lake boats ran to Nelson and the mining communities on the shores of Kootenay Lake. The Canadian service from Revelstoke was run by Columbia and Kootenay Steam Navigation Co. It had been organized by a group of B.C. businessmen, which included Captain John Irving, manager of the Canadian Pacific Navigation Co., F. S. Barnard of Victoria, son of the founder of Barnard's Express, and J. A. Mara, a leading Kamloops citizen.

The Columbia and Kootenay Steam Navigation Co. (C.K.S.N. for short) was a vital link in the growth of such communities as Arrowhead, Comaplix, Nakusp, and the mining settlements in the Slocan. The C.P.R., in 1893, built the 27-mile spur from Revelstoke to Arrowhead, making that point the terminus of the steamers. At Comaplix was a big sawmill, originally started by English interests, and then sold to S. H. Bowman, the St. Louis lumberman. Nakusp also had its lumber mills, a shipyard and the Nakusp & Slocan Railway underwritten by the C.P.R. to capture the traffic from the mines in the Slocan. Its competitor, the Kaslo & Slocan Railway, delivered its freight to Kaslo on Kootenay Lake where the American boats took it to Bonners Ferry and the Great Northern. The C.K.S.N. also ran boats on Kootenay Lake in competition and was a major factor in the building up of Nelson as a smelter town and distribution centre for the West Kootenays.

The millions of dollars pouring into the Kootenay mines, frenzied railway construction, and booming communities, plus the strong position held by James J. Hill and the Spokane businessmen in the trade of the Kootenays, prompted the C.P.R. to buy the C.K.S.N. in 1896 for $200,000. Along with the deal came Captain James W. Troup who was to be the future architect of the Princess fleet of the C.P.R.'s British Columbia Coast Service. The C.P.R. then set up a new division, the B.C. Lake & River Service, which was to contribute so much in the building of the communities in the Kootenays and Okanagan.

The emphasis was now not only on taking people from place to place, but also in transporting them in comfort. The new boats that the C.P.R. built and put into service had wide decks, comfortable cabins, lounges and dining rooms, and were tastefully decorated. The *Minto*, launched at Nakusp November 19, 1898, for the Arrow Lakes, served for 56 years and became a household word for comfort and reliability. The *Moyie*, launched at Nelson October 22, 1898, held the same reputation on Kootenay Lake. The C.P.R.'s long-range plans, to attract tourists to the Kootenays and the Okanagan (first formulated in 1906), stimulated considerable commercial activity, especially in the lake shipyards.. The first of the new breed of "super sternwheelers," the *Kuskanook*, was built in the east and assembled in the C.P.R.'s Nelson shipyard in May 1906. Then came the 1,700-ton *Bonnington* launched at Nakusp, April 24, 1911. The *Nasookin*, weighing 1,869 tons and the largest sternwheeler to run on B.C. lakes, was built at Port Arthur in 1913 and assembled at Nelson. She was the last of the line, and outshone all the other boats in the lake and, with her huge size, was licenced to carry 550 passengers. Simultaneously, with the coming of these boats, considerable activity arose in the building of resort hotels, such as the one built by the C.P.R. at Balfour on Kootenay Lake. The completion of the rail link to the coast via the Kettle Valley heralded the closing of the era of steamboating on the lakes of southern B.C. Most of the bigger ones were retired in the late twenties. A few, like the *Minto* and the *Moyie*, struggled on into the fifties, more for sentimental rather than economic reasons.

The railway had come to Okanagan Landing from Sicamous in 1892 and, in the following year, was leased to the C.P.R. Thus, the Okanagan had rail communications for the first time with the rest of Canada. What it lacked was a feeder line on the lake to bring transportation down to Penticton and the southern end of the valley. The Governor General, Lord Aberdeen, had recently purchased the Coldstream Ranch near Vernon, setting in motion a wide spread interest in Okanagan lands. The C.P.R., ever alert for new traffic, decided to build a sternwheeler (the *Aberdeen*) to ply Okanagan Lake. Built at Okanagan Landing, it slid into the water May 3, 1893. It was the first luxury sternwheeler seen in the interior. She possessed an observation lounge, a dining room complete with stewards and tablecloths, a bar, and staterooms. The schedule called for a tri-weekly service staying overnight at Penticton and coming back the next day. How much she contributed to the building of the lakeside communities is now beyond estimation. It is known that she brought tens of thousands of fruit trees for the new Okanagan orchards. In the mineral development to the south, she helped create half a dozen Boundary country communities such as Midway, Greenwood, Boundary Falls, and Grand Forks. The sternwheeler *Aberdeen* was the only way that passengers and much-needed machinery could be sent to the gold mine at Hedley.

In the 1900's more and more settlers came into the Okanagan. They were of an unusual type — Britishers with capital but little horticultural knowledge who came to establish a way of life full of sport and social graces which they had somehow been unable to do in the homeland. To meet the demands for this traffic the C.P.R. built another sternwheeler, the *Okanagan*. Then, railway construction days hit Penticton with the extension westward to Princeton, and ultimately to Hope. The town became a major distribution centre, with land prices rising three, four, and five hundred percent. In 1914, at Okanagan Landing was built the $180,000 *Sicamous*, the last of the luxury sternwheelers on Okanagan Lake, now a tourist attraction and restaurant on the waterfront at Penticton. The completion of the Kettle Valley Railroad in 1916 and the coming of the automobile roads terminated all steamboat services on Okanagan Lake. As with the Arrow Lakes service and the sternwheelers

54

on Kootenay Lake, the residents of those communities which these boats helped to build no longer hastened down to the wharves to welcome their coming.

From its formation in 1883 to its purchase by the C.P.R. in 1901 the dominant factor in the B.C. coastal steamboat scene was the Canadian Pacific Navigation Co. Ltd. Prior to this date coastal shipping (what there was of it) was the monopoly of the Hudson's Bay Company or in the hands of private ship owners who were mainly individuals of strong and eccentric personalities. Outside of the Hudson's Bay Company, none had the financial resources that would enable them to establish first-class scheduled services. It was the coming boom in railway construction that brought together the management of the Hudson's Bay Company, Captain John Irving of Fraser River fame, R. P. Rithet, leading commission merchant of Victoria, Peter McQuade, the ship chandler, and Robert Dunsmuir. For the first time, there was in British Columbia a group of businessmen who could command the credit or the capital to build and operate first-class modern steamers. The 14-vessel fleet that these entrepreneurs took over comprised all makes and sizes, from the 932 gross ton *Princess Louise* built in 1869, to the *Otter* of 291 gross tons built in 1862 at Blackwall for the Hudson's Bay Company. It was a shipping monopoly and, once the company was established, the principals were willing to retire some of the older boats and either purchase or build better ones. Thus, it came about that the company was the first in B.C. to build a modern screw steamer on its own account which was to serve as a prototype for successive generations of coastal passenger boats. The *Islander*, a steel twin-screw steamer of 1,495 gross tons with triple expansion engines and cruising speed of 12 knots, was built under the direction of Captain John Irving by Napier, Shanks & Bell of Yoker-Glasgow in 1888. It was the first of many vessels that, in after years, the C.P.R.'s B.C. Coast Service would build in Great Britain. Its building was financed by a loan from the Bank of British Columbia which would total $247,000 at the end of 1888. It incorporated many of the latest features in shipbuilding such as two screws instead of the usual one, the latest in marine propulsion triple expansion engines, and a hull of steel instead of iron. No expenses were spared in the interior fittings and her excellent dining facilities set a standard for many a later coastal ship.

Captain John Irving gave much thought to the arrangements for bringing the vessel out. It was a new venture which was to be

55

repeated dozens of times in succeeding years. The crew had to be very carefully picked with concessions made to their families. "If any of the crew feel inclined to bring their families and stay in this Country," wrote Captain Irving to Captain George W. Robertson on August 7, 1888, "I could give them a cheap rate and take it out of their salaries as earned in small installments, making a charge of £10.0.0 fare for full grown persons and one half fare for children under fifteen years of age." She came out via the Horn, in the late autumn of 1888. The first officer was Captain John T. Walbran, who became an authority on B.C. coastal matters and wrote a standard work on the subject under the title of *British Columbia Coast Names*.

The *Islander* created many precedents. Starting in 1890 and for succeeding summers, it made widely advertised tourist trips to the north. The clientele were mostly Americans and stops were made at Wrangell, Sitka, and Juneau. In July 1892, the C.P.R. sponsored their first Alaskan cruise on the *Islander*, forerunner of the hundreds of such cruises taken on C.P.R. boats up to the present day. Tragedy fell when the *Islander* struck a submerged rock or iceberg off Douglas Island, Alaska, about 2 a.m. August 22, 1901, and sank within 16 minutes. A similar accident happened seventeen years later when the *Princess Sophia* impaled herself on a reef in Lynn Canal in a hurricane and, two days after, slid off and foundered with all the 343 people aboard.

The Canadian Pacific Navigation had a motley fleet and although efforts were made to rationalize it and improve the services not much progress was made. The company always seemed to be short of money to build new ships. For most of the time in its career, it was in debt to the Bank of British Columbia or the B.C. Land and Investment Agency. It might very well have been that the shareholders were too anxious for their dividends. In the seventeen years of its corporate life, dividends were paid in fifteen. The fleet was mortgaged for considerably more than it was worth. Service, which was never superb in the first place, degenerated. Perhaps it was a wise move for them to sell out to the Canadian Pacific Railway in 1901.

The immediate benefit was the upgrading of services, particularly the Vancouver-Victoria run. In the early months of 1902, contracts were given for the building of two new boats. Of paramount interest to British Columbians was a contract for the construction of a single-screw wooden steamer for the northern coast and Alaska route. This was given to the British Columbia Marine Railway Co. (Bullen's yard) at Esquimalt. The other was given to Swan & Hunter, Newcastle-on-Tyne, for the Vancouver-Victoria run. Both Bullen's boat, the *Princess Beatrice*, and Swan & Hunter's *Princess Victoria* proved highly successful.

The fact that a major coastal passenger boat could be built in B.C. gave the provincial shipyards a considerable boost. It was a feat which was duplicated many times in the coming years. Eventually, the B.C. Coast Service of the C.P.R. had five more built in the province — two at Bullen's yard in Esquimalt — *Princess Royal* (1907) and *Princess Maquinna* (1913), one at Yarrow's — *Motor Princess* (1923), and two at the Burrard Drydock, North Vancouver — *Princess Louise* (1921) and the *Carrier Princess* (1923). In 1890, to supplement their fleet, the Union Steamship Co. of B.C. ordered the building of three new steel ships. These were built in Glasgow (in sections) and then shipped in the hold of a freighter around the Horn to Vancouver. They were then assembled on land purchased by the company on Coal Harbour, where the forest had to be cleared to make room for the ways. The *Comox*, as she came down the way, made marine history as the first steel vessel ever launched in British Columbia. Some of the benefits of an expanding coastal trade were well reported by the *News Advertiser* of October 25, 1891:

The Union Steamship Co. . . . have done a great deal of good for Vancouver, as they will not only work up trade to this port, but they are also giving employment to a large number of men, and thus put considerable sums of money in circulation.

The Union Steamship Co. continued patronizing local yards having four more boats built over the years — *Chehalis*, 1897 (False Creek); *Coquitlam*, 1901 (Coal Harbour); *Capilano*, 1919 (B.C. Marine Ways, Vancouver); and *Chilkoot*, 1920 (Burrard Drydock, North Vancouver).

The growth of the coastal trade stimulated much activity in the setting up of local ship repairing and shipbuilding facilities. The first of the modern yards was Bullen's in Esquimalt, better known to a couple of generations of shipping men as Yarrow's. By 1911, it was employing 300 men and, due to its proximity to the government drydock, was doing major overhauls. At the end of 1913, it was bought by Sir Alfred Yarrow, the great British shipbuilder of naval destroyers and other fast craft. Its sale to one of England's leading shipbuilders was a tribute to the strength and vitality of B.C.'s coastal shipping. The other great shipbuilding and repair yard was that of Wallace's, now known as Burrard-Yarrow's Corp. It was founded on leased land by Mr. Alfred Wallace as the Wallace Shipyards Ltd. at False Creek in 1894. Originially, it was a one-man backyard operation to make fishing boats. Business was booming, and he decided to go into tugboat and cannery tender construction. During the next four years, he received contracts for, and built, 14 good-sized boats including a Fisheries Patrol cruiser for the Canadian government and a ferry for the city of North Vancouver. In 1906, he moved to the foot of Lonsdale in North Vancouver and built machine shops and a 1,600-ton marine way. It is of interest to note that the first boat to come up on the slip was the Union Co.'s *Camosun*. For the first nine years of the twentieth century, the firm built 22 steamers, 14 motor vessels, 18 barges and scows, and two ferries. About 250 men were hired.

In the boom period of 1905-13, shipbuilding and ship repairing became important B.C. industries. In the abnormal war years of 1914-20, the industry broke all records. The output of B.C. yards, in the shape of steel and wooden cargo boats and auxiliary powered lumber schooners, reached the astonishing total of 98. Up to this point, no propelling machinery for cargo boats had been made in B.C. The Wallace yards were the first to set up foundries and machine shops to build ships' engines in the province. Thus, when the yard built the luxury liner *Princess Louise* for the C.P.R.'s B.C. Coast Service in 1919, the engines were built in the machine shops on the site and installed by yard employees. They were the first of their kind and the largest marine engines built in Canada up to that time.

During World War II over two hundred 8,000- to 10,000-ton cargo boats were built in B.C. as well as naval vessels of all types: frigates, corvettes, minesweepers, maintenance and victualling ships, and the conversion of 19 U.S.-designed and built hulls to small aircraft carriers for the Royal Navy at the Burrard Drydock. The biggest conversion job ever undertaken on this coast was done by Yarrows at Esquimalt to convert the *Queen Elizabeth* from a passenger liner to a troopship.

In the post-war years, the B.C. yards have done some outstanding work. A replacement for the Canadian National Vancouver-Prince Rupert Service was the *Prince George*. Construction of this 5,800-ton ship was commenced in 1946 and launched in October 1947.

Burrard Drydock built a passenger-freighter for the Canadian National's Halifax-West Indies service, the largest vessel to be laid down in a B.C. shipyard. To service the tug and barge industry, Yarrows, in 1950, switched from building barges of wood to steel. Four years later, B.C. naval architects, in co-operation with both Yarrows and Burrard, designed and built the first self-dumping log-barge, a technical innovation which revolutionized log hauling in the coastal forest industry. Barges are now being built well over 450 feet long, with a beam of 96 feet. To haul these, very powerful tugs are now necessary, with engines up to 3,600 to 4,100 h.p. Most of these tugs have been built in B.C. The first self-propelled, self-loading, and self-dumping barge, the *Haida Monarch*, was built by Yarrows in 1974 for the account of MacMillan-Bloedel at a cost of $8.2 million. Barging is now done by B.C. firms on the Pacific down to Los Angeles and up to Alaska. At the government drydock in Esquimalt, Burrard-Yarrows is now handling repair and overhaul work on the largest of vessels — giant oil tankers and bulk carriers of 80-100,000 tons and over.

A new floating drydock, built by Mitsubishi in Japan and towed across the Pacific, accommodating vessels up to 75,000 tons, is now in service (1982) at the North Vancouver yard of Burrard-Yarrows. This marks a major step in providing Vancouver with ship repairing facilities so necessary to a major port. The industry has come a long way since W. F. Bullen established his business in 1893.

One of the lasting benefits given by the creation of these two big coastal shipping companies (B.C. Coast Service of C.P.R. and the Union Steamship Co.) was reliable and frequent access from coastal points to the metropolitan areas of Vancouver and Victoria. Prospective settlers came to make their homes on the islands. Through the regular and reliable services, coast settlements became established and prospered. Loggers, cannery operators, and lumber companies relied upon these coastal services to supply them with workers, provisions, and supplies. The great wholesale houses in Vancouver and Victoria depended upon the coastal shipping for much of their business. A great provincial expansion of trade occurred in the boom years 1905-13. It also witnessed the greatest growth in the coastal fleets. The C.P.R. increased its fleet by nine vessels, the Union Steamship Co. doubled its fleet from five to ten. The Grand Trunk Pacific Railway entered the coastal trade in 1910 by opening up a Vancouver-Victoria-Prince Rupert run with the *Prince Rupert* and *Prince George*. Both these ships were markedly

59

superior to any that had as yet seen service on the northern run. From Prince Rupert, the G.T.P. inaugurated a new service to the Queen Charlottes.

The quality of service offered by the C.P.R. ships on its premier run (Vancouver-Victoria-Seattle) was superb. It commenced on September 23, 1908, and was to create an increasing amount of traffic between these cities for the next fifty years. Thousands of American tourists were attracted to B.C., creating demand for additional hotel and tourist facilities in the two coastal cities. To cater to these ships and other coastal services, the C.P.R. built extensive wharves and terminal buildings on the property that they had acquired from the C.P.N. on Belleville Street, Victoria. The head office building of the B.C. Coast Service, designed by Francis Rattenbury, is still one of the outstanding buildings in Victoria's inner harbour. For the short Vancouver-Nanaimo run, the C.P.R. purchased a fast Clyde excursion steamer, noted in marine history as the second passenger ship equipped with turbine engines. Renamed the *Princess Patricia*, she did the trip in 2¼ hours, a vast improvement on the service previously offered. On the northern run were the older ships — *Princess Royal, Princess May,* and the *Princess Beatrice*, covering the coast from Vancouver to Skagway.

The C.P.R. ran the prestige routes, but it was the Union Steamship Co. that operated the work boats. From the company's dock at the foot of Carrall Street, Union ships serviced the logging camps and canneries. There was so much business on these logging and cannery runs that it was not unusual for a ship to dock in Vancouver in the afternoon, load up with freight, and be out again in the evening. So close were the logging camps that in a four hours' watch, ten or eleven stops would be made. Union ships made history. The *Camosun* was the first steamer on the coast to install a wireless (June 1905). In the fall of 1907, she arrived in Vancouver with 6,000 cases of salmon, and on the next trip, with the closure of the canneries, brought down 400 passengers who slept on the deck or in the corridors. In October 1909, she landed at the dock in Vancouver from Swanson Bay with 106 bales of pulp for transshipment to Kobe, Japan — the first of many millions of bales of pulp exported from B.C. All this brought increasing trade to Vancouver, and was a factor in the rise of the great wholesale houses, like Malkin's and Kelly Douglas on Water Street, Fleck Brothers on West Pender, and McLennan & McFeely on Cordova. In the inter-war years, the company went into the excursion and summer resort business. Hotels, dance pavilions, and parks were built on Bowen Island and at Selma Park on Sechelt Peninsula. The three "ladies," *Alexandria*, *Cecilia*, and *Cynthia*, were brought out from England to run as excursion ships and this side of the business was built up.

It is impossible to estimate the extent which these coastal ships contributed to the build-up of the coast economy. Without adequate transportation, the industrial towns of Powell River, Port Alice, Ocean Falls, and Swanson Bay could not have survived. The building of Prince Rupert and the Grand Trunk Pacific Line eastward depended on men and supplies brought up by coastal steamer. The mines at Stewart, Anyox, and Princess Royal Island could not have been developed without steamship links with the south. In pre-World War I days, innumerable hand loggers used the ships to keep them in supplies and to take them down to Vancouver for their monthly or semi-annual celebrations. Without them, the bigger lumber companies could not have kept their logging camps supplied with loggers, provisions, boom chains, etc. The ninety-odd salmon canneries, situated on the coast, depended upon the shipping companies to bring up the help when the season opened and bring down the canned salmon when it closed. All these activities encouraged a great expansion of trade in the metropolitan areas of Vancouver and Victoria. This, in turn, sparked more people, more building, and more growth.

Today, the road and airplane has taken away the trade of the coastal steamers. The great fleets of the C.P.R.'s B.C. Coast Service, the Union Steamship Co., and the Grand Trunk Pacific, have disappeared. Government ferries now shuttle back and forth and are merely water extension of the provincial highways system. With the exception of the B.C. Ferries northern run to Ocean Falls and Prince Rupert, no passenger service is offered by boat to the coastal points. The freight that is shipped by water is barged. Air services and roads now take care of their transportation needs.

Street Railways and Inter-Urbans

Between 1888 and 1900, a revolution in urban transportation occurred in North America. Previously, there were street railways but the cars, with few exceptions, were hauled by horses or mules. The street railway was the answer to the needs of the rapidly growing cities. For a majority of their citizens, the work place was the city core. Thousands required transportation to and from the central core daily, and horse-driven streetcars could not meet the demand. Thus, necessity compelled the majority to live near their work places, creating dense overcrowding and slum conditions within the vicinity of the core. The problem was to find a better means of urban transportation.

The answer seemed to be in electrically-driven streetcars. Electric street railways had been operating in U.S. cities in a small way from about 1883, but the technical problems were either unknown or unsolved. It was not until the success of the electrically powered Richmond, Virginia, street railway had become apparent that capitalists and business entrepreneurs showed any interest. The Richmond street railway was the first large system to be electrified. Forty cars, together with 12 miles of track, was by far a greater installation than any of the other electric railways running at that time. In the space of the next two years, over 200 electric street railways were projected either under construction or in operation in the United States.

This was the background to the promotion and construction of the first street railways in British Columbia. David Higgins, prominent Victoria journalist and politician, Joseph Hunter, civil engineer who built Dunsmuir's Esquimalt & Nanaimo Railway, and Thomas Shotbolt, Victoria merchant, who, under the title National Electric Tramway and Light Co., reached an agreement with the city of Victoria to "construct a street railway within the city limits." Work was to start October 1, 1889, and was to be completed by July 1, 1890. By February 1890, the original installation had been laid down — four miles of track with a fleet of four electrically driven cars. A year later, the mileage had grown to 11½ with 11 cars. This was the first electric street railway in the Canadian west and the third in Canada, with only the cities of Windsor and St. Catharines preceding it. The benefits were realized early, as shown in the following editorial published in the *Colonist*, February 23, 1890:

The establishment of the streetcar service will, at once, considerably increase the area of the city and make available many lovely spots which were considered, a few months ago, too distant from the centre of business to be valuable for the sites of residences.

The emergence of the electric street railways was closely tied to two trends that were very evident in nineteenth-century history — the growth of the cities and urban land development. To the real estate promoter it was a technological innovation of surprising appeal. It quickly became evident that, if a real estate developer could persuade a streetcar company to put a line through his property on the outskirts of a city, then his fortune was made. In the eighties, the potentials in British Columbia had attracted some of the best promoters in the real estate business. Vancouver became a mecca for them. In 1894, the directory listed 62 real estate firms doing business in Vancouver. The leaders, including C. D. Rand of Rand Bros., David and Isaac Oppenheimer, Henry V. Edmonds and John Wulffsohn of Wulffsohn & Bewicke, held large property interests in Vancouver and vicinity, and were active in promoting electric street railways in the lower mainland. David and Isaac Oppenheimer, along with C. D. Rand, were major boosters of the Vancouver Electric Railways and Light Co. and financially interested. David Oppenheimer, in partnership with Henry V. Edmonds, were the major backers of the Westminster and Vancouver Tramway Co. which built the inter-urban line between these two cities. It turned out that they were more interested in selling real estate along this route than in operating an electric railway.

As explained earlier, interest in electric railways was high in the early nineties. The public viewed the new technologies being created by this new source of energy (electricity) as the forerunners of a golden age. Not only in the lower mainland were businessmen laying plans for the construction of electric railways, but also in the interior. In 1893, Colonel John M. Burke, a former governor of the state of Idaho and now a private banker in Kaslo, formed the Kaslo & Slocan Tramway Co. to build tramways on the streets of Kaslo and, if funds permitted, to extend them up the valley of Kaslo Creek.

Two years previously, the Okanagan Land and Development Co., with the financial support of John Wulffsohn of Vancouver, was given power by the provincial legislature to construct and operate tramways in the towns of Enderby and Vernon. On the coast, George Norris, publisher of the *Nanaimo Fress Press*, and his local associates, which included both a real estate and an insurance agent, incorporated the Nanaimo Electric Tramways Co. Ltd. "to operate a single or double track street railway . . . along such streets within the City of Nanaimo as the Mayor and Council of said City of Nanaimo may direct." When the C.P.R. looked into the advantages of building a branch across Lulu Island to Steveston and set up the

Vancouver & Lulu Island Railway Co. (1891), even they stipulated that "such line of railway to be operated by steam, horse, or electric power."

All these plans proved premature, as neither the capital nor the traffic was forthcoming. The only scheme to blossom into construction and operation was a small installation set up to service the needs of Nelson. British investors were keenly interested in the Kootenays, the silver-lead mines of the Slocan and the smelter at Nelson. It was Sir Joseph Trutch, provincial road builder and engineer, who was one of the organizers of the Hall smelter at Nelson. The commercial potential of the Kootenays was well known in London financial circles. Therefore, it was not surprising to find the dominant company in the street railway industry in Great Britain, British Electric Traction, looking with favour upon a proposal put forward by Captain T. J. Duncan and a group of Nelson businessmen. The result was the incorporation of the Nelson Electric Tramway Co. and an agreement with the city council of Nelson. Construction started in the summer of 1899, with regular service commencing December 27 of that year. The inducement which had prompted E. Garcke, the chairman of British Electric Traction, was anticipation that the tramway company would be able to sell West Kootenay Light & Power electricity to the city of Nelson. This was where the profit was to come from. The city council took the opposite way, setting up a municipal generating plant. The tramway company soon ran into difficulties and the British owners asked the city to take over its operation. In the spring of 1909 they sold the installation to the city of Nelson for $10,000. As the only town outside of the lower mainland in B.C. with a streetcar system, the city acquired a certain status symbol which was "none finer west of Winnipeg." Lured by generous concessions including free power, tax exemptions, and guaranteed bonds, it was turned back to a group of local businessmen. They could not make it profitable and it finally ended up again in the hands of the city. It was municipally run until 1949 when buses took over. The population of Nelson, throughout these years, never climbed over 11,600. The significance of the Nelson street railway was that it was the only one outside of the B.C. Electric system that was actually constructed and put into operation in British Columbia.

In the late nineties, the Boundary country enjoyed a copper boom, and a tramway between Greenwood and Phoenix was promoted by several mining men in the area. The Greenwood-Phoenix

Tramway Co. Ltd. opened offices in Greenwood. In 1901 or 1902, the company closed its doors, but the two mining executives who were behind the venture, Duncan McIntosh and George Collins, remained to pursue more profitable avenues.

In the winter of 1910, in Nanaimo, another mineralized area on Vancouver Island, a Vancouver engineering firm spoke for a group of business people under the name of B.C. Hydraulic Power Co., to seek municipal and provincial assistance for a proposed street railway in Nanaimo and its vicinity. To make an intercity connection, it was planned to extend the line to Ladysmith. The provincial government was asked to provide a bonus per mile for this track, with "additional privileges for distribution of energy and exemption from taxation." Needless to say, Premier Sir Richard McBride tactfully replied, "I regret very much that it has not been possible to grant your request."

The intimate connection between real estate development and urban transportation is well illustrated by the activities of the Oppenheimer brothers, David and Isaac. In Vancouver's pioneer days, they had their financial pulse in practically every commercial enterprise of any importance. As large property owners, they were interested in seeing that a street railway network would pass either through or near their land. Thus, the location of the original streetcar tracks laid out in 1889 reflected their desires. They held much property east of Main Street; the Powell Street line to Campbell Avenue was of major interest to them. In the depression of 1893, this route, along with Fairview, had to be abandoned. The Main Street and Powell Street lines joined and continued via Cordova to Hastings Street; then up Granville to a stop between Drake and Pacific. It was opened to the public on June 28, 1890. Originally, it had been planned as a horse-drawn operation. The directors had been in touch with several of the electrical manufacturing companies, asking for their best terms for supplying equipment. Finally, they were persuaded that electrical traction was the coming thing, mainly on the advice offered by James F. Garden, a professional engineer and later mayor of Vancouver. The half-built horse stables were scrapped; the rails were bonded and the horse cars built by the famous New York firm of John Stephenson & Co. (builders of horse-drawn streetcars since 1832) were changed to electric drive. Finally Angus MacDonald was appointed as a lineman, the first of many hundreds who have worked in this capacity for the B.C. Electric or the B.C. Hydro.

In 1892, the Fairview section was completed — the famous belt line which was a circular route through residential Fairview and downtown Vancouver. In the autumn of the following year, a severe business depression struck North America, culminating in an almost complete stoppage of trade. As the depression deepened, property values fell and the real estate market collapsed. Land became valueless and unsaleable at any price. Forty-five real estate firms either went into bankruptcy or withdrew from the business. The tramway, like other businesses, got into serious difficulties. Traffic declined because people no longer had any money to pay for streetcar rides. They either stayed at home or walked to work. Service on the Fairview line was suspended. The C.P.R., which had promised to hand over 68 lots in the district to the street railway company for their efforts in bringing in the line, refused to hand over the title. The tramway company was unable to raise money for a bond to be held in custody by the C.P.R. for continuation of service. The street railway properties were offered to the city for a price, but the voters turned down the bylaw. In this desperate situation, the Yorkshire Guarantee & Securities Corporation (an English mortgage and financial house recently established in Vancouver through the good offices of C. D. Rand) came to the rescue by buying debentures of the street railway company at a discount. One condition of this transaction which was to have far reaching effects was that the Yorkshire Corp. should have one director on the board. But still traffic declined. The Powell Street route was abandoned, causing greater strain on the Oppenheimers. The people of Vancouver had neither the money nor the credit for car fares. The Bank of British Columbia refused to extend any more credit and the bond holders took over.

The Vancouver Loan & Securities Corp. was one of many pioneer Vancouver commercial enterprises sponsored by the Yorkshire Guarantee Corp. In fact, they held the largest number of shares in that corporation, 16,500 against 13,387 held by W. G. Johnson and only 10,000 by Henry Town (who was chairman) out of the original issue of 80,000. The Vancouver Loan & Securities also had a financial interest in the Vancouver Improvement Co. but not the controlling interest which was held by G. P. Norton and the Yorkshire Guarantee. The two firms had close ties, William Farrell, the Vancouver manager for the Yorkshire Guarantee, was a director of the Vancouver Loan & Securities; William Sully, the Vancouver director of the Vancouver Loan & Securities was in frequent touch with G. P. Norton and the directors of the Yorkshire Guarantee in Huddersfield.

William Sully and W. C. Johnson of the Vancouver Loan and Securities were approached in the summer of 1893 by a Mr. War-brick who represented a group of Scottish capitalists.

"This gentleman," wrote William Sully, September 7, 1893, "is arranging a scheme for the reconstruction and amalgamation of the Vancouver Light and Street Railway Company and for placing the bonds of a new company in Europe."

The deal would involve the raising of between $1,000,000 and $1,500,000 with a strong local board of directors, including J. J. Trapp of New Westminster, David Oppenheimer, William Farrell of the Yorkshire Guarantee, and William Sully.

Back of all this can be seen the hand of Bruce Peebles Co. Ltd., a manufacturer of electrical equipment of Edinburgh. Originally makers of meters, etc. for the gas industry, they had recently entered the field of manufacturing electrical equipment. They were anxious to acquire overseas contracts and had interested a group of prominent Edinburgh businessmen who would be prepared to raise money to start overseas enterprises in the new field of electric traction and electric light.

The situation in Vancouver appeared ideal to take over the near bankrupt utilities and re-equip them with the latest in new machinery made in Edinburgh.

The proposal had the firm support of William Sully. In a letter dated September 9, 1893, to Mr. M. Milne, an English director of the Vancouver Loan & Securities, he wrote: "I have carefully considered the proposal and think it is one that should be entertained."

In spite of the high standing of the sponsors in the Scottish business world, the proposal never really got off the ground and it fell to the two major creditors of the tramway company to stage a reorganization at depression prices.

The two major creditors were the Bank of British Columbia and the Yorkshire Guarantee & Securities Corp.; G. P. Norton, the Huddersfield accountant (the man behind the Yorkshire Corp.), interested R. M. Horne-Payne, partner in the London stockbroking firm of Sperling & Co. Between them they raised enough money in England to buy the property from the street railway company at fire-sale prices. The Westminster & Vancouver Tramway Co. and the National Electric Tramway & Lighting Co. of Victoria were acquired under similar circumstances. These three companies were then joined together to form the British Columbia Electric Railway Co. which was to dominate the utility field in southwestern British Columbia for the next sixty years. Due to the fact that the Yorkshire Corp. held such large financial stakes in both Vancouver Street Railway and Westminster & Vancouver Tramway, its holdings in the B.C. Electric Railway Co. were considerable. G. P. Norton became an influential director of the new company. The property owners who had originally promoted the railway companies, the Oppenheimers and Henry V. Edmonds, lost out entirely. Much of their extensive holdings reverted back to the city for non-payment of taxes.

For the new owners, it was an opportune time to approach British investors in street railway matters. In the year previous to the formation of the B.C. Electric, British Electric Traction Co. Ltd. had been created. It was a giant corporation based in London which had been established to build a country-wide network of tramways. Electric tramways, in the eyes of British investors at that particular time, constituted a new technological-based industry with a vast potential for profit. Thus Horne-Payne, when he appealed to his London clientele, and G. P. Norton, when he appealed to the woollen manufacturers of the West Riding of Yorkshire, both received favourable responses. The money to launch the B.C. Electric came from these two sources, if not with enthusiasm, at least without undue effort. It is to be noted that in 1897, when the B.C. Electric was formed, only one major English city, Liverpool, had electrified its line. The changeover did not come in Bradford until 1898. Manchester was not completed until 1903 and Huddersfield, G. P. Norton's hometown, not until 1901. It was quite an adventurous step for any English group to take, especially in a place so far away as British Columbia.

The faith of Vancouverites in the growth of their city is phenomenal. It is based on a firm conviction that real estate values will appreciate. When lots began again to be sold in Fairview around 1897-98, confidence began to be restored. Extensions were made to existing lines. Pender Street was extended to Stanley Park, as was a new line, Davie Street.

Real estate was the key to the opening of new routes. In 1905, an agreement was reached with the C.P.R. which had far reaching effects on the future of the company. Under this arrangement, the

Roads

The technical work of the Royal Engineers in surveying, locating, and building the wagon roads so that the miners in the interior of B.C. could carry on their work was of inestimable value. Above is a picture of a plaque commemorating that work.

PHOTO: GOVERNMENT OF B.C.

Third and present Alexandra Bridge.

PHOTO: B.C. DEPARTMENT OF HIGHWAYS

Traction engine as built in 1865. The type ordered by Joseph Trutch for the Cariboo Road and never sent. Built by John Fowler and Sons, Leeds, England.

PHOTO: FOWLER PAPERS, UNIVERSITY OF READING

Thomson Road Steamer on streets of Glasgow, 1919.

PHOTO: SCOTTISH TRACTION ENGINE SOCIETY

Thomson Road Steamer and train as used on Cariboo Road.

Travel to the Cariboo in Edwardian days. A Winston 6-cylinder automobile of the B.C. Express Co. at Ashcroft.

Laying tracks by Onderdonk's crews in the lower Fraser Valley, 1884.

PHOTO: CANADIAN PACIFIC RAILWAY

First Safety Switch on the Big Hill, six miles east of Field, as it appeared in 1898.

PHOTO: CANADIAN PACIFIC RAILWAY

C.P.R. Engine No. 315, built by Baldwin in 1886, on the Big Hill between Hector and Field, 1890.

The Royal Train carrying the Duke and Duchess of York (afterwards King George V) at Field, British Columbia, October 1901. Note the use of five engines to haul ten cars.

River, Lake, and Coastal Steamers

The steamer *Islander* of the Canadian Pacific Navigation Co., creator of many precedents and the prototype of generations of coastal passenger boats.

PHOTO: FROM THE BOOK "CALIFORNIA AND ALASKA" BY WILLIAM SEWARD WEB, NEW YORK, 1890.

Bound for Atlin, the steamer *Gleaner* on Taku Arm, 1900.

PHOTO: B.C. DEPARTMENT OF MINES

Head Office B.C. Electric Railway Co. and Inter-urban Terminal, Vancouver, 1929.

PHOTO: B.C. POWER CORPORATION LTD., ANNUAL REPORT, 1929

City streetcar, Vancouver, 1929 model.

PHOTO: B.C. POWER CORPORATION LTD., ANNUAL REPORT, 1929

Air Transport

In a passenger car of a Zeppelin between Vancouver and Prince George as proposed by a group of Vancouver businessmen in 1910.

ILLUSTRATION: HARMSWORTH ENCYCLOPEDIA, 1915

A Curtis seaplane of the Royal Canadian Air Force at Alert Bay, 1920.

PHOTO: B.C. FOREST SERVICE

Grant McConachie, pioneer bush pilot and first president of C.P. Air.

The man who organized the first telephone company
in B.C., Edgar Crow Baker.

PHOTO: B.C. TELEPHONE CO.

Hammond Exchange of the B.C. Telephone Co., 1910.

PHOTO: B.C. TELEPHONE CO.

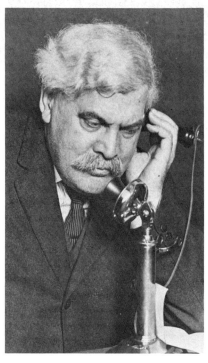

Switchboard, main office, B.C. Telephone Co., Empire Building, Vancouver, 1905.

PHOTO: B.C. TELEPHONE CO.

William Farrell, pioneer businessman of Vancouver. A founder of B.C. Telephone Co. and its chief officer for many years.

PHOTO: B.C. TELEPHONE CO.

Satellite receiving station of Teleglobe Canada, Cowichan Lake, B.C.

PHOTO: B.C. GOVERNMENT

Arthur Thomas Busby, Registrar of the Supreme Court of British Columbia and Acting Postmaster General without remuneration, from 1866 until Confederation in 1871. Never officially appointed to the later position but only under the verbal order of the Honourable Arthur N. Birch, administrator of the government, in 1866.

PHOTO: PROVINCIAL ARCHIVES, VICTORIA

A carrier of overseas mail from Vancouver. Royal Mail Steamship *Aroangi* at Pier B-C, Vancouver, October 1948.

PHOTO: COLLECTION G.W.T.

B.C. Electric was to lease and operate the Vancouver & Lulu Island line as an electric railway. Also, the streetcar company was to handle all C.P.R. traffic designated for or originating in the area. This gave the B.C. Electric a new function — that of a terminal railway which would provide a source of considerable income in the future years. The agreement provided streetcar access to Kitsilano Beach over C.P.R. lines, a district which that railway had long wanted to develop as a residential area.

The period 1905-13 witnessed the greatest boom in B.C. history and also saw the greatest expansion in the lower mainland streetcar network. The main thrust in this period by the B.C. Electric was to obtain liberal franchises from the surrounding municipalities to operate streetcar lines connecting with the Vancouver city routes. North Vancouver, in 1905, was protected by a fifty-year franchise and a perpetual monopoly for lighting; South Vancouver, in 1908, had a forty-year franchise with municipal tax exemptions on company property for ten years. Point Grey proved the most difficult. A line south on Granville to 25th Avenue was built under the impression that the council would be prepared to grant a forty-year franchise. It turned out that the councillors were thinking in terms of 15 years. Service was suspended until the council came around to the company's way of thinking. In the western section of Point Grey, the 4th Avenue extension was held up for four years because, in the words of H. R. Sperling, B.C. Electric's general manager, "it was impossible to reach a reasonable arrangement with the Municipality."

The end of this period saw the completion of the streetcar and inter-urban network in the lower mainland. There were three inter-urban lines built in this period, two of which had private right-of-way access into Vancouver. In 1913, with liberal franchises, restrictive clauses prohibiting competition in both Vancouver and Victoria, and inter-urban lines outside the jurisdiction of municipal control, the B.C. Electric was in a position of great strength.

The use of electric power for intercity transportation was recognized almost simultaneously with its use in electrifying street railways. The first intercity electric railway in British Columbia was sponsored by David Oppenheimer of Vancouver and Henry Y. Edmonds of New Westminster, both large land owners. As it had been with the proposed street railways, this was to be a means of helping to sell some of the promoters' real estate. The objective of the Westminster & Vancouver Tramway Co., incorporated April

26, 1890, was "to construct . . . a single or doubled track tramway . . . between the limits of the said cities." It was the first inter-urban to be built on the Pacific coast and the second in Canada, preceded only by the seven-mile line between St. Catharines and Thorold in southern Ontario, which was electrified in 1887. The transmission of electric power was in its experimental stages and, to carry it 14½ miles as proposed between New Westminster and Vancouver, was almost beyond the technical capacity of the time. A special powerhouse had to be built at an isolated spot in the forest named Edmonds, some three miles from New Westminster. The equipment consisted of four steam engines driving Edison dynamos. In a province blessed with abundant water power, it is surprising to find that the early electrical installations were steam-driven. Its isolated location is shown by the fact that the company had to erect a boarding house for its workers, no other accommodation being available. When fire broke out in one of the dynamos, the company could not raise enough money for a replacement, and this was one of the contributing factors in its subsequent bankruptcy. Among other technical innovations was the installation of a telephone system with portable instruments provided in each car so that, in case of emergency, instant communication could be made with either the powerhouse or the office. This seemed to be a necessary step since the only other stopping place outside of the two city terminals was Central Park. The whole length of the line ran through a 100-foot right-of-way slashed out of dense forest. The depression of 1893 killed any land sales and the technical difficulties forced the company into bankruptcy, the major creditors being Yorkshire Guarantee & Securities and the Bank of British Columbia. The properties were auctioned off by Sheriff J. D. Hall of Vancouver and T. J. Trapp of New Westminster and sold at reduced prices to the representative of J. Horne-Payne and G. P. Norton. Henry V. Edmonds' holdings of land were sold by the sheriff on December 14, 1894, in an effort to recover over $150,000 he owed to banks and real estate companies. Oppenheimer Brothers Ltd. was forced into receivership for debts in excess of $163,000. The original promoters lost out completely. On its formation in 1897, the B.C. Electric Railway Co. took over the line, the first of several inter-urban routes acquired by this company. Known as the Central Park line, it was double tracked; construction commencing in 1906 and completed in 1912 on the second track. Service was discontinued in 1954 and the line abandoned.

The second step in building up the inter-urban system was taken in 1905, when the B.C. Electric leased the Vancouver and Lulu Island Railway from the C.P.R. By this time, the industry in Canada was well established. The 25 miles of electric intercity railway operating in Canada in 1891 had grown to 270 in 1905. Thus, the company was not taking the speculative risk that the original promoters had in 1890. On the Lulu Island line, the C.P.R. had been running a steam service for several years. Farmers were taking up land in Richmond, and there was a considerable cannery trade with Steveston as well as the lumber business which was provided by the Eburne Sawmill in Marpole. Vancouver to Marpole came to be the most popular section of the line. Vancouver residents came out to Kerrisdale to make their homes. As the line ran on its own right-of-way, it was not subject to regulation by the Point Grey council. In 1908-09, the C.P.R. built the extension from Marpole to New Westminster and leased it to the B.C. Electric. This provided a second inter-urban connection between the cities and opened up prime industrial sites on the banks of the Fraser.

The Burnaby Lake inter-urban was built in the old tradition — to open up residential land. The construction was largely financed by donations from the property owners. General Manager R. M. Sperling hired a real estate agent to "canvas owners along the routes for bonuses and free rights-of-way with a view to constructing a route where the largest bonuses and the most rights-of-way were offered." It is estimated that lands, worth $111,000, were acquired this way. The company went heavily into the real estate business. Its arm in this field, St. Nicholas Estate Co., purchased 736 acres on the north side of Burnaby Lake. For various reasons, including a decline in the real estate market after 1913, the Burnaby Lake land boom never reached the heights anticipated. The company still had hundreds of acres unsold in 1916 which they were anxious to get rid of.

The biggest venture into the inter-urban field came with the decision to build on the south side in the Fraser Valley. This turned out to be, not so much an intercity line, but a mini-railway with all its problems of construction and operation. It held the proud position of being the longest inter-urban line (64 miles) in Canada. The idea of a railway on the south bank of the Fraser was of long standing. In 1891, plans had been laid to build a steam road from a connection at Abbortsford with the C.P.R.'s Mission branch to Chilliwack. The promoters of the Chilliwack Railway Company obtained the promise of a Dominion subsidy and tried to sell to the

C.P.R. The senior railway was not interested and the deal fell through.

In the great expansion period of 1905-10, two other railways became interested: the Great Northern (which had already built a line from Tsawwassen to Cloverdale) and the Canadian Northern. The Great Northern wanted to extend its line at least to Huntington and, hopefully, to Hope. The Canadian Northern was scheduled to come through the Fraser Canyon and wanted a right-of-way through Chilliwack to New Westminster. It seemed pointless to build an electric railway in the same locality that would be serviced by two steam roads. Local B.C. Electric officials, no doubt after consultations with the marketing staff of the Canadian Northern, concluded that enough local traffic (mainly in logs and lumber) could be generated to make an electric line possible. Z. A. Lash, chief legal advisor to the Canadian Northern and an intimate of MacKenzie and Mann, advised that the company build under provincial charter. Surveys were started in 1908 and the 21 miles to Cloverdale were built in 1909.

The B.C. Electric now mounted a vigorous campaign in England to attract settlers to the Fraser Valley, stressing the advantages of fruit and dairy farming. Their office in London was swamped with enquiries.

From an engineering standpoint, the section from Abbotsford to Chilliwack was the toughest. It passed through the marsh country bordering the Sumas Lake, now reclaimed into some of the finest dairy land in the country. The railway had to take a wide circle, down to the U.S. border at Sumas, and then cling to the mountains on the south side of the lake. Obstacles included muskeg with drainage problems, dense forests, solid rock, and mosquitos and flies to torment the workers. Actual costs far exceeded estimates and caused much tension between the Board in London and local management. Finally, after riding up from New Westminster in the comfort of one of the latest inter-urban cars, Sir Richard McBride drove in the last spike. Business lived up to expectations. Within 18 months of completion, there were 15 logging camps, shingle mills, and sawmills stretched out along the line. Farmer-settlers took up land and, before long, the company had to put on a daily milk and vegetable train to bring their produce to New Westminster and Vancouver. Industries came in such as a fruit cannery and a brickyard. Unfortunately, competition for traffic was so keen that the brickyard gave its business to the Great Northern because they were willing to build a spur to the plant. In spite of these setbacks, the company was able to operate three daily trains and freight interchange between the American roads at Sumas grew year by year.

It was another story at Saanich on Vancouver Island. The interurban from Victoria to the end of the Saanich Peninsula at Deep Cove was not built for the land speculators or traffic, but primarily to keep competition away from the Victoria streetcar system. The B.C. Electric had signed an agreement with the city of Victoria to spend $250,000 in capital expenditures over a period of years if the city would guarantee there would be no competition in the fields of transportation and lighting. This was one of the famous protective clauses which the utility company signed with the major municipalities in order that the return on the investment would be assured for a certain number of years. One of the results of the Victoria agreement was the building of the Jordan River hydroelectric generating plant; another was the building of the Saanich inter-urban. The two projects are closely linked. Jordan River would generate more power than there was a market for at the time. Therefore, part of the surplus could be used in running the interurban. The preliminary arrangements for building the line were started by the local management before any sanction for the project had been given by the London board. The local management was very anxious to get as many bonuses and free rights-of-way as possible. A very extensive canvas of the property owners was undertaken, with the result that the land donations totalled over $60,000 in 1911 real estate prices. When the slump struck in 1913-14, that value had dropped to $17,215. There was no hope in generating enough traffic; the population of Saanich at the time was about 6,000. There was no chance of extending the line to other centres of population, as Saanich was a peninsula with just one exit to Victoria. The line never recovered and was abandoned ten years later, in 1924. Perhaps the only lasting benefit was the establishment of the Dominion Experimental Farm on 50 acres of land donated by the company near Sidney. It is a striking example of the wide latitude of powers which the London board gave to its local management.

By 1913, the transportation pattern for both streetcars and interurbans had been basically established. No major construction change would take place, although equipment was constantly upgraded. As automobile competition intensified, bus services became more and more frequent until the last streetcars were replaced by trolley coaches and buses in 1955. In the inter-urban field, the company decided, after World War II, to gradually eliminate passenger service in favour of buses. Elimination of passenger service on the Fraser Valley line came in 1949; Lulu Island from Marpole in 1952; the Burnaby Lake line in 1953; Central Park in 1954; and Vancouver-Marpole in 1958. The whole operation was dieselized, much of the track being retained for freight service. What is left of the inter-urban now acts as a terminal railway, moving considerable tonnage to and from the main line railroads.

The capitalists at the head of this giant utility corporation, R. M. Horne-Payne and G. P. Norton, were part of a business elite which had grown up around the activities of the great railroad builders Mackenzie and Mann. R. H. Horne-Payne was chairman of the British Empire Trust, the fund-raising agent for both the Canadian Northern and the B.C. Electric. Mackenzie and Mann had large business interests in British Columbia. They owned the largest sawmill in the province, the Canadian Western Lumber Co. and Comox Logging and Railway Co. which was the largest logging outfit with the greatest mileage of logging railroads in the province. On Vancouver Island, they owned Canadian Collieries (Dunsmuir) Ltd. with coal mines at Extension and in the Cumberland-Comox area. Mackenzie and Mann's Canadian Northern Railway was building hundreds of miles of new railways in B.C. under provincial guarantees in the height of the 1905-13 boom period. Sir William Mackenzie and Sir Donald Mann were influential in shaping Sir Richard McBride's railway and economic policies. Through the good offices of Mackenzie and Mann, R. M. Horne-Payne had direct access to the Premier's office in Victoria.

G. P. Norton, partner with Horne-Payne in the B.C. Electric, was head of the Yorkshire Guarantee & Securities Corporation, a pioneer mortgage and financial institution of Vancouver. This company was interested in real estate and a wide range of commercial enterprises in the lower mainland. He was a recognized financial authority, a great fund raiser, and either he or his chartered accountants' firm was auditor or had business relationships with all the leading woollen manufacturers of the West Riding of Yorkshire.

It is not surprising that men of this calibre and knowledge were able to make substantial contributions to the building of the B.C. economy. Partially responsible for making Horne-Payne and Norton so successful was the high level of managerial talent in the men they picked and sent out to administer these properties. William

Farrell, the first manager of the Yorkshire Guarantee & Securities Corp. in Vancouver was chosen by Norton. He handled the difficult negotiations involving the Vancouver utility companies prior to the formation of the B.C. Electric. He became an outstanding British Columbia businessman, founder of the B.C. Telephone Co., director of Evans, Coleman, Evans Ltd. and several others. His successor, Robert Kerr Houlgate, also appointed by G. P. Norton, directed the important interests of the Yorkshire Corp. for many years. He held valuable real estate holdings and, at one time, was a director of the Union Steamship Co. of B.C.

H. Sperling was the son of R. K. Sperling, Horne-Payne's partner in Sperling & Co., the London financial house that raised the original money to establish B.C. Electric. He came to Vancouver in the service of the new company in 1897 and was appointed general manager in 1905, on J. Buntzen's retirement. The close relations between management in Vancouver and the board in London was a factor in the successful expansion of the company during the period 1905-14. Succeeding H. Sperling was another hand-picked London office man, George Kidd. He came to the company as a secretary in the London office in 1907 and was well known to both Horne-Payne and Norton. The training of these men, with the exception of Sperling, was in banking or accountancy, reflecting the preference of G. P. Norton who was a chartered accountant himself.

So closely united were the interests of the lower mainland with the B.C. Electric that the development of one would have been slower and much more difficult without the co-operation and assistance of the other. The streetcar company had access to pools of technical help only available to the few nation-wide companies operating in B.C. Horne-Payne's British Empire Trust was one of the best staffed and best equipped fund-raising institutions in England. It was able to raise, through private placement, debentures and shares issued on the London Stock Exchange, millions of pounds for a variety of commercial enterprises in Canada.

Through Mackenzie and Mann, the B.C. Electric had access to the best legal talent in the field of Canadian transportation. Z. A. Lash, intimate business associate of these two great entrepreneurs, held the reputation as the best corporation lawyer in Canada. The advertising campaign, waged in England by the B.C. Electric to attract settlers to the Fraser Valley, was modelled after those so successfully mounted by the Canadian Northern Railway. In railway engineering, advice was sought and freely given from the engineering department of the Canadian Northern regarding muskeg and drainage problems in the Sumas-Chilliwack area.

The physical benefits to the B.C. economy were great. An integrated system of supplying both power and transportation had changed the lower mainland from a land of forests and small river settlements to a metropolitan area with all modern conveniences within a generation. An expanding network of city and inter-urban lines had fostered growth well beyond civic boundaries. City lines created the conditions which encouraged the building of homes and attracted more and more people. The role that the inter-urban played in making the B.C. Electric a terminal railway opened up prime sites which industry was quick to utilize.

The lower mainland has grown because of many factors outside the control of an urban transportation company. But without the orderly development and business shrewdness as exemplified by B.C. Electric management, it might have been more a "boom-and-bust" situation which characterized other western Canadian towns such as Moose Jaw, Calgary, or Prince George.

Air Transport

It all started on Easter weekend, 1910, when Charles K. Hamilton, an American barnstorming pilot, made the first manned powered flight in British Columbia from the racetrack of Minoru Park in Richmond. Two years later, from the same location, on the same Easter weekend, Bill Stark, Vancouverite and graduate of the Curtiss Flying School at San Diego, took a man up in his Curtiss biplane. This first air passenger in B.C. was James T. H. Hewitt, Sports Editor of the *Vancouver Daily Province*. The same day Bill Stark took up his wife, Mrs. Olive Stark, who became the first B.C. woman to travel by air.

Meanwhile, a group of Vancouver businessmen of German extraction got caught up in the aviation fervour that was sweeping Germany. The enthusiasm in that country for Zeppelins had prompted several people including Albert Ballin, head of the Hamburg-Amerika Steamship Line, to set up a commercial company whose objective was to provide passenger service via airship between certain German cities. Tickets were sold in the steamship line's offices. It had proven a great success; 10,197 paying passengers were carried over a four-year period on 1,588 flights. If this could be done in Germany, it could certainly be done in B.C., these Vancouver businessmen concluded. The Vancouver syndicate chose one of the most heavily travelled routes in B.C. Due to the railway construction boom, the route from Ashcroft to Prince George was the most frequently travelled. Their idea was to buy a Zeppelin and put it on the Ashcroft-Prince George run. In the summer of 1910, an agent was sent to Berlin to inquire about buying a Zeppelin and the requirements for establishing such a service. Needless to say, neither the airship nor the technology was available for export and the matter was quietly dropped.

In 1914, a group of solid B.C. citizens organized a club to promote flying — the Aero Club of B.C. Among its founders were such names as Judge Shultz, H. B. Bell-Irving, H. H. Stevens (later a federal cabinet minister), Mr. Justice Duff of the Supreme Court of Canada, George Cowan, the lawyer, and Colonel Merritt. Bill Stark was appointed instructor. During World War I the club sponsored an air training school at Minoru Park with Bill Stark and William Templeton as instructors.

Nothing was done commercially during the war, but afterwards much thought was given to the use of the airplane in civilian roles. It was quickly realized how effectively it could be used in forest fire protection, aerial mapping, and in transportation of prospectors and surveyors to remote areas. These functions were not economically viable at the time, however. The forest branch in Victoria under the Honourable T. D. Pattullo, strongly advocated for the establishment of a seaplane base in B.C. In 1920, the federal government agreed to set up a base in Vancouver at Jericho Beach on land donated by the provincial government. A large concrete platform for handling flying boats with a slipway for launching was built in 1920-21; and permanent hangers and workshops were erected in 1922.

This R.C.A.F. squadron had many tasks and many masters. The Federal Customs and Fisheries Departments — geodetic and water surveys; forestry work for both federal and provincial governments; and other assignments of national importance. For example, an escort had to be provided to see the *Empress of Asia* out of port when it was suspected that an attempt would be made to smuggle narcotics from the liner to power boats cruising in the bay. The

R.C.A.F. squadron also embarked on a four-day trip to co-operate with H.M.C.S. destroyer *Patrician*, and the coast patrol boat, *Armentiers*, in an effort to apprehend a smuggling boat suspected of hiding on the coast of Vancouver Island. In the field of forestry, the first patrol undertaken for the B.C. government took place January 21, 1921, to evaluate storm damage over some 5 million acres in the Vancouver Forest District. The first flight in the interior on forestry work was done by a Curtiss flying boat on November 3, 1920.

There were few private firms engaged in commercial flying in B.C. until the late twenties. The first experimental commercial flight from Vancouver to Seattle took place February 17, 1919; the first from Vancouver to Nanaimo on August 16, 1919. Captain Ernest Hoy made the first flight over the Rockies — Vancouver-Vernon-Calgary — on August 5, 1919, a feat that was not repeated until the inauguration of the Trans-Canada airmail service in 1938. The one route that was a commercial success was that underwritten by the U.S. Post Office from Seattle to Victoria. It was the first foreign airmail route established by the U.S. Post Office and was set up to connect with the trans-Pacific steamers calling at Victoria. Under contract to the private firm Barnes & Gorst of Seattle, this service commenced October 15, 1920. It was not until 1925 that a small Vancouver firm, Pacific Airways, was organized to handle passenger and freight business. In that year, it only handled 26 hours of flying time. To keep itself alive, it had to contract out for forestry work for the B.C. Forest Service.

Without organized ground facilities, it was not possible to conduct air services effectively; the public was still unconvinced that such facilities were necessary. Outside of Jericho Air Station, none existed in B.C. Even at this early stage, though, Jericho was providing 27 permanent year-round jobs.

The first air service to northern B.C. was not due to the efforts of Vancouver businessmen, but to a group of Yukon residents based at Whitehorse. The Yukon Airways & Exploration Co. was capitalized at $50,000, mainly provided by local residents, and was incorporated in late 1927. "Its main purpose," according to Clyde Wann, the president, "was to open up unexplored country inaccessible by dogteams or packhorses." It operated a Ryan four-passenger monoplane between Whitehorse-Carcross and Atlin, B.C. Traffic was not sufficient so the company lasted only two years.

Vancouver International Airport had its beginnings in the actions taken by a private company, the British Columbia Airways Ltd. In the summer of 1928, they tried to establish a passenger service between Vancouver and Victoria with a tri-motor Ford airplane, and rented 40 acres for a landing strip north of Landsdowne Park in Richmond. They ran into difficulties both traffic-wise and financially and within a few weeks had to suspend the service. The city of Vancouver stepped in, purchased the property, and made use of it as a municipal airport from 1928 to 1931.

The story is told by William Templeton and others that Vancouver was pushed into upgrading its airport services because Mayor L. D. Taylor had sent an official invitation to Colonel Charles Lindberg to visit the city. He received the reply that it was impossible to come "because there is no airport there fit to land in."

This prompted the city council to place a bylaw before the voters to raise $300,000 "to purchase land on Sea Island . . . for the purpose of an airport and seaplane harbour."

The bylaw was passed by a large majority and the city then purchased 480 acres. William Templeton was given the task of designing and constructing a suitable airport. Drainage was a problem, but an inexpensive system of using B.C. cedar boxes to collect the water proved effective. The water was then diverted into open ditches. Everything was primitive — no meteorological station (all weather reports being received by telephone); no landing controls; and no night flying as there was no lighting system. It was not until 1934 that the Dominion government provided radio and meteorological services. The staff consisted of three men and a horse — manager William Templeton, two assistants, plus the beast which had been purchased for $35. They used a wagon built of odds and ends found around the city's repair shop. There were no commercial buildings in the vicinity until the end of 1935 when Coates Aircraft Ltd. built an aircraft repair shop on land leased from the city; the first commercial building erected by private enterprise to serve the aircraft industry.

This was the era of the bush pilot. The airplane, it was said, was useful only to open up the north. As Lieutenant-General A. G. L. McNaughton said before the Canadian Institute of Surveying in 1937: "For the north country, the air has wiped out a frontier and opened up new lands for economic development." This period saw the springing up of small independent bush passenger and freighting outfits such as Grant McConachie's Yukon Southern and

United Air Transport. For the first time, they tried to give scheduled but irregular service to isolated settlements like Fort St. James, Fort Nelson, or Manson Creek from the railhead at Prince George; or Ginger Coote Airways from Vancouver to Fort St. John.

These small lines were much helped by getting mail subsidies from the Canadian Post Office.

Their flights were sometimes very dangerous. On October 11, 1930, pilot Paddy Burke and two companions started out from Atlin in a Junkers all-metal plane. They had to land on the Liard River and ripped the pontoons. Consequently, they were stranded and ended up waiting without food except some cariboo meat which they had killed. They were found and picked up on December 6 by pilot Wasson flying a Yukon Treadwell's plane.

In the south, passenger services using the Vancouver Civic Airport were initiated to Victoria in 1932 by Canadian Airways and to Seattle in 1934 on a ten-passenger Boeing by United Airlines. On March 2, 1939, the service between Vancouver and eastern Canada was commenced by Trans-Canada Airlines.

World War II showed the massive contributions which the airplane could make in the development of B.C. The thrust of the Japanese into the Aleutian Islands after Pearl Harbor had alarmed the American government who feared for the security of Alaska. It was essential to build up the military forces there, primarily in air power. Thus, the route, which had been pioneered by Canadian Airways from Edmonton to Whitehorse, became of prime importance. In 1938 and 1939, surveys had been made and airstrips built at Fort Nelson, B.C., and Watson Lake, Yukon — intermediate stops on what would become the Northwest Staging Route for American military planes bound for Alaska. Consequently, it turned out that Canadian pilots and operating staff of Canadian Pacific Airlines were the only people possessed of intimate knowledge of this route. C.P. Air was in a good position to provide the Americans with hangars, accommodation, communications, and training. When the U.S. government decided to build the Alaska Highway along this route, it was C.P. Air's personnel and equipment which flew in men and material in the spring of 1942. Throughout the entire period of its construction, C.P. Air was the only commercial airline flying a scheduled service between Edmonton and Fairbanks.

The contributions that C.P. Air has made to the building up of the economy of the lower mainland has been substantial. The company, a subsidiary of the Canadian Pacific Railway, was a merger of ten airline companies operating across Canada, three of whom were based in B.C. The decision taken in 1947 to move the head office from Montreal to Vancouver was of major importance. It was not done without careful consideration. Both Edmonton and Winnipeg had offered inducements. The case in favour of Vancouver lay in its location; that of being the natural geographical meeting place for half a dozen or more international routes. The international routes have shown the greatest growth. These flights bring thousands per week into Vancouver International Airport making it the third largest airport in Canada.

C.P. Air has created thousands of jobs in the metropolitan Vancouver area. The big planes eat up millions of dollars worth of fuel per year which is refined in B.C. and millions more are spent in maintenance and spare parts at the great C.P. Air overhaul base on Sea Island. The purchasing department does business with over 700 B.C. suppliers, creating many more jobs not directly related to running an airline. It is the only major airline with a head office in Vancouver.

World War II brought added facilities to the B.C. aviation industry. Two new airports on the Lower Mainland (Abbotsford and Boundary Bay) were results of the British Commonwealth Air Training Plan. Abbotsford fitted well into the civilian picture, after the war, as an alternate airport to Vancouver when that location was fogged in. It also has served as the scene of the annual Abbotsford Air Show which, according to general manager R. Thornber, "is the greatest stimulator of air tourism in B.C." In the war period, new R.C.A.F. bases were built, for example, at Holberg, north of Quatsino Sound, Vancouver Island. New civilian airstrips were built or old ones upgraded. There was much activity from Prince Rupert east to Prince George. At Vancouver Airport, Boeing set up their seaplane manufacturing plant which, after the war, was turned over to C.P. Air as their overhaul and maintenance depot.

To meet the demands of the jet age, new terminal buildings and runways have been built at Vancouver International Airport. The terminal building itself cost $30 million.

The growth of the aviation industry since 1945 has been spectacular. Public demand has ensured that all major B.C. communities have adequate airport facilities. Scheduled airlines now serve all major centres of population in the province. This has helped to create a minor boom in airport construction in the shape of runways, terminal buildings, maintenance depots, access roads, and other facilities. The airports have now taken over the role of the railway stations, which were the hubs of activity in the twenties. Not only have the passenger carriers expanded but there has been an upsurge in air freighting and the use by commercial corporations of their own planes. It can now be said that there is very little in the way of routine commercial freight that cannot be airlifted. In 1951, Central B.C. Airways Ltd. had a $1,000,000 contract with Morrison-Knudson Co., the major contractor of the aluminum project at Kemano, to fly in materials and passengers. Ten years later Pacific Western Airlines provided a supply line to the construction work at Granduc copper mine. The west's most unique airlift was from Terrace where the plane, a DC-3, would fly 150 miles north to the Leduc Glacier. The landing strip had been bulldozed out 3,000 feet up the glacier. These supplies had formerly been packed in by snow train.

Greater and greater use of planes has been made by commercial companies, many possessing their own. Construction companies like Emil Anderson & Co. of Hope, who did so much work on the highways in the boom periods of the fifties and sixties, owned a Piper so that their executives could rush from job to job. An equipment company, Finning Tractor, who supplied so much of the equipment for the great construction jobs of the time, owned and flew a De Havilland. Sawmill and logging companies were prime prospects for their own individual planes. Ainsworth Lumber Co. of 100 Mile House flew a Cessna as did the D. & A. Logging Ltd. of Revelstoke. The Canadian Forest Products Ltd., with interests in pulp mills at Prince George, operated a Grumman and Cattermole Tretheway when engaged in building a mill at Mackenzie, used a Piper. Some of these planes were engaged in rather unusual work, like the one owned by Nelson Bros. Fisheries Ltd. who, in season, hunted and located schools of fish; or the Cessna which used to be owned and flown by the Vancouver Television Services Ltd. to service cablevision customers on the Gulf Islands and logging camps and mining sites to the north end of Vancouver Island; or even the helicopter fleet which engaged in logging the more inaccessable stands of timber on the coast. Helicopters are also used to erect power transmission towers and in the inspection of pipelines in B.C.

The number of planes operating in B.C. had grown substantially over the years from six in 1921, to 963 in 1964, to 1,314 in 1967, to 2,948 in 1976, and to 4,576 in 1981.

The growth of Vancouver International Airport has been sustained and rapid. It is now the terminus of more than a dozen international routes. From a staff of three in 1931 it has grown to provide on-site jobs for over 12,000 (1981). It is estimated that there are another 5,000 jobs outside the vicinity of the airport which are directly dependent upon airport activities. The payroll of employees connected with the aircraft industry or air transportation in metropolitan Vancouver goes well over $300 million per year.

Job creation, resulting from the purchase of materials and supplies in construction projects, which initiated and completed the aviation industry in B.C., has contributed a great deal in the building up of this province since 1918.

Pipelines

Major events on the Canadian prairies have always had an impact on British Columbia. The settlement of Alberta and Saskatchewan in the early years of this century created the conditions for a healthy and prosperous lumber industry in B.C. When oil was found in commercial quantities in central Alberta it was not long before this fact was felt in B.C. The producers in Alberta were anxious to find markets for their oil. There were three areas where Alberta crude, if able to be delivered, could find buyers: eastern Canada, the American mid-west, and the Pacific coast. By 1950 the east had been connected by the Interprovincial Pipeline stretching 1,100 miles from Edmonton, Alberta to Superior, Wisconsin at the head of the Great Lakes. It was not long before the line was extended to the petrochemical centre of Sarnia and the province of Ontario.

The Pacific Northwest was unique in being one of the few areas in North America not connected by pipelines to oil producing fields. The refined products were shipped by tanker up from California. In the case of Vancouver, the crude came to the refinery at Ioco by tanker from either California or South America. If a pipeline was built over the Rockies, it at least could supply Vancouver and the lower mainland. If refineries could be built on Puget Sound, the pipeline could also supply Western Washington. The question was: is it technically possible to build a pipeline over the Rockies? Could it be financed? Several groups were studying this problem, including the Bechtel Corporation, a giant U.S. construction and engineering firm that had already built many thousands of miles of oil pipelines throughout the world. Field surveys and engineering and marketing studies were undertaken.

Two giants in the industry, Imperial Oil and Gulf Oil, along with Bechtel Corporation, agreed to set up a company, the Trans Mountain Oil Pipe Line Co., to build the project. Shell Oil and Standard of California became involved later. Initially, the pipeline was only to supply the requirements of Vancouver and the lower mainland through the facilities at Imperial's refinery at Ioco. The long-term view was that refineries would eventually be built in the Puget Sound area and could be supplied via the pipeline with Alberta crude. Up to this time, there were no major refineries on the American west coast north of California. It was a gamble, as expressed very clearly in the prospectus issued by the company for their first public share offering in the late winter of 1951.

"It should be expressly understood however," the prospectus reads, "that the shares to be sold by the Company are a speculation. As the figures in the table above indicate the Canadian market on the west coast is restricted and the earnings will therefore be limited unless an export market is obtained. Before such development occurs many problems, not all within the control of the Company will have to be resolved."

Both federal and provincial governments were in favour of the project. The Board of Transport Commissions said that "the construction of the proposed pipeline appears to be in the public interest." The government of Alberta stated that "it is in the best interests of the national economy that the Pacific coast area be supplied with oil produced in Canada." There was very little difficulty in getting permission to construct the pipeline.

It was a tremendous construction job. The actual length of the line from Edmonton to Vancouver via the Yellowhead Pass and the Fraser Canyon is 718 miles. U.S. Steel Corporation and Kaiser Steel mills in California supplied most of the 155,000 tons of steel piping required. Construction equipment ranged from mechanical ditchers, tractors, jeeps, and cranes to ambulances. The work force at its peak numbered more than 2,500. Even clearing the right-of-way was a big job. A fifty-foot-wide strip had to be cleared of all trees and stumps. This was done mainly by local British Columbia firms that specialized in the laying out of logging roads and electrical power transmission lines. An engineering feat of considerable magnitude was the crossing of the Fraser River at Port Mann. The width of the channel at this point is 2,500 feet. The pipe had to be laid in a trench dug out by a dredge 15 feet below the river bed. The job was done in winter when the water level was lowest. Most of the well-known contracting firms that have done so much towards the building of B.C. made their contributions. Mannix Ltd. built 220 miles of pipeline as well as several pumping stations. Northern Construction and J. W. Stewart, with a history going back to railway construction days, were involved in the erection of several pumping stations. Marwell Construction Co. Ltd. were prime contractors for the Burnaby Tank Farm and the marine loading dock at Vancouver.

Construction started in the spring of 1952 and after a winter shutdown was resumed in March of 1953. The first crude was delivered to Imperial's Ioco refinery on October 20, 1953. It was a construction job worth almost $100 million, one of the biggest up to that date in British Columbia's construction history.

British Columbia, through the efforts of the Trans Mountain Pipe Line Co., is now no longer dependent upon foreign oil. The hopes of the promoters have been fully realized as refineries have been built on Puget Sound, one at Ferndale outside Bellingham, another at Anacortes. Up to the time when Alaskan crude became available these refineries were supplied with Alberta oil. Conditions have changed and they now use very little Alberta crude.

Today, the basic function of the Trans Mountain Pipe Line Co. is to supply the four refineries in the Vancouver area and one at Kamloops. The marine dock in Vancouver, originally built to service the offshore trade, is now used in emergencies to ship oil to refineries in the United States or the eastern seaboard of Canada.

The only major developments up to the present in oil and gas in British Columbia have occurred in the northeastern section of the province. The presence of oil and gas had long been suspected in the Peace River country. Royal North West Mounted Police reports of 1907-09 told of large natural gas spouts which burned constantly. Imperial Oil made a small gas discovery at Pouce Coupe, six miles southeast of Dawson Creek on the Alberta side of the boundary in 1921. Economically it was of no significance and no further work was done. Oil and gas exploration was discouraged by the almost continuous reserves put upon the leasing of crown lands by the provincial government from 1919 to 1947. In a period from 1935-36 when the reserves were temporarily lifted, Frank McMahon, financially supported by a group of Vancouver businessmen, Colonel Victor Spencer, Norman Whittall, and others undertook a drilling program. Encouraging results were found but all progress was blocked by Premier Pattullo reinstating the reserves. In 1942 the provincial government under Premier John Hart started exploration on its own but nothing substantial was found. By 1948, natural gas wells were producing in the Pouce Coupe area and in 1950 Dawson Creek was the first town in British Columbia to use natural gas. It was the discovery of the well on the Wilson farm near Fort St. John by Pacific Petroleums in November 1951 which set off the oil and gas boom in the Peace country. It was in part due to Frank McMahon's faith, held through many years of disappointment and discouragement, in the oil and gas potential of the Peace country. Frank McMahon was one of the most colourful entrepreneurs ever to appear on the British Columbia scene. He was a lifelong optimist, a great booster of the west, and one who was always ready to take high risks. He had a personality that portrayed, to a marked degree, the aggressiveness, the energy, and the faith displayed by the pioneers who built the province. He was a native son, born in the little mining community of Moyie in the East Kootenays. In his youth he worked at various jobs including a small contract diamond drilling firm which he owned. The Great Depression wiped him out. In the late thirties he started drilling in the Flathead country of the East Kootenays looking for gas. Nothing of any interest was found and, as previously mentioned, he turned his attention to the Peace River country. In the early post-war period he founded Pacific Petroleums for oil and gas exploration, and in 1947-48 launched a major exploration program in the Peace River country.

In 1949 Frank McMahon incorporated the Westcoast Transmission Co. Ltd., a company designed to build large pipelines. The objective was to bring northern gas to southern B.C. and the American Pacific coast states. It took six years of struggling to get the authorization from the various governments. Even then it was a calculated risk, as there were not enough proven reserves of gas in the British Columbia section of the Peace River country to justify the building of such a large project. However, the outlook became promising as more and more producing wells were found. In 1952 the province of Alberta gave permission to Westcoast to export gas into B.C. from its Peace River wells. It was a time when great interest began to be shown in the north. W. A. C. Bennett had just

86

assumed office as premier of British Columbia and he, like John Diefenbaker, had a vision of the greatness of the north. The Wenner-Gren interests were undertaking studies looking towards the development of 40,000 square miles of land in the Rocky Mountain Trench. It was not gas and oil which they were looking for, but forestry wealth. The development of the forests, the building of pulp mills, and the influx of workers all created a demand for gas, but the whole scheme of piping gas south depended upon finding an American purchaser. Eventually one was found (the Pacific Northwest Pipeline Corp.) and after many disappointments approval was given by the Federal Power Commission. Pacific Northwest would take the gas at the border and then resell it to distributing companies. The price had to be very attractive; one third of that charged to the B.C. customers (B.C. Electric and Inland Natural Gas). Even though throughout the years renegotiated prices steadily rose, the deal nonetheless stimulated steady growth. In more recent years the situation has changed and the prices now set by the National Energy Board are as high or higher than American gas.

Construction of the southern end of the pipeline commenced in October 1955 in the Fraser Valley. This was to bring in American gas to the lower mainland until the complete line from Taylor was finished. The prime contractor was Canadian Bechtel who, two years previously, had completed the Trans Mountain oil pipeline. Construction presented no serious difficulties. The vast scale of the project ($200,000,000) created much local business. Six hundred and fifty miles of pipe were laid using some 230,000 tons of steel, 96,000 tons of which came from South Durham, England. The work force at its peak was 2,200.

The financing was by the largest private arrangement made without government support up to that date in western Canada. Most of the bond issues, totalling $83 million, were taken up by the leading North American insurance companies. A certain amount of stock was sold to the general public. Leading American banks provided loans: the First National City Bank of New York $10 million, the Mellon Bank of Pittsburgh $7.5 million, and the National Bank of Commerce of Seattle $1 million.

The Westcoast Transmission Co. has made several important contributions to the industrial history of the Canadian west. It built the first major natural gas pipeline in Canada and concluded the first major interchange of natural gas between Canada and the United States. In B.C. much construction and many investment dollars have been spent in the northeastern section in building feeder lines to its terminal at Taylor. Here, in co-operation with Phillips Petroleum and the Jefferson Lake Sulphur Co., a $30 million refinery, scrubbing plant, and a sulphur recovery unit have been built.

British Columbia has three big purchasers of northern gas: B.C. Hydro for Vancouver and the lower mainland, Inland Natural Gas Co. Ltd., and Pacific Northern Gas Ltd. The B.C. Electric Railway Co. (predecessor of B.C. Hydro) had, from the earliest times, a gas manufacturing and distributing system. Gas manufacturing by the burning of coal was one of the oldest established industries in the province. When natural gas became available in late summer 1957 the gas manufacturing plants and the gas meters, long outstanding features of downtown Vancouver, were dismantled. The comparative cheapness and ease in handling promoted much growth in the use of natural gas in the lower mainland which has continued to this day.

The Inland Natural Gas Co. Ltd. serves the central and southern interior. It is a factor in the profitable operations of pulp mills from Prince George to Skookumchuck in the East Kootenays. It supplies natural gas to the copper mines in the Highland Valley, the coal mines of Sparwood and Elkford, and 60 communities stretching from Hudson Hope to Cranbrook, with 92,000 customers and 2,000 miles of transmission lines.

West of Prince George lies the line of the Pacific Northern Gas Co. which supplies natural gas to the towns and villages along the Canadian National Railway line to Prince Rupert. Along this route are situated major sawmills, two pulp mills, and the aluminum smelter at Kitimat.

One of the more unusual achievements of Westcoast Transmission was the sponsorship of the 505-mile oil pipeline from Taylor to Kamloops. Westcoast was not really in the oil business and the deal was due to the pressures exerted on Frank McMahon by W. A. C. Bennett. As early as 1954 the premier had voiced his views that an oil pipeline from the Peace to the south would be desirable. In 1959 four applications had been received at a public hearing to build pipelines from the oil fields to Taylor and ship the oil by tank car over the Pacific Great Eastern to Vancouver. Many expressed the opinion that sufficient reserves of oil were not yet found and the project was premature. W. A. C. Bennett persisted, however, and the government invited several companies to submit proposals in

1960. One of these companies was Western Pacific Products and Crude Oil Pipeline Ltd., fifty percent of which was owned by Westcoast Transmission. Western Pacific's plan was to build using Westcoast Transmission's right-of-way, thus saving all the major expenses of surveying, grading, and clearing. In addition, when the line became operative, it would be more economical because of the joint use of transportation equipment, communication systems, and maintenance staff. Furthermore, on the controversial question of reserves, the directors stated "There is general agreement in the Canadian oil industry that substantial additional reserves of oil and gas will be found through intensified exploration following construction of the Western Pacific pipeline." Dut to the uncertainties no major oil company was prepared to submit proposals and Westcoast Transmission got approval almost by default.

The line was built within a year and, as anticipated, there occurred a marked expansion in exploration. In the summer of 1961, there were only 47 oil producing wells in the Peace area. By the end of 1962 the number had risen to more than 300. But in the long run it has proved a disappointment. Oil has not been found in huge quantities in northern B.C. and today the line is carrying just about the same amount of oil as it did when it was first completed: some 27,000 to 30,000 barrels per day.

In the quarter of a century since the emergence of the gas boom in the Peace River area hundreds of miles of pipe have been laid as feeder lines to bring the gas from the outlying fields to Westcoast Transmission's main line. A 200-mile extension was made to tap the fields in the vicinity of Fort Nelson. The gas wells in the Grizzly Valley now feed into the $98 million dollar gas processing plant at Pine River (one of the biggest projects built in 1979 for the Canadian gas industry) and then, relieved of its by-products, the gas flows into the main line near Chetwynd. There are two more big gas processing plants, one at Taylor and the other at Fort Nelson. Here the gas is cleaned of its by-products: butane, propane, and sulphur. Millions of dollars have been invested in northern B.C. in such facilities, by Westcoast Transmission and other companies.

British Columbia is now tied into the oil and gas pipeline grid which spans the American west. The Westcoast Transmission system is an integral part of an immense pipeline grid which extends from the Northwest Territories through the Western States to the Mexican border. Thus the technical facilities for a continental system in North America for gas production and distribution are now in place. Outside of Vancouver Island, all the important communities and industries in British Columbia are now supplied with northern B.C. gas. This has all happened within the space of a quarter of a century, and has played a major part in the expanding growth of B.C.'s economy.

CHAPTER THREE

COMMUNICATIONS

Telegraphs

In these days of rapid communications when messages bounce off a satellite and are received half way around the world almost at the moment of sending, it is hard to visualize conditions a hundred years ago when it took weeks for them to arrive at New York from London. The wonders of rapid communication as exemplified by the electric telegraph and the submarine cable had yet to be proven. The first commercial use of a telegraph line took place in 1837 and the first effective submarine cable (made possible by the discovery of the insulation properties of gutta-percha) came into operation in 1851. The following decade saw the rapid increases in the telegraph systems of both Europe and America; yet the Atlantic Ocean still had to be crossed. Brilliant minds on both continents worked on this problem. Electronic communications were still in their infancy and success had not yet been achieved.

It was in this environment that American promoter and entrepreneur Perry McDonough Collins suggested connecting New York and London by an intercontinental telegraph line: from St. Louis in the mid-west to San Francisco, then northward through Oregon, Washington, through the wilds of British Columbia and Russian-America (now Alaska) to the Bering Strait. By a 40-mile submarine cable it would cross into Siberia and proceed 3,300 miles eastward to link up with the Russian telegraph to St. Petersburg.

Little is known of Collins; his name does not appear in any of the *Who's Who* of the period. Details of his early career are obscure. It is known he came to California in the gold rush days and set up as a banker and dealer in gold dust. He then apparently became interested in the possibilities of extending American trade over the Pacific. In 1856-57 he made an adventurous journey across Russia from St. Petersburg to the mouth of the Amur River, though there is no evidence that he was promoting an overland telegraph line at this point. His concern seemed to be to find ways of extending American trade into Siberia.

When he returned to the States, all conversation was about the recent attempts to bridge the Atlantic by electric cable. Repeated failures and expert opinion of its impracticality led him to consider the possibility of connecting the two continents by an overland line.

He approached the governments in both Washington and in London with his scheme and received favourable replies. For several years he continued lobbying and finally got authorization from the Russians to construct a line through Siberia and Russian-America. In the meantime, the Western Union Telegraph Co., a group of upper state New York telegraphists and businessmen, had constructed a line across the west from St. Louis to San Francisco with the assistance of the government in Washington. It was an age of great commercial expansion in the States and the stockholders of the Western Union (by this time all men of wealth) saw no reason why they should stop in California.

Both parties got together. Collins was asked to submit his terms formally, upon which he would be willing to sell his concessions and privileges. He asked for $100,000 in cash, a like amount in the Western Union Extension stock, and an insider's right to subscribe for any further issues, "as compensation for eight years service in securing the grants."

These terms came before the Board on March 16, 1864, and were accepted. In return the company undertook to build a telegraph line through British Columbia, Russian-America, and across the Bering Strait to the mouth of the Amur River.

What kind of a company was this who undertook to build a line 5,000 miles long through unknown and unexplored country? The Western Union Telegraph Co. was a leading American corporation in the telegraph field with headquarters in Rochester, N.Y., whose chief shareholder was Ezra Cornell (founder of Cornell University in Ithaca, N.Y.). Cornell at this time was one of the most powerful men in the industry. He had worked with the telegraph since the building of the original line from Baltimore to Washington in 1844 as contractor, company promoter, and owner. He not only knew the technical side thoroughly, but as a businessman had originated and managed many of the pioneer lines in the eastern and middle western States. The Western Union, his creation, was brought together in 1855 to combine seven major and several minor companies in the middle west — hence its name. This started the company on its road to expansion so that in later years it dominated the whole American industry. Western Union grew up with the railways and adopted their monopolistic practices. Company policy from its creation was to acquire its competitors either through ruinous competition or by buying them out at bargain prices. If the Atlantic cable failed they would be in a position of monopoly control over the traffic between the two continents.

To finance this venture a new type of stock was created named the Western Union Telegraph Extension stock — an issue almost entirely taken up by that small group of Rochester and Ithaca men owning the Western Union. As was customary then (and still is) a small number of shares was to be set aside for diplomats, government officials, and "others whose influence it may be deemed necessary to secure." The Russian Minister at Washington was given 300 shares, while in St. Petersburg, Cassius Clay, the American Minister, received a package of several hundred to give to influential officials. There is no record of any being given to English officials either in London or New Westminster.

The cost of the line was estimated at $1,500,000 or $300 per mile for the 5,000 miles. Revenue was anticipated to reach $25,000 per day (a thousand messages at $25 per message). Annually some $9,000,000 of business would be transacted. These were large figures in the business world of that day, and Western Union officials expected this intercontinental overland route to be very profitable. They had some justification for their optimism, as their western line to San Francisco had cost one half of the contract price and was in great demand by both eastern and western businessmen.

The organization of the actual exploration and construction was entrusted to Colonel Charles S. Bulkley, an experienced telegraph engineer, who was in charge of the United States Army's telegraph system in the southwest. He was given leave of absence from the army; this clearly illustrates the close co-operation between the Western Union and the American government. In fact, all the plans were made "under the instructions and with the approbation" of the State Department.

As a military man Colonel Bulkley set up his organization along army lines. "My organization is military in its character," he wrote to the executive committee of the Western Union at Rochester July 25, 1865, "requiring officers and men in the land and marine service to wear uniforms without cost to the company and our system of accounts is similar to the Quartermaster's Department of the Army."

The operations were divided into three vast geographic divisions — British America (British Columbia), Russian-America (Alaska), and Siberia. There were to be two distinct organizations, the Marine service and the Land service. The Marine service operated in all geographical divisions, owned or chartered over two dozen boats, and was responsible for the shipment and arrival of men, equipment, and supplies to their appointed places. The Marine service made its contribution to the British Columbia economy. Its vessels made many a voyage to western Alaska or Siberia stocked with Vancouver Island coal, and telegraph equipment picked up at Victoria from the holds of British ships which had arrived there from England.

Two distinguished American telegraph engineers were appointed to the British America division. Franklin L. Pope of New York, later to become a partner of Thomas A. Edison, became Chief of Explorations, and Captain Edmund Conway became Chief of Construction Parties.

Captain Edmund Conway, at this time twenty-three years of age, had acquired his training by working as a telegraphist on the Grand Trunk Railway in Quebec. On the outbreak of the Civil War, he had gone south, joined the Union Army in the Department of Military Telegraphs and served with distinction in all the campaigns in northern Virginia. Like all his fellow executives on the construction and exploration side, he had been picked by Colonel Bulkley from the technical corps of the Union Army.

The first telegraph line into British Columbia was not, as many think, a Western Union one. Before any practical steps had been taken on the overland route, Horace W. Carpenter, president of the California State Telegraph Co., had come up to British Columbia to ask permission to extend his line (which was then in Oregon) into New Westminster. Permission had been given by the council with the approval of Governor James Douglas and was set forth in an ordinance known as the "First Telegraph Act — 1864." This gave the California State Telegraph Co. the building and operating rights, within the colony, for a period of 25 years and free custom entry, "for wire, submarine cable and materials necessary for the construction of the said telegraph line."

Thus there was a telegraph line being built northward that would eventually reach New Westminster before Captain Conway or any other Western Union man could put up any of their lines. On September 4, 1864, the line became operative to Olympia, Washington Territory, and one month later, it was ten miles north of Seattle.

In that month, Captain Conway made his first visit to New Westminster. He wined and dined Governor Seymour, members of the Colonial Legislature, and government officials with the objective of obtaining approval to build in the colony. It resulted in the passage by the Legislative Council of the International Telegraph Ordinance of February 21, 1865. It gave the same privileges to Perry McDonough Collins as had been given, in the earlier ordinance, to the president of the California State Telegraph Co. with one minor difference. The concession was to run for 33 years, not 25 as granted to the California company. Construction was to commence January 1, 1867, and was to be completed by January 1, 1870, whereupon, New Westminster was to be kept "in complete and continuous telegraphic communications with the whole telegraphic systems of the United States and Russia."

Governor Seymour appeared interested and made arrangements to have an extension put in from the telegraph office, in the town, to Government House, a distance of about one mile. This was completed on March 6, 1865. On the 17th of March, the U.S. Navy ship *Shubrich* arrived with cable for the river crossing at New Westminster along with Colonel Bulkley, the engineer-in-chief. It was then brought to the attention of Colonel Bulkley that the right to construct a line in B.C. had been given to Perry Collins and not to the Western Union people. To straighten things out, Colonel Bulkley instructed Conway to write a letter to Governor Seymour stating that it was the Western Union which would be doing the job by sending in their men and money.

"I regret," Conway wrote, "that the company has no agent with instructions to attend to this matter or that the government was not informed that the company had already been formed and incorporated"; this is a typical attitude held towards the government by powerful American corporations which have done business in B.C. in the last one hundred years. The result was a new ordinance transferring the privileges granted Collins to the Western Union Telegraph.

On Tuesday, March 21, 1865, the cable of the California State Telegraph Co. was laid across the Fraser River, connecting the town of New Westminster with the Surrey side. Two weeks later,

95

the first message was sent between Sehome (Bellingham Bay) and New Westminster, completing a period of feverish construction activity by telegraph construction foreman John Henry Fravel.

The line entered British Columbia near where the Peace Arch now stands. It continued westward to Mud Bay, where it connected with the Kennedy trail which stretched northward to the Fraser. The line's most dramatic moment came on April 18, when the message came through of President Lincoln's assassination.

Both Colonel Bulkley and Captain Conway were unsatisfied with the California State line. Falling trees, heavy rains, and high winds caused frequent interruptions. Thus on March 30, 1865, we find Conway exploring the old Whatcom-Fort Hope trail. He started from the Fraser near Sumas Mountain at 6 a.m., over a very rough path strewn with fallen timber, and arrived at Whatcom at 4 p.m. after a tough hike of 28 miles. Next year the Western Union built their own line along this trail, connecting with the main overland telegraph at Chilliwack. It was abandoned in 1867, reactivated in 1870 due to the interest shown by the Northern Pacific Railway in Bellingham Bay as its Pacific terminal, and then fell again into disuse.

In the meantime Conway had been busy with the colonial officials in New Westminster and had reached an agreement with them. The government agreed to "forthwith lay out and construct from New Westminster to Yale a sleigh Road of uniform width of twelve feet." Two thirds of the cost was to be paid by the Colonial government; the company agreed to pay the other third, to a limit of $8,000. By using the existing Cariboo Wagon Road and the agreed upon government road to Yale, the Western Union had obtained its right-of-way for its first 435 miles at practically no cost.

Construction started immediately. N. R. Burrage, the quartermaster for the British American division, opened an office at Yale in April 1865. Conway instructed Thomas McClure, a Royal Engineer who had elected to stay in the colony, to locate and survey the trail up through Sumas Prairie. John Fravel (who had brought the California State line from Bellingham to New Westminster) entered the employment of the Western Union in charge of the construction gangs in the Fraser Valley.

The line was to follow the south bank of the Fraser from opposite New Westminster, through Port Mann, to Langley, where it cut into the Hudson's Bay Brigade trail to Hope. On June 27 the Western Union's own cable was laid across the Fraser near the present railway bridge at New Westminster and it was then possible to keep in instant touch with the work gangs. On August 17, the line was completed to Hope, although some difficulty had been experienced in crossing the Chilliwack River, and on the 26th it came into Yale. Further up country, Conway opened an office a few miles from Ashcroft at Cornwall's ranch, and two days later another at Clinton. Construction gangs followed closely and on September 14 the line reached Quesnel. Always on the alert for business, Conway contacted the *Cariboo Sentinel* and sold the owner a package of weekly telegraphic news reports.

It had been comparatively easy to build the line along an existing road, in a country where there was adequate transportation to bring up supplies. It was another problem to build north of Quesnel into an unexplored country; trails had to be made and materials packed in at immense cost and time. Only a few unco-operative Hudson's Bay Company employees knew what obstacles would be encountered in northern B.C.

To tackle the all important job of northern exploration, Colonel Bulkley set up a three-fold plan. A party was to sail under Robert Kennicott from San Francisco to St. Michael at the mouth of the Yukon River, to travel up the river, then turn south as far as possible. In British Columbia, Franklin Pope was to start from Quesnel and explore northward with the ultimate object of contacting the Kennicott party. The third prong was to explore from the sea the Skeena, Nass, and Stikine rivers to gain knowledge of the country as a supply route to the various parties that would be surveying the interior. It was left to Conway to make arrangements for the river explorations.

After some correspondence, he was able to obtain the services of Captain Horace Coffin, owner of a small sternwheel steamer named *The Union*. Captain Coffin was an old-time steamboat captain on the Fraser. Things had been tough on the Fraser in 1864 and he had taken his boat on a trading expedition up the northwest coast. On this trip, he had ascended the Skeena for a few miles, the first steamer to do so. Therefore, when he took this Western Union assignment, he had some experience of northern waters.

The season was late, but, as Conway reported to Colonel Bulkley:

Capt. Coffin left New Westminster on the 30th of August 1865 and entered the mouth of the Skeena on the 15th of Sept. The steamer ascended the river 90 miles, at this point two canoes were loaded with supplies. They succeeded in getting them up to Agglegate village on

97

the 28th of Sept., distance from the mouth of the river 216 miles. . . .
The steamer entered the Nasse river on 9th of October and ascended
43 miles. . . . Capt. Coffin considered it too late in the season to explore
the Sticken so he returned to New Westminster.

It is interesting to note that this expedition (the pioneer exploration
of the northern rivers by steamboat) only cost the Western Union
$2,860.

Pope's land party (25 men and 40 mules) left Quesnel July 4.
Due to supply difficulties, he sent the mules with ten men back from
Fort St. James. Dr. J. T. Rothrock, with a picked party of eight,
continued on and established winter quarters at the northern end
of Takla Lake. Here, with the help of George Blenkinsop, an old
Hudson's Bay Company man, he built Bulkley House — the first
house built by white men in northern British Columbia.

At a cost of $850, including wages and provisions, Conway, with
four men and ten mules, set out from Quesnel to Bulkley House
on September 20, 1865, "to see for myself the country through
which we proposed constructing the line." Another of his objectives
was to find a way to the Stikine, but he was unable to get a guide
and returned to New Westminster on November 20.

Telegraph construction engineers were looking for certain things
— preferably open country, but with enough timber to cut poles
from. Rock locations were to be avoided, as well as heavily timbered
sections, which would entail considerable cutting. Creeks could be
crossed without too much trouble, but rivers of considerable width
presented serious problems. Conway found a country not impossible
for telegraph lines but very difficult to supply with provisions and
telegraphic equipment for large parties of men. This was to be a
major problem for the next year and one half.

Matters rested as the men were paid off and construction ceased
for the winter. The first season saw New Westminster tied in to the
whole telegraph systems of the United States, 435 miles of line built
and in operation to the Cariboo, the newspapers of the colony supplied for the first time with weekly telegraphic news reports of happenings in the United States and Canada, and the Western Union
firmly committed to a gigantic construction program in B.C. in the
coming year.

Construction started north of Quesnel in May 1866. This involved a work force of 200 to 250 men in the bush. The procedure
was as follows: the line having been selected, a surveyor went ahead
with two or three axemen who blazed the trees. Then came the

choppers, a gang of some 80 men, who cut down the trees to make a pathway from 12 to 20 feet wide. Next there came a man to measure the distances; at the end of each 70 feet he drove a stake into the ground; after him came another gang which dug holes where the stakes had been driven; then a party of axemen who cut the poles upon which to string the wires; next the pole setters whose job it was to nail the bracket on the pole, place the insulator in the bracket, and set the pole upright in the hole, filling in the earth and stones, and stamping it well down; finally came the wire party which strung the wire on the poles. In addition, other parties were engaged in building the stations — log cabins with chimney, doors, and windows, 25 miles apart — making trails, building bridges over streams, and constructing rafts to cross the bigger rivers. Then there were the packers — 25 men or more with 150 to 200 mules and horses — engaged to bring up supplies over the completed trail from Quesnel.

Work continued all summer. At the end of the season in September, it was halted on the Kispiox River, 50 miles north of where it flows into the Skeena at present-day Hazelton (then known in Western Union records as Fort Stager). In the season, 378 miles of wire had been strung north of Quesnel, 15 stations built, 440 miles of trails for horse or mule travel constructed, 9,200 poles cut and placed in position, and construction crews from 200 to 250 kept in the field.

On the sea side the steamer *Munford*, specially built on Puget Sound for the Western Union, travelled up and down the British Columbia coast taking in material to the supply stations established on the Skeena and Stikine rivers and at Wrangel. Parties of explorers were also sent in from the coast to try and find suitable ways of crossing the coast mountains. A party of 23 men, under J. L. Butler, left Victoria July 5 and ascended the Skeena to Fort Stager where they left 150 miles of telegraphic material. They also went up the Stikine and between Telegraph Creek and its mouth cached wire and other equipment for 200 miles of line.

Exploration parties were in the field all summer, trying to find a way behind the Coast Mountains from the Skeena to the Stikine rivers. Attempts were made both from the land and the sea side. Conway, in his report to Colonel Bulkley on the season's activities, wrote, "I started Byrnes back for Aquligit (on the Skeena) to make explorations towards the Stikine. He tried in different directions to find a good route but owing to want of time and food he was unable to get through. I also started two men from Shakesville (on the Stikine) to try and come down to the Nass River keeping near the coast but they got snowed in in the mountains and were compelled to put back. I also attempted to get in from the head of the Portland Canal but was prevented by the lateness of the season and the impossibility of procuring a guide."

Messrs Scovell and Barrett left Victoria on the 15th of March, ascended with great difficulty the Stikine to Shakesville, mostly on broken ice, arranged for a guide, and travelled about 50 miles towards the Nass; owing to the want of food and the difficulty of travelling through the soft snow they returned completely worn out. Scovell started out again in July and a month and a half later reached the Skeena, describing his route as passable for a telegraph line.

Several members of the exploration parties stayed and wintered in the Stikine country, and in the spring and early summer of 1867 continued their explorations. On reaching the coast they met N. R. Burrage, the paymaster, who had come up from Victoria in an Indian canoe to tell them that the project had been abandoned by the orders of the directors of the Western Union in Rochester.

Three events occurred in the autumn of 1866 which were to materially affect the activities of the Western Union in British Columbia. In August, the fifth attempt to connect America and Europe by cable had been successful. Not one, but two cables were now effective and in constant use, and messages were passing between New York and London at an increasing rate. The impossible had been accomplished. The second event was the consolidation of the Western Union with two of its main competitors. The Western Union emerged as predominant in the telegraph industry and as America's first great industrial monopoly. Thousands of miles of telegraph lines were now redundant, including what had been built for the overland intercontinental lines. Telegraph revenues due to the new Atlantic cable increased considerably; most of it came into the Western Union treasury, as it controlled the majority of the domestic lines. Therefore another connection with Europe was not necessary to the financial health of the company.

The third event was the refusal of the Russian government to grant a 40 percent rebate to the Western Union on all messages passing over their wires to and from America. This special concession had been agreed upon by the president of the Western Union and the responsible officials in the Ministry of Posts and Telegraph before any construction had actually started. This would have given the American company the competitive edge, which it hoped would blunt the effectiveness of a successful Atlantic cable. The Russian government found that it contravened the European Telegraph Convention of which both themselves and the British government were signees; thus, they had no alternative but to disallow it.

This had become apparent in the autumn of 1866 and the directors at that time made preparations to cut their financial loss on the overland route. Provision was made to convert Western Union Extension stock into bonds of the Western Union Telegraph Co. If converted, this gave the large shareholders a guaranteed income on stock which within a year would become worthless. Over $3,000,000 was thus converted, leaving the small stockholder, who was without inside company policy information, with valueless certificates. Hundreds of local Rochester and New York people who had bought in good faith and on the good earning reputation of the Western Union were left holding the bag. As quoted by the *Boston Traveller* newspaper, "The affairs of the company are managed solely with a view to the interests of a few large stockholders."

Officially the Board of Directors voted in March 1867 not to expend any more money on the Russian extension but unofficially in the winter of 1866 no plans were laid for the coming year's construction. What it meant in B.C. was that at the end of the 1866 construction season all the staff north of Quesnel were laid off, the line abandoned, stocks of telegraph material left in the woods, and the telegraph trail untended. The tons of iron wire, the thousands of glass insulators, and the many hundreds of poles left to rot in the wilds proved a source of much profit to the Indians. The wire was fabricated into spears, fish traps, nails, and the building of bridges; the insulators became drinking vessels and many an Indian warmed himself by a pole fire.

The benefits to B.C. were many; it aided materially in opening up the northern country. The old telegraph trail north of Quesnel was for many years the main thoroughfare to the northern interior. The explorations undertaken by Michael Byrnes and Vital LaForce, while employed by Western Union, influenced the Cariboo miners to send them up again in search of gold — a move which sparked the Omineca Gold Rush of 1869-70.

At a time when the first excitement of the Cariboo gold field had dulled, it provided much needed employment to many like Royal Engineer Thomas McClure and Robert McMicking who became telegraph operators at Quesnel. In later years, they introduced further wonders of electricity to the citizens of B.C. in the shape of the telephone and electric lighting.

The telegraph from Quesnel southward was a powerful isolation breaking force. It made rapid communication possible between widely separated settlements. To the citizens of British Columbia, who were thousands of miles from the main centres of activity, it gave a prospective of what was happening in the outer world through the telegraphic news reports in their local papers. As the telegraph lines became more extensive within the province, it became a significant factor in the development of spheres of influence of the coastal and interior cities.

This was the first time that the people of British Columbia had been exposed to the activities of a giant American business corporation. It was a novel experience — sometimes costly in terms of government concessions and subsidies; other times profitable to the private sector in terms of jobs created and money spent.

Like other American business enterprises, the decisions were made outside of B.C., based upon factors which took no account of local interests or needs. Government officials had to remember that the corporation was in a position to mobilize certain resources of the American government and use them for its own purposes. Its closure of operations in B.C. was a hard-headed dollars and cents business decision, based on the economies of the telegraph industry in the eastern and mid-western United States. Furthermore, Western Union's decision to lease its lines in B.C. to the Colonial government was not a goodwill gesture in recognition of help received, but was an act to get rid of an unprofitable operation which had no potential, as far as contemporary opinion was concerned.

In the 80's, the Dominion government purchased all Western Union facilities in B.C. for $24,000 — assets which had originally cost the company well over $1,000,000.

The dismantling of Collins Overland Telegraph did not mean the end of telegraphic communications in B.C. The line from New Westminster to Quesnel was first kept open by the Western Union, then by the Colonial government. At the time of Confederation, it became a Dominion government's responsibility. Robert McMicking, an Overlander of '62, became superintendent, manning some 16 offices from Sehome on the American border to Barkerville in the Cariboo. "It was never profitable," explained R. McMicking to B. N. Pearse, the resident Dominion government engineer in

Victoria. "In British Columbia nearly all the population is at either extremity, 600 miles distant, and not a sufficient population to keep a line engaged half the time." Typical of other years was the annual loss of $25,125 in 1872. Operating conditions were severe and in many cases unique. "Operators suited to the country and the profession are remarkably scarce," wrote R. McMicking to petitioners at Quesnel Mouth, complaining about the service on December 1, 1872. Near Chilliwack, an Indian cutting timber broke the telegraph line and when questioned said that "it was of no importance." Writing to Dr. I. W. Powell, Superintendent of Indian Affairs, concerning this incident on May 20, 1873, R. McMicking asked, "When opportunity offers, will you be kind enough to set the Chief right?"

Much of the systems business originated from the sawmill run by S. P. Moody & Co. at Moodyville on Burrard Inlet. The line had been put in by the Western Union at the behest of the sawmill company. When it fell into disrepair, Sir Joseph Trutch, on behalf of the Dominion government, refused to have repairs made. Consequently, S. P. Moody & Co. accepted all responsibility for its upkeep. Additional revenue was found by R. McMicking in supplying provincial news to Victoria, New Westminster, and Barkerville papers.

The telegraph network in the rest of the province grew slowly. Victoria was served by a branch which left the Portland-New Westminster line some 15 miles south of Bellingham Bay and proceeded by way of Fidalgo, Lopez, and San Juan Islands. There were 13 miles of submarine cable supplied by Messrs Glass, Elliott & Co. of London, England. H.M.S. *Forward*, a Royal Navy ship stationed at Esquimalt, was turned into a cable ship to lay the nine miles between San Juan and Vancouver Island. It provided, over the years, a highly unsatisfactory service as the cables were always breaking.

In 1879, Victoria was linked to Nanaimo by wire. Over the years, this line was extended to Alberni, then to Cape Beale, which provided an alternative circuit to the direct Victoria-Cape Beale line. The lighthouse at Cape Beale, at the southeast entrance to Barclay Sound, was an isolated spot situated some three days of arduous journeying away from Victoria. It was also the scene of many shipwrecks. Lack of communications prevented the lighthouse keeper from obtaining assistance in such circumstances, so the Dominion government in 1889 agreed to build a telegraph line. Construction started in the autumn of that year but, due to the wet weather, the men refused to work and returned to Victoria. A new gang was sent out in the spring of 1890 and completed the job. The line was in operation for 16 years but proved very unreliable as trees continually fell, breaking the wire. In one winter's storm, 80 trees fell across the line within a distance of ten miles. It was superceded by the wireless station established on Pachena Point in 1907.

As the railways spread throughout the province, their telegraph systems were opened to the public for commercial use. First, the Canadian Pacific telegraph in the southern sections; then the Canadian Northern and Grand Trunk Pacific telegraphs in the north-central interior. By 1914, all the inhabited localities were connected by telegraph. The Canadian Pacific Telegraph was the predominant factor. It functioned as a wire news service which brought news that was national in scope to the provincial papers. Its connection with the Associated Press provided world coverage for the first time in B.C.

Some of the great days of telegraphic achievements were reinacted in the building of the B.C.-Yukon telegraph line. This was a Dominion government project to provide adequate communications between the Yukon and the rest of Canada. It followed the path laid out by Major Pope in 1865-66 for the Collins line from Quesnel to Hazelton and Telegraph Creek. Here it met the line coming down from Dawson City via Atlin. There were 44 stations on the line in one of the most rugged and remote parts of B.C. It was abandoned in 1936, but not before it became a legend in telegraphic lore.

The telegraph has been replaced by the telephone and the radio. Telegrams no longer play a vital role in the business, educational, and social life of the people. But if it had not been for the telegraph, British Columbia would have been more isolated than it was from the centres of investment and learning. Technology and its progress might also have been less spectacular.

Telephones and Telecommunications

When the telephone appeared on the commercial scene, it was viewed by the leaders of the telegraph industry as an extension or modification of the telegraph. To the public, the telephone was a curiosity: a novelty to attract attention, but of no real practical value. Its workings were more akin to the telegraph than any other technology of the day. It was, therefore, the more progressive telegraphists who took up the idea, formed telephone companies, and promoted its use.

In British Columbia, the most prominent member of the industry was Robert McMicking. Trained as a telegraphist, he had come to B.C. with the Overlanders of '62, become an operator on the Collins Overland Telegraph, and finally superintendent of the government telegraphs in B.C. In January 1878, while still serving as superintendent of B.C. Telegraphs, McMicking accepted the position as agent of the Bell Telephone Co. in B.C. He received a consignment of telephones and set up a line between the telegraph office in Victoria and the *Colonist* newspaper. For two years, he promoted the use of the telephone among his friends and business acquaintances. The Reverend William Duncan picked up two telephones from him in Victoria and set up a line in the Indian village of Metlakatla on the Skeena River from the village store to the sawmill, a quarter of a mile away. This was the first telephone installation on the mainland of British Columbia. In 1879, the first commercial telephone on Vancouver Island was set up by order of Frank D. Little (chief engineer of Dunsmuir Diggle & Co.) to run between the company's office in Wellington and the loading wharf at Departure Bay.

Finally, Robert McMicking's telephone activities got him into trouble with his superiors in the government telegraph service. Telephone purchase had been made through the government telegraph account and the amount now stood over $4,000. A Victoria businessman, Edgar Crow Baker, came to his financial assistance with the help of the Masons, but the Minister of Public Works refused to overlook his telephone activities and he was dismissed from the service on March 31, 1880. McMicking was now out of a job and Edgar Baker again came to his assistance by offering him the job of manager of his newly created Victoria & Esquimalt Telephone Company.

This company had been formed early in March 1880 by Edgar Baker and five of his business associates to provide telephone service between Victoria and Esquimalt. The amounts of money involved were really quite small — each sponsor contributing $500. Customers were slow in coming forward. On March 10, the company had 11 customers. In July, a telephone was ordered by the prominent lawyer and future premier, Theodore Davis. In September the police station was connected. By the end of the year the company had 50 subscribers.

For many years, the telephone was not a full-time occupation for those in the business. Edgar Baker was secretary to the Pilotage Commissioners and the greater part of his time was spent on shipping matters. He was also a company promoter interested in B.C. mines and mining stocks. Robert McMicking served as electrician to the city of Victoria looking after the electric generating plant and the street lighting. He was very careful to state in his letter of acceptance to the mayor, "that it does not interfere with my business as Electrician and Electrical dealer in other directions." He also held the reputation of being the foremost authority on electrical matters in the province, and was widely consulted by those who had electrical problems. As an additional sideline, he was an inspector of wiring for the insurance industry (the Board of Underwriters).

The first major commercial telephone system on the mainland was set up in 1880 by McMicking for the railway contractor Andrew Onderdonk to connect his Yale house to the construction sites and boarding houses that lined the 15½-mile stretch of building activity in the Fraser Canyon to Spuzzum. Railway construction was also responsible for the organizing of the first telephone company on the mainland, the New Westminster & Port Moody Telephone Co. It was the need of the railway construction personnel at Port Moody to communicate with New Westminster merchants that promoted the building of that line. When the railway was extended down Burrard Inlet to Hastings Mill and Gastown, the telephone company did likewise and changed its name to the New Westminster & Burrard Inlet Telephone Co. It was not long before Vancouver businessmen became interested in it. In 1887, Dr. J. M. Lefevre, C.P.R. surgeon, W. P. Salsbury, and John Wulffsohn of Wulffsohn & Bewicke, became shareholders. It is to be remembered that in those early days, telephone companies were very small. Five hundred dollars would buy a substantial interest in any company as Edgar Baker discovered when he purchased a fourth interest in the Kamloops Telephone Co. for that amount.

John Wulffsohn was one of the leading pioneer entrepreneurs of Vancouver. His firm, Wulffsohn & Bewicke, ran a real estate business, "advanced money on approved security," acted as a stockbroker, company promoter, and fund raiser. At the company's offices, corporation bonds, debentures, mining stocks, gas, and other company shares could be bought and sold. He became very active in channelling investment capital from his British and continental connections into local companies. He was one of the promoters of the Vernon townsite, and either he or his clients held interests in many townsite developments in the mining centres of the Kootenays. Therefore, it is not surprising that he was able to interest Dr. J. M. Lefevre and other associates, including Frank S. Barnard of Victoria, in the formation of the Vernon & Nelson Telephone Co. in 1891. In the next few years, this company was to provide telephone service to the West Kootenays by buying into or acquiring local ones. On Vancouver Island, the Lefevre group bought into the locally sponsored system in Nanaimo and revitalized it under the name of the Nanaimo Telephone Co.

Raising the money for expansion or takeovers always presented problems. This was why the involvement of John Wulffsohn in the telephone company's affairs was so important. Through his company, Wulffsohn & Bewicke, contacts had been made with investors in Edinburgh to either float a debenture or to sell the business. But sufficient guarantees could not be given and the deal fell through. There is also evidence to show that G. P. Norton, head of the Yorkshire Guarantee & Securities, submitted plans to raise funds. Then the depression of 1893-94 struck, and the confidence of the overseas investors in Wulffsohn & Bewicke faded. It was not until the upsurge in business, triggered by the Klondike boom, re-established investors' faith, and English money was again attracted to the telephone business. John Wulffsohn dropped out of the picture, and G. P. Norton and associates in the Yorkshire Guarantee & Securities Corp. entered the business; first by the creation of the Western Canada Telephone Co. and then a large holding company, the B.C. Telephones Ltd. With funds raised in Huddersfield among the Yorkshire woollen manufacturers, all the major companies in B.C. were bought under one ownership. The amounts involved were quite substantial — £62,500 in comparison with that furnished to float the original companies ($3,000 for the Victoria & Esquimalt). Edgar Baker writes in his diary that this sale of his share in the Victoria & Esquimalt Telephone Co. netted him a profit of $70,000.

The consolidation with the accompanying ability to raise additional capital in England sparked further expansion. Connections had been made with Seattle via Blaine in 1894; to Chilliwack by leased Canadian Pacific line (the old Collins telegraph) in 1896; Rossland to Spokane in the same year. But between Vancouver and

Victoria, there were no telephone connections until the laying of the submarine cable through the San Juan Islands in 1904. This was accomplished by an American corporation (the International Telephone Co.) created by American citizens, but financially underwritten by the newly organized British Columbia Telephone Co. Ltd.

G. P. Norton and his business partners in Huddersfield set out to dominate the telephone industry in British Columbia. For four years, 1898-1902, they exercised complete control. Then the minority of Canadian shareholders under Dr. J. M. Lefevre and William Farrell approached the Huddersfield group to attempt to buy back the control. Surprisingly enough, they were successful and the majority of the Huddersfield group agreed to sell. This was a startling change of policy, for it was this group that had reorganized the Vancouver Tramway & Light Co. and had been largely instrumental in creating the British Columbia Electric Railway Co. With their agent in Vancouver, R. Kerr Houlgate, they had expert and detailed knowledge of conditions in B.C. The B.C. Electric was a good and profitable investment with a great future and apparently they never had any intention of withdrawing. Didn't the telephone company have the same potential? At that time the telephone had not won public acceptance in Great Britain. To the urban dweller, tramways were essential but the telephone was not. Furthermore, telephones could not be used to develop and sell real estate like streetcars could. Whatever the reason, it was a major step and the telephone system in B.C. once more became locally owned.

William Farrell soon had plans under way to consolidate the operating companies into one province-wide corporation. This was accomplished in 1904 by the creation of the present company, the British Columbia Telephone Co. Ltd. The area covered was southern British Columbia from Vancouver Island in the west, to Nelson and the Kootenays in the east. Signifying the smallness of the operation, there were not more than 4,500 phones in the total system.

Up to this point, there had been no telephone connections between the lower mainland and Victoria, or Vancouver and the interior — two vital missing links in a province-wide telephone network. In the spring of 1904, the Vancouver interests behind the B.C. Telephone Co. Ltd. decided the time had come to connect Vancouver Island with the mainland. The route chosen was a land and submarine cable line through the San Juan Islands landing on the mainland near Bellingham. The submarine cable stretched from Telegraph Bay just north of Cadboro Bay on Vancouver Island to San Juan, then by cable and land wire over Shaw, Orcas, and Lummi islands to Mariette on the mainland. Here it connected with the Pacific States Telephone & Telegraph line to Bellingham and the Canadian-U.S. border. It was very similar to the route taken by the telegraph line in 1866. To come through American territory, William Farrell and his associates thought it advisable to set up an American corporation, the International Telephone Co. To create this corporation, the Vernon & Nelson Telephone Co. gave $50,000 of their debenture stock to serve as bank collateral in order to raise money for the project. They also agreed to pay the International Telephone Co. a rental of $3,000 per year for a period of 20 years. This line not only gave Victoria telephone access to Vancouver, but also through the Bellingham exchange to Seattle, Portland, and numerous points in Washington and Oregon. Due to the influx of American businessmen into B.C. in the next few years, it proved highly successful. The other vital link in the telephone system between Vancouver and the interior had to wait until 1931 before it was completed.

In the boom years 1905-13, telephone expansion in B.C. was substantial. There had been objections to its use when the lawyers considered it below their dignity to communicate by telephone with their clients, or doctors and dentists feared that professional advice sent over the telephone could not be charged for. More and more people were turning to the telephone for business or pleasure. To cater to the increasing business, the B.C. Telephone Co. Ltd. went into the real estate business to build its first building in 1906 — a brick and concrete structure at 555 Seymour Street (still standing in 1982). It was the first complete fireproof building erected in Vancouver. The Vancouver exchange, which had been in rented quarters in the Lefevre block at the corner of Hastings and Seymour since 1890 was moved to the new location. A major building program was initiated in 1909-10 which was to have considerable impact on construction in Vancouver. Three new brick and concrete buildings were erected to house the Highland, Fairmont, and Bayview exchanges.

On the outskirts of Vancouver, medium-sized wooden framed buildings were erected to serve as exchanges and commercial offices: Aldergrove in 1912, Port Coquitlam in 1913, and West Vancouver in 1914. Between 1907 and 1911, phones in the Vancouver area

109

doubled from 5,000 to 11,000. The staff jumped from 25 in 1893 to 700 in 1911.

During this period, three events occurred which had major significance on the telephone industry in B.C. Because British Columbia lies sandwiched between continental United States and Alaska, communications between these two points had to pass through the province. The military planners during World War II understood this well. Up to 1904, Alaska had no telegraph or telephone connections with the states to the south. In that year, the U.S. government laid a submarine cable from Seattle through the Strait of Juan de Fuca and northward, paralleling the coast of Vancouver Island. Its destination was Sitka in the Alaskan panhandle and ultimately 750 miles further northwest to Valdez. This effectively blocked any attempt to extend Canadian telegraph or telephone lines along the coast northward to tap the Alaskan panhandle. The second event was the laying of a 32-mile submarine cable by the B.C. Telephone Co. from Point Grey to Newcastle Island. For the first time this gave direct Canadian connection between the lower mainland and Vancouver Island. Consequently, Nanaimo, not Victoria, became the island's communication centre. The cable was laid by the Henley Telegraph Construction Co. of London, England, at a time when its success was not a certainty. For a number of years, it was the longest telephone cable owned by a private company. The third event was the formation on April 25, 1907, of the Okanagan Telephone Company. By default, B.C. Telephone had allowed this company to build up a vested interest in one of the most promising markets in B.C. In the early days, great hopes had been raised for the success of the Vernon exchange of the Vernon & Nelson Telephone Co., but these hopes were not realized. At that time, Vernonites had not been convinced of the necessity of the telephone so subscribers were few. In time, the office had been closed and the equipment abandoned. The Okanagan Telephone Co. went into Vernon and, by consolidating the local systems in the valley, was able to provide satisfactory service. By 1912, it had a long distance line in operation from Vernon to Penticton. The company was very progressive, and was supported by a local public who held it in respect and pride as a great regional institution.

At about the same time the Dominion Government Telegraphs went into the telephone business. It needed little modification to send telephone messages over telegraph wires, and one of the objectives of the Government Telegraphs was to provide communication services to communities which could not support commercial ventures. In the boom years before World War I, the growing communities in the Okanagan were just the spots where such service was needed. The Government Telegraph began to build up a long distance telephone network from Kamloops down through Merritt to Princeton, then eastward to the gold mines at Hedley, Keremeos, Penticton, Kelowna, and Vernon. From Vernon, the line extended back to Kamloops, some 400 miles of line in all. Some of it was composite (telephone and telegraph); some was worked as a telephone line only; some parts with the line strung from tree to tree. Only at a few places was local service provided. Local exchanges were situated at Merritt (65 subscribers), Princeton (35 subscribers), and Hedley (13 subscribers). Local service was left to private enterprise in Kelowna, Armstrong, Enderby, and other places. On Vancouver Island, the Government Telegraphs put in a 40-mile telephone line from Victoria to Jordan River in 1909 to service the Jordan River power project of the B.C. Electric. A line was also operative from Victoria to Sidney and, when the explosives plant was built, to James Island. From Nanaimo, Government Telegraphs had a telephone line to Gabriola Island. The main users seemed to be commercial companies such as the Canadian Puget Sound Lumber Co., which had a station on the Jordan River line, or Marcus Daly's mining company at Hedley. As early as 1905, a 26-mile line went over to Salt Spring Island and Ganges from Duncan.

World War I saw no striking innovations. A surprising number of male employees (101 out of a probable 400) joined up to serve overseas. Technology was ever extending the distances over which voice conversation could be carried. In 1915, calls were accepted for points as far south as San Francisco. In the next two years, service was extended from Vancouver to Montreal and New York via the United States. In the post-war years, one of the main characteristics of the world-wide telephone industry was its continuous growth. Irrespective of the economic climate, telephones became more and more of a necessity. Over the years, telephone plants became more automatic. The first automatic exchange in B.C. was installed by the Powell River Co. to service its newsprint plant and company town at Powell River in 1921. The B.C. Telephone Co. followed by installing their first automatic exchange at Hammond in 1928, and a major one in Victoria in 1930.

The inter-war years represented the golden period for the smaller locally owned telephone companies. At their peak, there were 45. In the Fraser Valley, Mission and Chilliwack had their own companies. Solar Telephones were in Revelstoke and the municipality of Summerland ran its own. Most of the rest of the villages and towns in the Okanagan enjoyed the services of the locally owned Okanagan Telephone Co. In the north, Prince Rupert and Prince George had their own installations.

At the height of the boom in the late twenties, there was a definite trend for eager out-of-the-province interests to buy up the major economic institutions in British Columbia. In 1923, F. N. Southam, a leading Ontario newspaper publisher, approached Walter Nichol to purchase the *Province* newspaper. Nichol sold out for $2,000,000 and these eastern interests have retained control up to the present day. In 1927, Theodore, Gary & Co., a Chicago-based telephone owning and management company, was approached by Gordon Farrell, the principal shareholder in the B.C. Telephone Co., to buy controlling interest in the firm. In 1928, control of the B.C. Electric Railway Co. passed out of the hands of the London-based group into those of an eastern Canadian syndicate, under the guidance of Sir Herbert Holt. Within five years, the three most influential economic units in B.C. had passed into eastern Canadian or American hands.

In the course of time, Theodore, Gary & Co. evolved into the General Telephone & Electronics Corp., one of the giants in the telecommunication field. With its 19 telephone companies servicing over 16 million phones and its vast manufacturing capacity, the corporate office was in a position to give the best in professional advice and technical know-how to any of its subsidiaries. There is no doubt that over the years the B.C. Telephone Co. has benefited materially from this connection.

Early in 1926, a group under the leadership of Major-General A. D. McRae appeared to be making the necessary moves to obtain control of the company. They included some of the Lefevre family who owned one third of the B.C. Telephone Co. stock. Gordon Farrell was utterly opposed to the idea and persuaded the directors to approach Bell Telephone of Canada. Paul Sise, president of Bell Canada, came out to look over the situation. He offered to pay $125 a share to Gordon Farrell and associates. They turned it down as a ridiculously low figure.

The B.C. Telephone Co. was not a big organization, and up to that time had relied upon the Pacific Telephone Co. of Seattle for technical advice. The U.S. company had run into trouble in this regard with both the American Telephone & Telegraph Co. and the Federal Communications Commission. They decided to cut off the service, and B.C. Telephone Co. became technically isolated.

This was the background which influenced the directors to approach the Gary interests. The Gary Corporation of Chicago was a large company which owned and managed telephones. They were strong in both the service and manufacturing ends of the industry. One of their manufacturing arms was the Automatic Electric Co. Ltd., makers of the Strowger switching equipment which the B.C. Telephone Co. was in the process of installing. The Gary Corp. took a 60-day option at $250 a share. A number of shareholders were not convinced and Gordon Farrell had a hectic time persuading them to sell. Eventually, enough shares were sold at $225 to give the Gary Corp. control.

Theodore Gary formed the National Telephone & Telegraph Corp. to finance the deal. It was a Delaware corporation set up as a holding company to acquire a majority of shares in the British Columbia Telephone Company. It is of interest to note that on the directorate were business executives from London, England, the most prominent of whom was Sir Alexander Roger.

Various factors induced the management of the National Telephone & Telegraph to transfer the assets to a new company incorporated in Canada, known as the Anglo-Canadian Telephone Company. One factor responsible for the change was that the greater part of the National Telephone & Telegraph Co. assets were in Canadian companies, creating legislative and exchange difficulties. Today the Anglo-Canadian Telephone Co. still owns the majority of the voting shares of the B.C. Telephone Co. and is itself a subsidiary of the giant General Telephone & Electronics Corp., a world leader in the telecommunications industry. The technical ties are still close between B.C. Telephone and its parent, General Telephone & Electronics Corporation. B.C. Telephone Co. has a service agreement by which it has access to the telephone technical expertise of the General Telephone.

The thirties saw the bringing in of the Trans-Canada Telephone System, a consortium of all major Canadian telephone companies. This, like the Trans-Canada Airlines, provides a direct Canadian link between eastern and western Canada. It was the responsibility of the B.C. Telephone Co. to provide the British Columbia link. This era also saw the creation of a radio-telephone service which was to link coastal shipping, lighthouses, and isolated settlements both on the coast and in the interior with one another and the metropolitan centres of Vancouver and Victoria.

In World War II, the B.C. Telephone Co. played a significant but undramatic role in providing communications to scattered military installations. The headquarters of the Pacific Communications Centre, the exchange connecting all military lines in the Pacific Command, was located in the B.C. Telephone building at 768 Seymour Street, Vancouver, from 1940 to 1945.

The great telephone story of World War II was the building of the line between Edmonton and Fairbanks, Alaska, by the U.S. Army Signal Corps in 1942. This was considered a military necessity by the planners in the Pentagon. It provided instant communication with Washington and all other military installations in the U.S., plus weather and other information to the air strips along the Northwest Staging Route to Alaska. The weather and the isolation caused great difficulty in its construction. Camps had to be set up before the construction of the Alaska Highway. Materials and men had to be flown in; the planes landed on uncharted lakes and the goods were then carried by pack horse to the sites. By May 1943, full telephone service and teletype service were in operation between Dawson Creek and Whitehorse.

The main thrust in the immediate post-war years came from an influx of population in B.C., proportionally greater than anywhere else in Canada. More people than ever before wanted telephone service. This increase was partially taken care of by automation. By the end of 1954, 50 percent of the telephones belonging to the B.C. Telephone Co. and 85 percent of the Okanagan Telephone Co.'s were automatic. In 1947, the Okanagan Telephone Co. had begun to fully automate its system, and by 1954, all the major exchanges had been switched over. During the same year, the B.C. Telephone Co. took over 1,000 miles of telephone lines from the Dominion Government Telegraph. Provision was also made through the construction of a coast-to-coast microwave chain by the Trans-Canada Telephone System to bring television and radio programs to British Columbia viewers.

The industry was moving from its traditional position of providing only oral telephone service to one of transmitting visual and high-speed data both nationally and continent wide. This meant spending huge sums on telecommunication equipment and its adequate housing. In 1956, almost one million dollars was spent on new buildings and additions to old ones, a considerable boost to the B.C. construction industry. On July 1, 1958, the world's longest single microwave system opened — from Sydney, Nova Scotia, to Victoria, B.C. The B.C. Telephone Co. constructed the section from the Alberta border to Vancouver Island, by far the most difficult of the whole system. On Dog Mountain near Hope, men and equipment had to be flown in by helicopter as the construction of an access road was impossible. An aerial tramway was then built from the base of the site, a rise of 4,900 feet.

The technical competence of the microwave system proved itself in one of the bigger news events in 1958. During the visit of H.R.H. Princess Margaret to Victoria in July of that year, the B.C. Telephone Co. supplied the television links for national and international coverage. Pictures were transmitted from Victoria to the William Farrell building in Vancouver and then on to the national network.

A major technological step was taken in 1961 by the introduction in Nanaimo of Direct Distance Dialing which enabled a customer to make his long distance calls without the assistance of an operator. This is now in province-wide use in British Columbia. That year also saw the introduction of the North West Telephone Company. This company provided services in many of the northern B.C. communities such as Prince George and the Peace River country. It also ran the radio-telephone system serving the coastal regions and the northern interior. It was the pioneer in the field of radiotelephones, having at the time of transfer some 4,000 phones in aircraft, coastal shipping, and road vehicles.

In 1962, the B.C. Telephone Co., in co-operation with the Alaska Telephone Co., placed in service a tropospheric microwave system between the lower mainland and points in Alaska. This provided a second channel between the United States and Alaska through B.C. This entailed the building of several relay stations. One of these was on Trutch Island, an isolated spot 150 miles north of Port Hardy, which had to have a small village built to house the maintenance staff.

In the seventies, the industry moved on to providing multi-purpose communications for many uses. Specialized devices were introduced for speedier and clearer messages between individuals, computers or businesses. Pictures were added to voice transmission. Marked increases were seen in computer use and the sending of business information to be collected at centralized spots. Daily business transactions, which in the past would have been recorded in Vancouver, are now sent through high speed data transmission to Toronto. Engineering studies are now fed directly by telephone wires into computers in Toronto, New York, or San Francisco. Business conferences (aural and visual to each participant) are now held via telephone wire between parties situated thousands of miles apart in the eastern United States, London, or Hamburg. This has meant tremendous increase in the transmission of business data and an expansion of the telephone business — undreamed of fifty years ago. In 1969, Telestat Canada Ltd. was established to build and operate a communication satellite providing channels for Canadian users. The B.C. Telephone Co. was one of the original sponsors and is part owner. This has resulted in an earth station being built by B.C. Telephone Co. near Duncan, Vancouver Island, to receive and send communications for the Trans-Canada Telephone network. In the same locality the Canadian Overseas Telecommunications Corp., now Teleglobe Canada, has built its own earth station to send and receive telephone messages from the Pacific Rim countries. Up to this time, all Trans-Pacific calls had to be routed through Washington State or California.

Meanwhile, several years of searching for a new B.C. Telephone Co.'s headquarters location in downtown Vancouver proved fruitless. A six-acre site was then chosen on Boundary Road in Burnaby and construction began in 1975.

Because of inadequate earnings, B.C. Telephone Co. could not issue additional bonds to finance the project. The funds it might have been able to provide were designated for customer service requirements. A separate subsidiary, 70,074 Ltd., was incorporated to handle the headquarters building as its sole asset and provide the security for its financing.

In the U.S., interest rates were lower and the $25 million needed could be obtained from a single lender rather than the many which would be required in Canada. B.C. Telephone Co. obtained the funds from John Hancock Insurance Company.

Today B.C. Telephone Co. provides telecommunication services for the whole province from the 49th parallel to the Yukon border. Its only competitor is the Canadian National-Canadian Pacific Telecommunications owned by the two major railways. Its microwave networks in B.C. handle high-speed digital business data, news, television, and radio transmissions from the major provincial centres.

This is the vehicle used by the Canadian Press to send news dispatches to its member papers.

B.C. Telephone Co. has access to the telephone expertise from the GTE Service Corporation, as is typical with other telephone operating companies under the ownership of General Telephone and Electronics Corp. In turn, GTE decentralizes most of these services from Stamford, Connecticut, headquarters to three U.S. regions.

The contributions that the communications companies have made to the building of British Columbia are impressive. The telephone industry in its early days was labour-intensive. It created much needed work, especially for women. The industry was and is a great user of the building contractor. It requires and has built many outstanding structures to house its equipment and staff. The $32 million head office building is a "masterpiece of architectural design," according to Mayor Tom Constable of Burnaby. Today many of the high technological components of the telephone industry are made in B.C. in the factories of B.C. Telephone Co.'s subsidiary, AEL Microtel Ltd. Through the work of many thousands in the industry, British Columbians now enjoy one of the best telecommunications networks in the world. Canada is now a world leader in this field, and B.C. has contributed much to its achievements.

Postal Services

The first letter sent in British Columbia was written by the explorer, David Thompson, from a point on the Columbia River to the officer-in-charge at Fort St. James in 1811. Handed from Indian band to Indian band, it arrived eight months later. The province's postal needs were met by the good offices of the Hudson's Bay Company until 1858. What negligible correspondence there was came by way of the company's annual fur brigades or with employees travelling on official business between the forts. In 1849, Vancouver Island had become a Crown Colony and thus, came under the provisions of the Imperial government's Colonial Postal Act. Nothing seems to have been done at this time to set up a postal administration. Governor Sir James Douglas wrote to Earl Grey, Secretary of State for the Colonies, on July 25, 1855, "I have the honour to inform your lordship that no general postal arrangements have ever existed in this colony."

Letters mailed from eastern Canada or Great Britain came via New York and Panama to San Francisco through the courtesy of the United States Post Office, and then by boat to Portland or Fort Vancouver on the Columbia River. Hudson's Bay Company employees then brought them by horseback and express canoe twice a month up Puget Sound to Victoria. The whole process took at least two months. As more people settled on the island, there was growing dissatisfaction with such arrangements, and the Legislative Assembly petitioned the governor for remedies.

There was no money available for postal services, but on his own responsibility Sir James Douglas appointed the Harbour Master, Captain Sangster, as Victoria's first postmaster. The efforts of the company were appreciated, as shown by a resolution passed by the Legislative Assembly in 1857: "That the Assembly acknowledge the Colony to be under great obligations to the Hudson's Bay Co. for the kind and liberal manner in which they have carried gratuitously the letters from the American shores to this island."

The influx of the gold miners in 1858 pointed out the need for better arrangements. With them came the express companies, which had served their postal requirements so well in California that they had virtually taken over the government mail services. They were to play the same role in British Columbia. The early colonial officials tried to set up a postal service. It was not a monopoly as in other countries, as they had to contend with fierce competition from the express companies. The express companies' couriers went everywhere — over the roughest trails, into the remotest of creeks. The miners trusted them as they never trusted the colonial post office; the expressmen became the postmen, and the express offices the post offices. Basically, it was that the Colonial government was after the same revenue sought by the expressmen, who also wanted the privilege of delivering mail without government prosecution. An agreement was reached so that the express companies could carry the mail; but to each letter was to be attached a colonial stamp in prepayment of the proper postage. The expressmen could do this because their charges were high, $1.00 or $2.00 per letter according to the distance carried.

No official postal regulations were ever instigated in the Colony of Vancouver Island, but in 1864 her sister Colony of British Columbia passed a Postal Ordinance to try to set up a more effective system. W. R. Spalding was appointed to head the department as the first Postmaster-General of British Columbia. When the two colonies amalgamated in 1866, this system and its regulations became operative in both. The losses were so heavy (£6,664 in 1865) that Spalding was relieved of his duties and Arthur T. Bushy, Registrar of the Supreme Court, was told to handle the postal affairs without salary along with his court duties.

The postage stamps issued by the two colonies have been the objects of admiration and treasure for successive generations of collectors. The first issue of 1860 is unique in that it is the only issue of British Colonial stamps that could officially be used in more than one colony. They bear the title for both the Colony of Vancouver Island and the Colony of British Columbia.

In the spring of 1864, Governor Frederick Seymour initiated the first door-to-door delivery of mail in British Columbia. For a small consideration, a Chinese man would deliver letters to the New Westminster homes after the Victoria boat arrived.

Sending or receiving mail which originated outside the colonies had to rely upon the United States Post Office. There were two routes used. One was by steamer from Victoria direct to San Francisco; the other was by way of Olympia and Portland, Oregon, to San Francisco. From Portland to New York, it would take 40 to 45 days via Pony Express to the Missouri River, and then by rail. Accidents to the mails were frequent, so most business houses would send their letters in duplicate. One would go via Pony Express, the other by way of Panama. This materially slowed up business, not only in British Columbia but in the entire Pacific Northwest.

The situation continued until Confederation, with poor service, high rates (it cost 25 cents to send a letter from New Westminster to Barkerville), and heavy losses. By the Terms of Union, it was stipulated that the Dominion government would take over and run the postal service in British Columbia. This meant bringing colonial postal services up to par with those provided for the rest of Canada. Whatever disadvantages the citizens of British Columbia laboured under due to other aspects of the Union, they benefited immensely by this one. Fundamental to the change was the different attitude which the Canadian public and the Canadian postal officials held regarding the role of the post office in society. Successive British governments in the nineteenth century had seen the post office as a commercial venture; something which had to be self-supporting, and also return a handsome profit into the British treasury. The results were that postal rates were high, wages low, and working conditions abominable. This attitude was reflected in the colonial postal administrations, including that of British Columbia.

The Canadian viewpoint was that the post office was not only a business but a national service — an instrument which should be used to advance the educational and cultural opportunities of the people. Annual losses were heavy, but postal rates low. Services were given in localities where it was not economically justified, and concession was given to the mailing of magazines, newspapers, and other religious and educational material. First of all, the monopoly of the express companies was broken. By law, the post office was the only organization in the country authorized to carry mail; any private firm so doing would be prosecuted with the risk of incurring heavy penalties. Secondly, "On all letters transmitted by Post for any distance in Canada — there shall be charged and paid one uniform rate of 3 cents." Reductions were also announced on newspapers and periodicals. There was such an upsurge in postal business that the contractor serving the Cariboo had to be reimbursed for the cartage of additional volume. Within the space of six years, the number of post offices almost doubled from 25 in 1871 to 49 in 1877. Registration and money order offices were established in many locations where the business did not warrant it. People found that the purchase of postal notes was the most satisfactory way of paying bills. In 1885, there were 18 registration and money order offices in the province. The Canadian post office had postal conventions or arrangements with practically all the civilized countries of the world. Through the Universal Postal Union, it had access to a world-wide network of post offices. There was practically no country where a letter could not be sent. Through its amalgamation with the Dominion post office, British Columbia was now part of this network.

With the mineral boom of the nineties and the influx of population, the post office expanded rapidly. In 1898, there were 311 offices in B.C.; by 1900, the number had grown to 364. It also meant expansion in staff, creation of new jobs, and a building program to provide new postal facilities. In 1871, there were only three postmasters on salary in all of B.C.; in 1898 there were 78. At the time of Confederation, post offices were housed in stores, commercial establishments, or in the offices of government agents. By 1900, a major public building had been erected to house the post office in Victoria. Designed by Thomas Fuller, Chief Architect of the Department of Public Works, it had all the modern conveniences such as electric light and elevators. In 1898, it was finished by general contractors Elford & Smith, and outfitted with post office equipment supplied by Weiler Bros. at a cost of $55,000. It became a landmark on Victoria's inner harbour and served at headquarters for the Victoria Postal Division for over 65 years. Major new public buildings were also built to house the post offices in Nelson, Rossland, Grand Forks, Greenwood, etc. In fact, in the growing towns of the interior, the most imposing building was often the new post office.

The Canadian Pacific trans-Pacific steamship services, which has been most beneficial to the economy of B.C., was brought about in part by the mail contracts given by the British Post Office. G.P.O. London gave the Canadian Pacific Railway an annual subsidy of £45,000 to carry Far Eastern mails from Halifax to Hong Kong. This service (once every four weeks) was carried via Vancouver for over half a century. It was the deciding factor that prompted Sir William Van Horne to build the first of the famous Empress liners. These ships carried thousands of travellers to Vancouver and gave the city world-wide publicity.

Another famous overseas route prompted by mail subsidies out of Vancouver was the Canadian Australian Line to New Zealand and Sydney. It was started by James Huddart, a Melbourne shipowner, on an annual subsidy of £25,000 given by the Canadian government, and £10,000 by New South Wales. The British Post Office took a great interest in the new route but was under contract to the P. & O. and the Orient Line for its Australian mail and was unwilling to subsidize an alternate way. For over 60 years, Canadian mail for the South Pacific was sent through Vancouver on these ships.

It only became possible to build up these overseas mail routes through Vancouver when the Canadian Pacific Railway made its through-connection to eastern Canada. Postal mail cars were introduced early on the main line when it was built through the Rockies. As early as 1886, mail cars were operating on trains between Calgary and Donald, British Columbia. By 1890, postal cars were running from Vancouver to Calgary and on the Island from Equimalt to Wellington. Each car would have two or more mail clerks who would receive, sort, and distribute mail as it was taken on at the stations or picked up from the mail catching posts. On the local runs the post office would pay the railway to have the baggageman handle the mail. By 1898, seven local British Columbia railways were receiving money from the post office to handle the local mail. These railways included the Victoria & Sidney, the Red Mountain, the Kaslo & Slocan, and the B.C. Electric for its Central Park line. As the transportation network grew, so did the post office. On every train, river, lake, or coastal steamer, somebody was appointed to look after the mail. On the trains, it was the baggageman; on the boats, the purser; in more remote areas it was the boss of the pack train, or an Indian with a canoe. The post office had agents everywhere.

From its establishment, the Vancouver Post Office has handled the Oriental and Australian mails and a goodly portion of that for the northern coast, as well as all for Vancouver and vicinity. In 1890-91, the first stone post office building was erected at the corner of Granville and Pender. It was here that the post office savings bank, the dead letter office, and the parcel post came into being. Here was arranged the placing of the first street letter boxes (first introduced in Toronto in 1859). The first house-to-house delivery in Vancouver was organized from here in 1895, copying that which had been running in eastern Canadian cities since 1875. In those early days, the atmosphere in the post office was relaxed and informal. The staff acted as a bureau of information, or as a general reference department for everything. Strangers would drop in to ask about houses to rent, places to stay, or job opportunities. The hours were as informal as the conversation, depending of course, upon the arrival of the trains and boats.

As business developed, a contract was signed on August 22, 1905, for a new post office at the corner of Granville and Hastings. It was to be one of the most imposing buildings in Vancouver. It was designed by the Chief Architect of the Department of Public Works and the contractors were the well-known Winnipeg firm of Kelly Bros. & Mitchell Ltd. This firm also held the contract for the new Canadian Bank of Commerce building across the street. The post office was to be a four-storey building costing $100,000, built of stone from local quarries with a clock tower. The upper storeys would house government departments such as customs, fisheries, etc. It took over three years to build and is today one of the landmarks of downtown Vancouver.

By the start of World War I, the post office in B.C. was big business. There were postmasters or agents in every part of the province. The mail was carried by every means of conveyance from the most modern steamers to Indian canoes — from express trains to dog teams. The northern post offices at such places as Atlin, Lake Bennett, Telegraph, or Manson Creeks, which had been established during the Klondike Gold Rush of 1899, always presented problems. Mail for Atlin came in from the north from Lake Bennett or Log Cabin on the White Pass & Yukon Railway, then via river, lake, and land trail in summer; and dog team in winter. Telegraph Creek was served in summer from Wrangel in the Alaskan panhandle, and in winter by courier from Atlin. In October 1906, the mail from Hazelton to Port Essington was lost in the Skeena River "owing to the upsetting of the canoe in which it was conveyed." In the same year, mail from Camp McKinley in the Boundary country was stolen by burglars while in the Midway post office with "no clues," as the Postmaster General reported.

No outstanding event occurred during the war years which affected the postal service in the way the lumber industry was influenced by the opening up of the Queen Charlotte Islands to obtain spruce for the building of airplanes. Enlistment was heavy; the volume of mail increased to a marked degree, especially to the Armed Forces overseas. Mail was censored somewhat, particularly from aliens and prisoner-of-war camps in the interior. The war was far away, and outside of manpower registration and other government wartime regulations, the work load of the post office was routine, but heavy.

The Canadian postal administration had been watching progress in aviation with interest. Many pioneer flights had been partly financed by the transport of letters. Though the cost was high and the reliability of the service much in question, the advantages were great. The United States Post Office was a pioneer in this field and by 1927 several successful airmail routes were in operation, including one from Seattle to Victoria (as described in chapter 2). This was the year the Canadian Post Office officially went into the airmail business, alloting $75,000 in its budget for this purpose. One of the first semi-official arrangements was made with the Yukon Airways & Exploration Ltd. to carry the mails from Whitehorse to Dawson. In 1928, it was extended from Whitehorse to Carcross and Atlin, and in December of that year the first flight was made to Telegraph Creek. These flights carried the first letters ever to be flown into northern British Columbia. In the south, there was a short-lived, semi-official service between Vancouver and Victoria provided by British Columbia Airways Ltd., only in the summer of 1928. To help pay for the services, the Post Office Department allowed these companies to print and sell their own semi-official stamps which had to be attached to all letters along with the regulation postage. These semi-official stamps are now collectors' items. Gradually, connections were made to Seattle by United Airways in 1934 and to eastern Canada by Trans-Canada Airlines in 1939.

It was the mineral development in northern B.C. which sparked the greatest activity. In the summer of 1937, mail contracts were given to Grant McConachie and his United Air Transport Ltd. for flights to and from Prince George, Fort St. James, Takla Landing, and Manson Creek. As the *Vancouver Sun* printed on June 3, 1937, "The inauguration of the two regular services from Prince George will give impetus to development of the north. For the first time a mail service will enable the rapidly increasing number of miners and trappers to keep in touch with civilization."

In the same year (1937), airmail service was established between Edmonton and Whitehorse with an intermediate stop at Fort Nelson, British Columbia. This crossed northern B.C. near the B.C.-Yukon border and was the forerunner of the North West Staging Route of World War II. Vancouver-Williams Lake-Quesnel-Prince George were connected for the first time by airmail August 4, 1938. By the next year, most of the post offices north of the Canadian National rail line (Prince George-Prince Rupert) were served by airmail. In the Peace district, the mail still came through Edmonton by air to Grande Prairie, Alberta, and then by surface mail to Pouce Coupe and Dawson Creek. Airmail was not in universal use as it is today but had to be specified by the sender of the letter and extra postage was required.

Until the 1970's, the post office was a "manual" operation which employed many people, and was housed in many types of buildings. In terms of jobs created and capital expenditures (buildings and equipment), the post office ranks as one of the major businesses in B.C. At the present time (1982) there are 6,800 full-time postal employees in the province, 2,900 of whom work in Vancouver.

A new central building devoted entirely to postal use was erected on Georgia Street in Vancouver. The site was cleared in 1953, construction started two years later, and it was finally completed in 1958. This building is the main distribution point for the B.C. and Yukon Postal District, and handles all foreign mail for the Pacific Rim countries.

At the Vancouver International Airport, a post office building has been erected to handle the arrivals and departures of all airmail, both domestic and foreign. This is a new concept for the Pacific coast, as up to that time airmail was taken directly to planes from the general post office building downtown. In Victoria, a new mechanized mail handling plant distribution centre has been built at a cost of $9.4 million on the outskirts.

The post office has been slow to mechanize, but has now installed letter-sorting machines, letter shakers, optical scanners, and coding machinery, all computer controlled. This machinery is designed in Germany, Belgium, and Japan, and is now installed in Vancouver and Victoria. It will eventually result in a factory-like system which processes the mail mechanically.

The post office now faces direct competition from the telecommunications companies such as the B.C. Telephone Co. and Canadian National-Canadian Pacific Telecommunications. One of the main innovations of the future post office will be electronic mailing. The letter is scanned at the receiving point, sent via satellite to its destination, recovered in its original form, and delivered. Letters can thus be written and delivered within hours instead of days.

The functions of the post office are central to the maintenance and development of British Columbia society. Over the years, B.C. postal services have provided one of the most vital links in the field of communications, and this has played a significant role in the building of the province.

CHAPTER FOUR

GROWTH OF METROPOLITAN CITIES

Victoria

Cities dominate their geographic regions for many reasons. In the case of Victoria, it was the only British port in the North Pacific in the early days. Through it was funnelled all merchandise for both Vancouver Island and the mainland. The commission merchants stationed in Victoria anticipated most of the needs of the two colonies' miners and townspeople and then met it through San Francisco or London. The greater proportion of this trade had to come through Victoria. To service it, merchants and their employees, transportation men, bank clerks, and professional people like accountants, doctors, lawyers, and civil engineers congregated in Victoria. Thus, the influence of the city spread to every settled part of the country.

The city grew from a settlement of transients living in tents to a more settled community of wooden stores, warehouses, and homes. Within a few years, more substantial brick and stone structures were built with a permanent population of over 6,000 and 1,500 buildings. At the close of the Cariboo Gold Rush, Victoria had become a town with substantially built business establishments and many tasteful, small homes. It was also the capital of the united colonies of British Columbia and Vancouver Island and held the political and the economic power of the region.

The decade 1870-1880 was a period of business stagnation in British Columbia; population had declined from the previous years. According to the census taken by the provincial government in 1871, there were now only 4,350 whites living in Victoria or vicinity. But it still continued to be the dominant economic, political, and social centre for the province. The most prominent buildings erected during this period were the Customs House on Wharf Street, which still stands today, and the beginnings of the present

City Hall. One of the factors which partially explains the "no growth" situation was that the population of Victoria in 1881 was almost the same as that of 1862. There was no land development because there was no influx of people. However, over the years, a significant shift had occurred in land ownership. In the early days the Hudson's Bay Company had purchased most of the land upon which the city of Victoria now stands from the Colony of Vancouver Island. Old-time employees of the Hudson's Bay Company like Joseph Despard Pemberton, Dr. John Sebastian Helmcken, Sir James Douglas, or John Tod purchased large blocks of this land from the company.

For centuries, the wealth of the gentry in the United Kingdom had rested upon ownership of land. Influenced by this tradition, these employees began to accumulate large landed estates. In their lifetime there was very little demand for this land and in many cases these blocks passed intact to their descendants, so there were a number of estates bearing family names: Pemberton, Douglas, Tod, etc.

When the country was opened up by the railway contracts, much business activity arose, and the economy began to take shape in a form which was more lasting. These years witnessed the establishment of many important Victoria firms. It was in 1881 that Robert Ward started his commission, cannery, and insurance business which eventually would be housed in the Temple Building on Fort Street, one of the few commercial structures designed by Samuel Maclure. It still stands today. On the north side of Bastion Square a red brick building was erected in 1880 by Turner-Beeton & Co. — cannery owners, commission and insurance agents, and manufacturers of clothing. Its importance in the Victoria business hierarchy might be gauged by the fact that its managing director, J. H. Turner, was to be a future premier of British Columbia. This was the time that R. P. Rithet & Co. moved into their new building on Wharf Street which they occupied for the next sixty years, and is still in use as the offices of the Provincial Ministry of Tourism in 1982. It also saw the erection of the head office on the Pacific coast of the London-based Bank of British Columbia at Fort and Government streets. Designed by architect W. H. Williams of Portland, Oregon, it is still a landmark of downtown Victoria.

This decade also witnessed the start of the millions of pounds of English money which poured into Victoria over the next 35 years. The B.C. Land and Investment Agency Ltd. under the London capitalist, Thomas Dixon Galpin, invested heavily in Victoria property and was the vehicle by which many English investors did likewise. The Yorkshire Guarantee & Securities Corp., which was to play so great a role in the development of Vancouver, was starting to encourage their clients to invest money in Victoria through their agent, Daly & Claxten.

On the manufacturing side, Albion Iron Works, the best equipped machine shop north of San Francisco, was filling an order for 60 thirty-ton rail cars for the Esquimalt & Nanaimo Railway, turning out engines and boilers for tugboats, and steel pipe for both the Victoria and Vancouver waterworks. This firm also carried on a large business in the making of stoves for the Pacific coast market. It was a large operation for its time covering some 3½ acres of ground and employing over 220 men. In another location, the Victoria Machinery Depot, well known to three generations of Victorians, was busy making machinery for the salmon canneries up the coast. In the consulting field, Braden & Stamford, civil and sanitary engineers of Victoria, were putting up gas works in Nanaimo, New Westminster, and Vancouver, installing plumbing in the original Hotel Vancouver and Jubilee Hospital in Victoria. They also had much work south of the border installing the gas, electric light, and waterworks plants in Port Angeles.

From 1890 to 1914, vast changes occurred in the economic life of the province. New methods in transportation had made travel easy and inexpensive, stimulating much immigration. New products appeared in the market place. In the industrial field there were improvements in the factories. In the field of consumer goods, there were bicycles, automobiles, and gramophones. The manufacturing and distribution of these new products created more business, an increasing number of new jobs and urban growth. It was reflected in the growth of the city of Victoria, and was symbolized by the crowning building achievement of the nineties: the new Parliament Buildings. It anchored beyond controversy the capital in Victoria and set the growth pattern of the city in two main directions; that of providing governmental services and acting as the main tourist attraction on Vancouver Island. It also brought onto the Victoria scene the architect, F. M. Rattenbury, who would exercise such an outstanding influence on the design of buildings erected in the province over the next 25 years. His great work in the first decade of the twentieth century was the Empress Hotel. Within this period the city acquired its streetcar system, telephones, and electricity. The boundaries of the city were extended twice, first in 1891 to take in most of James Bay, and east and northward to the boundaries of what was to become Oak Bay municipality, and secondly in 1912, when part of the Ross Bay area was taken in.

The keynote to metropolitan progress was land development. Typical of this was the development of Oak Bay as a residential area. Up to 1891, Oak Bay was too far away from Victoria to attract any of its citizens to build homes. The land was owned in large blocks by the Hudson's Bay Company or some of its employees. Joseph Pemberton owned some 188 acres, the Tod estate had over 400, and smaller parcels were owned by the Ross family. Beaumont Boggs, partner in the Victoria real estate firm of Crane, McGregor & Boggs, conceived the idea of forming a syndicate to buy some of the Oak Bay property and persuade the street railway company to extend its line. The property would then be subdivided and sold to wealthy people.

The street railway reached Oak Bay in June of 1891, one track providing a shuttle service every half hour. The syndicate also sponsored the building of a luxury hotel — the Mount Baker — which was famous on three continents for its patronage by the new leisured English middle-class travellers. Oak Bay became known as "a watering, bathing, and seaside resort." When the Victoria Golf Club rented part of the Pemberton Estate from the developer, the Gonzales Point Land Co., and laid out its course, Oak Bay became an exclusive residential district for the moneyed classes and people such as F. M. Rattenbury and Samuel Maclure began to build their homes there.

F. M. Rattenbury also had his hand in the most prestigious land development scheme ever undertaken in Victoria. Uplands was an exclusive residential district within the municipality of Oak Bay, and was built in accordance with long range plans and under strict controls on land purchased from the Hudson's Bay Company. The general layout and the landscaping was entrusted to Frederick Law Olmstead, the foremost American landscape architect and the man who designed the grounds of the Alaska-Yukon Exhibition in Seattle in 1909. F. M. Rattenbury was to be the architectural advisor to the developers. It is due to his influence that Uplands houses fit so well into their surroundings. In 1913, Victoria's land boom ended. Land became unsaleable and many Victorians lacked the money to pay their taxes. This had its effect on Uplands. The asphalt roads, the water mains, the sewerage system, and the ornamental street lights had all been built, but only a few lots had been sold and hundreds of acres remained in the hands of the developers. The underwriters, a group of French financiers, ran out of money. Then World War I came and by 1920-21 the company was owing the municipality of Oak Bay some $80,000 in back taxes. Uplands' prosperity never really recovered until after World War II.

The period 1890-1914 saw not only growth in the suburbs but in the city itself. Even before the opening of the Empress in 1908, Victoria had become noted for its hotels. The seven-storey addition to the Driard Hotel in 1892 (now part of Eaton's department store) made it the first hotel of its day in Victoria. Anyone of note had to stay at the Driard Hotel — including Baroness Macdonald, widow of Sir John A. Macdonald. The Hotel Dallas near Rithet's Outer Wharves, remodelled by F. M. Rattenbury in 1902, the Mount Baker, and Oak Bay Hotel were the luxury hotels catering to the upcoming leisured class. Even the German aristocracy under the sponsorship of Alvo von Alensleben had ventured into the hotel business with the building of the Kaiserhof at the corner of Blanshard and Johnson streets. As late as 1912, Victoria entrepreneurs were building luxury hotels such as the Belmont Building which was originally erected as a hotel. Unfortunately, with the collapse of the boom in 1913, plans were changed and it became an office building. But Rattenbury's creation, the Empress, outshone them all. It is hard to estimate the contributions this hotel has made to the business and social life of Victoria, through three quarters of a century. The creation of such grand hotels helped to set the trend that has made Victoria a tourist city throughout the years.

The erection of business establishments also made a contribution to the growth of the city, which it still enjoys. When the Bank of Montreal opened its first office in Victoria in 1892, it was in a Rattenbury-designed building which still stands and is still used for its original purpose. Substantial office blocks were erected like the 160-office Sayward Building in 1910, the Pemberton Building (now Yarrows) and others. In commercial buildings and warehouses, one of the finest examples is the Pither & Leiser warehouse of 1905 at the corner of Fort and Wharf streets, now used as provincial government offices.

By 1914, Victoria had lost its metropolitan status as the first city of B.C., but still had a dominant position as the business centre for southern Vancouver Island. Furthermore, it was the political capital of the province, housing the headquarters of all provincial government departments. It was fast becoming the administrative centre of B.C. and a tourist city of world-wide repute.

These are the characteristics of Victoria today. Tourism brought the building of many hotels and motels and tourist attractions like the provincial museum. As the centre of government, there was need for office space which was initially filled by the erection of the Douglas Building and temporary offices around the Parliament grounds. In recent years the government has erected several office buildings in downtown Victoria. The biggest business in Victoria today is government, and it is housed in many public and private office buildings in the metropolitan area. Because Victoria is a retirement centre, the developers have erected dozens of high-rises and two- and three-storey frame apartments and condominiums. To service these people, shopping centres have been built such as Mayfair, Town & Country, and Hillside. These have spread out into the neighbouring municipalities so that today there are more people living in the surrounding districts than in the city itself.

New Westminster

Until overshadowed by Vancouver at the turn of the century, New Westminster exercised considerable economic and social power. In gold rush days it was the trans-shipment point for goods destined for the gold bars on the Fraser or the mines of the Cariboo. For nine years, 1859-68, it was the seat of government for the Colony of British Columbia and housed the civil servants and their governmental departments. It also had close ties with the great lumber export mills (Moodyville and Hastings) on Burrard Inlet. When the Cariboo gold boom collapsed and the capital moved to Victoria, it lost much of its influence. But even in the stagnant seventies, it possessed aggressive businessmen, Henry V. Edmonds and T. J. Trapp, who advocated and built a railway to the south — the New Westminster & Southern. The Dominion government also expended large sums in New Westminster in the building of the penitentiary and the asylum for the insane.

Over the succeeding years, houses were built and businesses established so that in the early nineties, New Westminster for a short time enjoyed metropolitan status with a population of 7,000. It was the natural commercial centre for the Fraser Valley and the 20-odd salmon canneries situated on the lower reaches. Although many of the canneries were Vancouver or Victoria owned, they looked to New Westminster for their wooden fish boxes, some cannery machinery, and other supplies. Many wealthy entrepreneurs such as McEwen the salmon canner, Irving of shipping fame, and owners of sawmills had their homes on Royal Avenue. The city was becoming a large sawmill centre with two important mills within the city itself, the Royal City Planing Mills and the Brunette sawmill, and the big Ross-Mclaren one at Millside, now Fraser Mills. The sawmill owners like Sewell P. Moody, J. A. Homer, and James B. Kennedy wielded much influence in provincial as well as federal affairs.

In the field of manufacturing, New Westminster was not insignificant. In 1890, there were five machine shops within the city which could make machinery for the sawmilling and cannery industries, and boilers and steel pipes for waterworks and irrigation projects. At the time, the McGilliveray Pipe Co. of New Westminster was making pipe for the hydraulic mines in the Cariboo. Donald McGilliveray had a province-wide reputation as a builder and contractor. It was the boom period and in 1891-92 New Westminster built a new courthouse and a well-designed library with recreation rooms near the present post office.

Real estate was most active of all. Henry V. Edmonds was one of the first to see the potentials of Vancouver property. In 1884 before the coming of the C.P.R. he had bought property in Coal Harbour. He was the owner and developer of the district of Mt. Pleasant, subdividing the property and selling the lots for housing. He was one of the principal backers of the street railway in New Westminster and promoted the Westminster & Vancouver Tramway Co. as a means of improving the saleability of his holdings around Edmonds. The depression of 1893-94 wiped him out completely as it did to numerous other real estate operators.

This grave business setback affected New Westminster as it did Vancouver. There were many business failures, and vacant stores were a common sight on city streets. Thomas John Trapp, one of the greatest of New Westminster merchants, had to sign over his assets to his creditors. Machine shops went bankrupt. B.C. Iron Works of Vancouver bought one and shipped the machinery to the Kootenays to take advantage of the engineering business which was expected from the newly opened mines in that area. After 1900 New Westminster lost its metropolitan status to Vancouver. Business decisions were now being made there or in Victoria or London.

New Westminster was still pre-eminently the commercial centre of the Fraser Valley. This was true more than ever after the building of the B.C. Electric's inter-urban line to Chilliwack. All Fraser Valley roads on the south side led to New Westminster. As the province grew, the lumbering industry grew with it including that within the city boundaries. Enough work was available for its citizens and they grew very self-satisfied. The city became self-contained and the attitudes of its citizens parochial. They held great pride in their city but were adverse to change. These attitudes lasted until after the close of World War II. Good roads, the bus, and the private automobile changed work and shopping habits, so that New Westminster has become just another unit of metropolitan Vancouver.

Vancouver

The investment and speculation in land played a major role in the development of Vancouver. For many years previous to the coming of the railroad, land speculators interested in capital appreciation had been attracted to the area surrounding Burrard Inlet. A coal seam had been identified by George Turner of the Royal Engineers when he surveyed Lot 185 (the present West End) in 1863 on the instructions of Colonel Moody. The prospect of finding coal had resulted in "a flood of applications for pre-emptions" — one of whom was Colonel Moody himself who pre-empted 250 acres "on the upper end of False Creek," according to the *British Columbian* of June 25, 1862.

The building of Hastings Mill in 1865 created considerable employment and a demand for timber leases. The mill company applied for and was granted over 8,000 acres around English Bay that extended as far back as the Arbutus ridge.

In December of 1865, three Huddersfield youths (John Morton, Samuel Brighouse and William Hailstone) applied for and purchased from the Crown 585 acres comprising Lot 185 for £114. Bounded on the east by what is now Burrard Street, on the west by Stanley Park and on the other two sides by Burrard Inlet and English Bay, it is now known as the West End of the city of Vancouver — one of the most valuable pieces of real estate in western

133

Canada. When they bought it, they had no knowledge of its future value or the fortunes that it would bring them. It seemed to be suitable for farming and there was a bed of clay within the property from which rough pottery could be made.

In 1870, the little settlement of Granville was laid out as a townsite by the Colonial government. At that time, there were nine buildings on the site including a customs house and a jail. Sixteen lots had been sold. Over the next decade 30 more lots were sold by the government to private owners. In 1880, the permanent population fluctuated from 75 to 100; there were three hotels and several stores. The settlement also supported a large floating group of loggers and seamen. Three streets had been laid out: Water, Carrall and Westminster Road. Under the agreement made between the provincial government and the C.P.R. on November 26, 1885, Granville townsite was given to the railway as part of the land bonus to induce the railway to extend its line down Burrard Inlet. According to the government there "are no legal claims against the land." The C.P.R. found this to be the understatement of the year, as it had to purchase the land from the present occupiers. The railway set a limit of $200 per lot. Many were dissatisfied with this price and went to arbitration. Out of the 15 cases that went to arbitration, the judge found 13 of these valid. It finally ended up that the province had to pay.

The year 1882 saw the creation of the first major private real estate development in British Columbia, the forerunner of such vast projects as the British Properties and Annacis Island. David Oppenheimer and his associates, which included C. D. Rand, bought an interest in the Morton-Brighouse-Hailstone property in the West End and subdivided it into townsite lots. The surveys were undertaken by George Turner in a civilian capacity now. The whole of Lot 185 was staked out into individual lots and numbered — the streets were laid out on paper and the complete plan filed in the land registry at New Westminster. The promoters named the development the city of Liverpool and through the efforts of C. D. Rand, the lots went on sale. The C.P.R. had not yet announced its intention of extending the line westward from Port Moody and there was little interest. There must have been a few sales for its is known that H. V. Edmonds (who held large acreage in the east end of what was to be the city of Vancouver) owned property at Coal Harbour at an early date. As an early attempt to persuade the C.P.R., David Oppenheimer convinced John Morton and his partners to donate ⅓ of their holdings to the railway company. Morton's opinion was that this gesture was unnecessary as the C.P.R. would be compelled to extend its line down the inlet for technical reasons without any additional inducement. The time was premature; the Winnipeg land boom had just collapsed and there were no indications that the C.P.R. would build down the inlet.

Today the city of Liverpool appears on no maps and the scheme has been entirely forgotten. John Morton retired to Mission where he farmed for a number of years. Samuel Brighouse concentrated on his properties on Lulu Island where he became politically prominent in the affairs of the municipality of Richmond. William Hailstone seems to have dropped out of the picture and returned within a few years to England.

It was the coming of the railway in 1886 to what is now the city of Vancouver that sparked real development. Basically, it was in the hands of two groups. The Canadian Pacific Railway was obligated to build wharves, a station, railway shops, and other facilities consistent with the terminal of a great transcontinental railway. The other group consisted of private entrepreneurs whose main preoccupations were urban growth, construction of homes and commercial buildings, sale and speculation in real estate, and the financing of land purchases and commercial enterprises. It was in the field of real estate that the greatest growth and most feverish activity was seen.

One of the most active enterprises in this field was the Vancouver Improvement Co. Outside of the C.P.R., it was the largest land owner in Vancouver and was tied up financially and socially with three of the most active businessmen in the city, the Oppenheimer brothers (David and Isaac) and C. D. Rand of Rand Bros., real estate operators and agents for some of the most important out-of-town investment and financial houses. The Vancouver Improvement Co. was originally a Victoria-based company incorporated in 1886 under such names as Major G. T. Dupont, Frank S. Barnard, Edward G. Prior, Dr. Israel Powell, and the Oppenheimer brothers. Dupont, Powell, and the Oppenheimers already had large holdings in Vancouver real estate. In fact, as far back as 1877, Dr. Israel Powell had bought 330 acres (D.L. 183 and 192) from Judge Pellew Crease for $3,500.

The Vancouver Improvement Co. supplied the land upon which the B.C. Sugar Refinery was built. It also helped to establish the two pioneer engineering firms of Vancouver. The Vancouver City

Foundry and Machine Works was built on waterfront property adjacent to the C.P.R. tracks owned by the Vancouver Improvement Co. The capital to set up the B.C. Iron Works was raised in private offerings and public shares by Rand Bros. In its corporate capacity, Oppenheimer Bros. Ltd. subscribed for and held a block of these shares for many years. The Vancouver Improvement Co., along with David Oppenheimer, promoted the first street railway and the first electric lighting company in Vancouver. Through its vast holdings, it brought much business to Rand Bros., one of the two most important financial and real estate operators in the city. The close connection between these firms was shown in the fact that C. D. Rand, the senior partner in Rand Bros., was also secretary of the Vancouver Improvement Co. The volume of business transacted was immense for its day and location. In the six years from 1886 to 1893, it sold $330,000 worth of land and still had $450,000 more on its books. With such a bright future early in its career, it is surprising that several major shareholders, Dr. Israel Powell, Edward G. Prior, Major G. T. Dupont, were persuaded to sell to the group of Huddersfield woollen manufacturers who founded the Yorkshire Guarantee and Securities Corp. Thus, in 1890 control passed into their hands and remained until its liquidation some eight years later.

Throughout the years, John Morton and his cousin, Samuel Brighouse, were in constant touch with their families and friends in Huddersfield. Many were wealthy businessmen and woollen manufacturers with surplus money to invest. Particularly, they were all clients of the chartered accountant G. P. Norton. Thus, through long association they knew what was happening in Vancouver and vicinity. It has been mentioned earlier in this chapter how John Morton became associated with David Oppenheimer in his land deals. It is interesting to note that both men relied upon C. D. Rand as their agent to handle their real estate deals. Thus C. D. Rand, through John Morton, had come to know the wealthy group in Huddersfield who had money to invest. He persuaded them that Vancouver was the place to invest and that Rand Bros. was the ideal agent to do the job. It was not long before G. P. Norton, the leader of the group, organized a limited liability company based in Huddersfield to collect funds to be invested in Vancouver real estate or mortgages. Rand Bros. was to act as the Vancouver agent.

G. P. Norton's creation, the Yorkshire Guarantee and Securities Corp., was so successful in raising money from the manufacturers and professional people not only from Huddersfield, but from the neighbouring towns of Bradford and Leeds (where they established offices), that they decided to send their own representatives to Vancouver. The man they chose was William Farrell, a resident of the West Riding of Yorkshire with banking and accounting experience. He arrived in Vancouver in September 1891 to open an office of the Yorkshire Guarantee and Securities Corp. on the premises of Rand Bros. The new office was separated from the main office by a partition "which will leave no way of access from one office to the other." The rent was $50 per month.

Thus was established one of the most influential financial institutions in Vancouver in its pioneer days. It was mentioned in Chapter 2 how this firm, in times of great difficulties, kept the street railway and lighting companies afloat and was ultimately able to accomplish a reorganization resulting in the formation of the British Columbia Electric Railway Company. As described in Chapter 3, it also brought the telephone systems operating in B.C. under one ownership. For a number of years, this small group of Huddersfield investors exercised immense economic power in British Columbia since they controlled all major utilities and the most powerful financial institution in the province. They were also one of the largest land owners in Vancouver.

In the seven years from 1886 to 1893, the growth of Vancouver had been spectacular. In those years 62 real estate firms had become established. There were 32 practising lawyers, 10 architects, and many secondary manufacturing establishments had been built. The city was well supplied with utilities: a gas plant, electric lighting, street railways, telephones, and a water supply that crossed from the North Shore in one of the first underwater pipes laid in British Columbia. Numerous office buildings, stores, and homes had been built. The railway had been busy building terminal facilities, laying out the townsite on its land grant (although not very many houses had yet been built), and erecting the Hotel Vancouver "away out of town in the clearing." All citizens agreed that Vancouver's future was bright, even going so far as to say that its location guaranteed its future greatness. Outside money kept pouring in, especially in real estate. In fact, the buying and selling of land was the main preoccupation of the majority of the residents. Vancouverites were gambling on the future.

Then came the Depression of 1893-1896. The bottom collapsed from the real estate market. In his annual report for 1894, Henry

137

Town, chairman of the Vancouver Loan and Securities, wrote: "Land sales were impossible — and for the first time we have received no dividends" (from the Vancouver Improvement Co.). Real estate actually became valueless and unsaleable at any price. Much of it came back into the hands of the city for the non-payment of taxes. Grocers, hardware, and dry goods merchants, draymen and truckmen, stationers and printers, plumbers and electricians, wholesale produce dealers, jewellers, harness makers, boot and shoe manufacturers, hotel keepers, restaurant owners, real estate operators, and even a farmer, James W. Larson in the municipality of South Vancouver, were all forced out of business.

It reflects very highly upon the business sagacity, the financial skills, and the resources of that small group of Huddersfield investors behind the Yorkshire Guarantee and Securities Corp., that they were able to save the utilities of Vancouver. These included the streetcar line, the electric lighting, and the telephone. Once the worst was over, they were put on a sound financial footing. Their land owning companies never really survived the effects of this depression. The Vancouver Improvement Co. was liquidated in 1898; the tax bill alone on land which could not be sold was $18,600. The Vancouver Land and Securities Corp. closed its Vancouver offices in 1896 and was voluntarily liquidated in 1904. According to the annual report of August 31, 1898, "The holdings of the corporation are chiefly situated outside of the good business lots and choice residential property. A great deal of the property is at the present time unsaleable, there being in Vancouver an absence of demand for Real Estate."

The significant upturn in the economy for 1905 to 1913 marked the next phase in Vancouver's development. The emphasis now lay more in the commercial field than in real estate. The mining boom in the Kootenays, the opening up of the prairie markets to B.C. lumber, the building of two additional transcontinental railways all had their effects on Vancouver. It became the day of the merchant prince. The great wholesale houses, W. H. Malkin & Co., Kelly Douglas & Co., McLennen and McFeely, became the distributing centres for the logging camps, the salmon canneries, and the construction firms building the railways, the company towns and the great hydroelectric projects. Vancouver served as the shopping and wholesale centre for an ever-growing mainland market. These were the times when Vancouver received 2,000 or more newcomers every month. The wholesalers built large warehouses

138

adjacent to the C.P.R. track on Water Street which became in those days the busiest street west of Winnipeg.

Many notable buildings were erected in this period. The Winch building next to the post office was constructed of stone from a local quarry to house the financial commission and insurance company of that name. The Dominion Building was "an object of pride to every citizen" at the corner of Cambie and Hastings; the Roger's Building on Granville Street; L. D. Taylor's World Building which was the forerunner in style of the Woolworth Building in New York and the Smith Building in Seattle. Outstanding buildings of architectural merit included the Canadian Bank of Commerce at Hastings and Granville, which was designed in the classic Greco-Roman style by a Toronto architectural firm and built by a well-known Winnipeg contractor. The Vancouver Courthouse, a Rattenbury creation, billed as the most outstanding public building in B.C. outside of the Parliament Buildings in Victoria.

It was in this period that Vancouver first gained metropolitan status. It became the financial, distribution, shopping, and manufacturing centre of B.C., a position that it has never relinquished. Within the city limits, manufacturing became quite important. Prior to 1914, False Creek was the heartland of the B.C. sawmilling industry. On the outskirts, the north banks of the Fraser River were dotted with sawmills from Marpole to New Westminster. Dollarton on the North Shore and Barnet on the South Shore of Burrard Inlet were sawmilling centres. Great engineering works were situated almost within the core of Vancouver, the Vancouver Engineering Works on First Avenue and Dominion Bridge on False Creek.

The year 1914 brought business stagnation, and in August, outright depression when World War I was declared. For the first time since the middle of the nineties, the population of the city decreased. Business and industry was at a standstill. Only when the war industries got into their strides in 1915-16, did Vancouver experience a temporary revival.

With the return of peace and prosperity of the 1920's, the city again began experiencing growth. The business district started to spread west of Granville. Houses in the downtown area gave way to commercial buildings. Some notable achievements were the building of the new University of British Columbia at its new site at Point Grey in 1924-25 by the R. J. Ryan Construction Company, the opening of the first bridge linking Vancouver with the North

Shore at the Second Narrows in 1925, and the erecting of the Marine Building at the corner of Hastings and Burrard in 1928-29. This was built by the Toronto-based Stimson Developers, and was the most ornate of all Vancouver office buildings. When the Depression hit, they got into financial trouble, offering it to the city of Vancouver as a new City Hall at 40 percent of its initial cost. The city turned the offer down. Finally, it was purchased by the Guinness interests of England at a fire-sale price. Mention should also be made of the Union Bank Building (1919-20) opposite Spencer's Department Store on Hastings Street, for its architectural beauty. It now houses a branch of the Toronto-Dominion Bank.

One of the significant factors was the entry of the Guinness interests of England into Vancouver and North Shore real estate. The building of the First Narrows Bridge (a private venture of Guinness) and the development of the British Properties as a high-class restrictive residential area were to have major effects in Vancouver, and particularly the North Shore.

When the Great Depression struck, building came to a standstill. Factories closed down, some for well over a year. Breadlines began to form not only of unemployed Vancouverites, but thousands more who streamed in from logging camps, mining communities, and hundreds of towns and villages on the prairies where no work was to be found. Instead of expansion, it became contraction.

It was not until the war clouds had gathered over Europe and the nations were feverishly rearming with its demand for metals, that Vancouver came out of its apathy. The year 1939 saw the opening of the new Hotel Vancouver, an architectural landmark, and the completion of the First Narrows Bridge, an engineering achievement of the first magnitude.

The economic recovery that had been going on since 1937 was augmented by World War II. The city experienced growth of a transient nature. Thousands of extra workers were drawn into the city by the war industries, the shipyards, aircraft, and munition factories. They had to be fed, housed, and cared for. This provided a stimulus for business. The federal government built housing estates (Sea Island for example) which are with us today. The shipyards at False Creek and North Vancouver, and the Boeing aircraft plant on Sea Island, showed a healthy appetite for steel, machinery of all kinds, and other essentials. All this created a climate which was beneficial to Vancouver. By 1941, the city population reached 275,000 — almost a threefold increase over 1914.

The post-war prosperity which lasted with only minor breaks to the present day has seen vast changes in Vancouver. Industry has moved out from downtown Vancouver and it has become a place of giant office buildings. Whereas, in the 1930's, the Marine Building was considered the ultimate in office construction, today in 1982 there are in the city core half a dozen structures with twice the floor space, and rising to 34 and 35 storeys. One of novel construction is the Trans Mountain Pipe Line Building on Georgia Street, built on the suspension principle — the whole weight of the building being carried by wire rope suspended from a central tower.

After 1945, in the residential sections, a new development was the high-rise apartment. From the shores of English Bay in West Vancouver to Langley in the Fraser Valley, these can be seen in all the bedroom suburbs of Greater Vancouver.

A building concept which now enjoys wide acceptance in metropolitan Vancouver is that of the industrial estate. Some enterprising entrepreneur would buy up undeveloped acreage, put in the services, roads, sewerage, gas, electricity, water, and even railway lines if practical. He would then approach manufacturers, distributors, and warehousemen and offer to build a factory or warehouse to their specifications with all services supplied; then lease it to the potential occupier. Some of these industrial estates are set in beautiful surroundings, landscaped with boulevards and wide open spaces. They are models of how factories and warehouses should be built and situated.

The originator of the idea in western Canada was an Englishman, the Duke of Westminster. Hugh Grosvenor, 2nd Duke of Westminster, was a man of many interests, head of an old family famous in English history, one of the largest landholders in the country, a soldier of distinction in two wars and a businessman of extraordinary vision. He succeeded his grandfather in the dukedom in 1899 and for fifty years was a progressive factor in land development both in England and abroad. He early saw that economic growth in England was on the decline and that the more profitable investments were to be found in the Empire and Commonwealth. As early as 1906 he was interested in land development in what was then called Rhodesia and in succeeding years sent his agents into South Africa, Australia, and Canada to look for investment opportunities. He or his agent bought 1,200 acres on Annacis Island in 1950. Within the next two years he had decided to turn this property into an industrial estate based on the models which had been so successfully tried in England. But he died in 1953 and the executors of the estate gave the job to John Laing and Son, a contractor based in the city of Carlisle, England. They had done considerable work for the late duke on some of his English estates with gratifying results and were highly regarded by him as competent and innovative contractors.

Late in the summer of 1953, seven executives from John Laing and Son in Carlisle came over to start the project. By September 1954, there were 24 English executives and supervisors on the job. In July 1955, the estate was officially opened by the Honourable Ralph Campney, Minister of National Defence. It was a success from the start. Two years later there were 30 tenants employing over 1,000 people. In the next year and a half, John Laing and Son (Canada) Ltd. built a copper mill, employing 350 (in a period of 2½ months) and a fine paper mill for the Powell River Co. (now MacMillan-Bloedel) on the estate. There are now in service dozens of these industrial estates modelled after Annacis Island in and around metropolitan Vancouver.

John Laing and Son (Canada) Ltd. went into general construction business and made valuable contributions to the building of post-war Vancouver. They were awarded the contract in the face of stiff competition for the building of the new 21-storey B.C. Electric head office building in downtown Vancouver (now the head office for B.C. Hydro). They built a large proportion of Woodward's shopping centres in the fifties and sixties, including major work at Oakridge and Guildford. Their crowning achievement was building the new Government House at Victoria.

Since World War II, the physical face of Vancouver has changed from that of low-profile aging landmarks to high-rise city skylines. There has been a massive drive to build multi-storey office space in the city's core and high-rise apartments in the West End. People and industry have moved out of the heart of Vancouver into the suburbs, leaving it deserted at night and on holidays. In recent years, the trend has been partially reversed by the development of the south side of False Creek into a residential area of good homes and apartments, and the gradual spread of high-rise apartment blocks from the West End to Burrard Street. This has meant that there is a larger population living within walking distance of the city's core which keeps it vibrant during evening hours.

The move to the suburbs has sparked a proliferation of shopping centres such as Park Royal in West Vancouver, Richmond Square in the municipality of Richmond, and Coquitlam Town Centre at the corner of Barnet and Lougheed highways in Coquitlam. Gone are the days when downtown Vancouver was the transportation hub of western Canada, or when the Water Street merchants provided the fruit, the groceries, and other necessities for practically all of British Columbia, or when Cordova Street was the rendezvous of the up-coast loggers. Now the emphasis is on high-rise apartment blocks, cultural complexes, such as the new provincial government buildings in Robson Square, or new convention and trade centres like the one proposed on the site of Pier B-C.

GROWTH OF THE SMALL TOWNS

Most of the small towns in British Columbia have come into being to supply a particular need or some necessary function which could not be done in any other way. In the early days, it was to provide recreational and essential services to the gold miners. This was the function of Yale when the sand bars of the Fraser were being worked for their gold. Here were established the merchants who supplied the miners with their food, clothing, and simple tools of the trade, such as picks and shovels. Here were the bars, dance-halls, and hotels where the miner could socialize with his fellows and obtain liquor according to his ability to pay. Here were situated the magistrate, the constable, and the jail. As the miners moved up-country, the function of Yale changed to that of a trans-shipment point for goods destined for the Cariboo country. It was the southern terminus of the stagecoach, the packer, the roadbuilder, and those countless thousands seeking fortune in the Cariboo gold fields. The end of the journey was in the twin towns of Barkerville and Richfield. As those towns grew, hotels and eating houses sprung up, government offices were built, banks opened, and the Cariboo merchants established their stores and warehouses. Churches and hospitals were erected.

In those days, these towns contained some of the largest population centres in the colony and their influence was felt far beyond the boundaries of gold country. As the gold boom withered away, their powers declined until, as in the case of Barkerville, they almost became ghost towns. Only in recent years has Barkerville been revived as a tourist attraction by the provincial government. Successive gold rushes like Leech River on Vancouver Island or up in the Omineca country spawned other such towns which were abandoned when the mines became exhausted.

The next round of small town building came with the building of the main line of the C.P.R. through the Rockies. Revelstoke, Field, Golden, and Kamloops all graduated from construction camps or convenient places for retail trading into railway towns — divisional points where the engines were changed in the days of steam locomotion. In those early days, the principal employer was the C.P.R. and the town's activities were fashioned to the needs of the railway. Not that other economic interests were neglected. Smelters were built for the refining of ore from nearby mines in both Revelstoke and Golden. The first was erected in Revelstoke by the Kootenay (B.C.) Smelting and Trading Co. of London, England, in 1889. When it was blown in July 1891, it was equipped with everything but the ore. A few hundred tons were refined from the Monarch mine near Field and then the smelter was abandoned. The first one at Golden was built by Calgary entrepreneurs in 1891, smelted a trickle of ore from the Monarch mine, and then closed down indefinitely. In 1920, the machinery was sold for scrap and the bricks used to build local homes. The second built in Golden came on stream in 1904 and operated for one evening. Thirty-three years later, the property was sold at a tax sale and the machinery scrapped. In time, lumbering became as important as transportation in these towns and, in recent years, tourism has brought millions of dollars to their economies.

From a collection of cottages and shacks clustered around the railway track, Kamloops has grown into a fair-sized city with motels, modern office buildings, shopping plazas, and all the accoutrements of urban living. The economy is based primarily on forestry. The great pulp mill of Weyerhaeuser is kept supplied by chips and logs from a dozen or more satellite sawmills within a radius of 150 miles. The population has grown from 1,600 in 1901 to over 63,000 in 1981.

The mining boom of the nineties in the Kootenays opened up the need for a half-dozen small towns. Kaslo, Ainsworth, and Sandon depended upon the mines and when they closed, the towns became depopulated and in some cases like Sandon, were abandoned entirely. Nelson, with its Hall smelter, was slightly different. It was the distribution, shopping, and governmental centre for all of the West Kootenays. It was the only small town in B.C. that completed and successfully operated a street railway. It had the added distinction of having two buildings (the Bank of Montreal and the Courthouse) designed by F. M. Rattenbury. Its population has not kept up with the rest of B.C. In 1901, it had 5,275 people; by 1981 this figure had only risen to 9,031.

Rossland was the centre of a rich mining area. Mines like LeRoy, Centre Star, and War Eagle were known not only in B.C., but in the boardrooms of Toronto and London, England. It rapidly became known as the greatest mining community in B.C. Merchants and professional people, lawyers, doctors, and mining engineers all flocked in to serve the adjacent mines and their promoters. In its heyday, it boasted of 6,200 citizens. Today, it is a residential suburb for Trail smelter workers with a population of 3,900. In the winter season, many are attracted to the sports facilities on Red Mountain, in an earlier day, the treasure house of Rossland's wealth.

Trail, one of the three smelter towns remaining in B.C., has a history of expansion since E. S. Topping purchased 343 acres from the Crown where the smelter and city now stand. The business of the whole town depends on Cominco, the giant mining and exploration company owned by the Canadian Pacific. The smelter is one of the world's most famous metallurgical plants. Immense amounts of lead, zinc, and other metals are produced here every year. The population has steadily grown from 1,370 in 1901 to 9,500 in 1981.

West of the Kootenays lies the Boundary country where, at the turn of the century, the great smelter towns of Grand Forks, Greenwood, and Boundary Falls sprang up. They depended upon the low-grade copper deposits found in the district and were built to service the mines and refine their ores. All experienced real estate booms, but Grand Forks is unique in that the smelter was built upon funds realized from the sale of its town lots. Expansion came to a halt on collapse of world copper prices in 1919-20. The mines were closed down, the machinery in the smelters shipped elsewhere, and most of the residents left. A partial revival occurred when the lumber business expanded after 1945. Pope and Talbot was the pioneer Washington State firm that supplied much of the better grade lumber used in the building of early New Westminster, and now (1982) operates sawmills in Grand Forks and Midway. Still to be seen are the elegant post offices and government buildings erected in these towns in copper boom days.

Immigration to the Okanagan Valley was different. Lord Aberdeen, Governor General of Canada, purchased the famous Coldstream Ranch near Vernon in 1891. His enthusiastic endorsement of this purchase set in motion a stream of English families of the upper and middle classes to the Okanagan. The towns (Vernon, Kelowna, Penticton) which began in response to this flow were unique. They were rural towns of neat houses and well-kept gardens, in no sense commercially oriented. The only industrial establishments were those connected with fruit or dairy farming. Fruit canneries, apple warehouses, and creameries were practically the only signs of industrial life. It was not until after the end of World War II that industry began to move in. Today, each town has one or two industrial estates where is manufactured or distributed anything from heavy off-the-highway logging equipment to lightweight campers that can be fitted on to pick-up trucks. In forestry, Crown Zellerbach runs one of the most advanced electronically equipped sawmills in the industry at Kelowna. The towns which in 1901 had populations of a few hundred, have now blossomed into fair-sized cities. Kelowna is the largest with a population of 58,000. Each now possesses all the modern facilities associated with urban living — motels and restaurants, high-rise apartments, and office blocks, museums, and community colleges. The Peach Bowl in Penticton is one of the more popular British Columbia convention centres.

The boom years 1905-1913 witnessed not only expansion in the small towns around the province, but a comparatively new development — the company town. James Dunsmuir had experimented with this idea without much public acceptance in 1900 when he built Ladysmith. But the idea of building a factory and a town to house its workers on a site a hundred miles more or less from any other settlement, had never been tried in B.C. In this period, there were a number of such towns built — Powell River, Ocean Falls, Swanson Bay, Britannia Beach, and Anyox. All depended upon some basic industry — pulp, paper, or mining. All required massive inflows of outside capital. The pulp and paper towns were built because of the spread of education and the rising standard of living in the United States had created a great demand for these two commodities. Britannia Beach and Anyox were mining towns built as necessary items in the development of rich copper mines. The mine at Anyox was situated hundreds of miles from any main centre of population, and could not have been brought into production without providing modern housing and up-to-the-minute care for its workers. Some of these towns like Powell River, Britannia Beach, and Anyox were built by American capital. Others, like Swanson Bay, were built by funds supplied by English capitalists. Albert Reed of Reed Paper, a big publishing and paper company of London, England, put up and lost thousands of pounds in this venture. Wherever the funds came from, the promoters all agreed on one thing — to get the best technical and planning advice available in the building of their towns. They all excelled in that the towns were as well laid out as the ground permitted, the houses were well built, adequate services were provided, and the rents invariably cheap. Out of these five company towns, the only one to survive and progress has been Powell River. The rest have disappeared, or in the case of Ocean Falls, exist in a state of future uncertainty.

The last of the new towns to be built prior to World War I were those on the Grand Trunk Pacific's Prince Rupert line. Within a few years, Prince George grew from a small trading centre catering to the trapper and prospector to the hub of north-central B.C. It was the scene of some fantastic real estate deals and only emerged as an incorporated town in March of 1915. It was held back through many years by its distance from other centres of large population and the absence of cheap electric power. When Peace River power became available in the 1960's, it came into its own. The pulp mill explosion of those years saw two mills built in the town — Prince George Pulp and Paper, and Intercontinental Pulp. Forestry operations are now big business in Prince George and vicinity. It is also an administrative centre of the provincial government for north-central B.C. Secondary industry is now strongly represented — Q.M. Machine Shop in the B.C. Railway's industrial park, custom manufacturers for the forest industry. Prince George now has a growing export trade. It is a city of over 66,500 people (1981).

Prince Rupert was to be the terminal city of the second transcontinental railway — a mighty port of the Pacific Northwest and a rival to Vancouver. These dreams have not yet been realized. It is now certain that as the resources of the north-central interior become more fully developed, Prince Rupert will become a major coal export port. The Alberta Wheat Pool is also planning to move some of its grain through Prince Rupert to relieve the congestion in Vancouver. The population has not kept pace with the anticipations of the founders. In 1911, there were 4,200 residents; in 1981, there were only 16,000. Times have now changed with the development of the northeastern coal fields and Prince Rupert is on the verge of realizing her destiny as an important port.

The small towns of Vancouver Island are in a class by themselves. Some like Nanaimo, Chemainus, and Comox have been long established. Nanaimo, for example, dates well back into colonial times. It was a coal mining town and experienced the ups and downs of that industry. The Vancouver Coal and Land Co., the owners of the mine, decided very early to lay out the town as a townsite. The streets were named after company officials and directors. Originally, it was a company town with a difference. Miners were encouraged to buy their own homes which were surrounded with sufficient ground for them to grow their own vegetables, an insurance against slack times in the industry.

When they opened up the Wellington, and later the Extension mines, the Dunsmuirs provided the merchants of Nanaimo with much business. The town's growth was gradual and unspectacular. With the decline of the coal industry in the 1920's, came hard times offset to a certain extent by its emerging role as the distribution centre for central and northern Vancouver Island. The ferry link provided by the C.P.R. to Vancouver made it a transportation centre of considerable importance. As coal mining declined, the forest industry took its place. Today (1982), it is a great pulp-making and sawmilling centre. MacMillan-Bloedel's Harmac mill ranks as one of the great pulp producers of the province. In recent years, it has again sprung into prominence as a port; enormous quantities of pulp and lumber being shipped to the States or overseas. The population, since its incorporation in 1874, has increased manyfold from 1,500 (1874) to 46,500 (1981).

Chemainus has always been a one-industry town relying entirely on its sawmill, now owned by MacMillan-Bloedel. Comox was a coal mining town expanded by the Dunsmuirs in the nineties of the last century. Like all other towns of northern Vancouver Island, it has gone heavily into forestry.

Alberni, the settlement around Anderson's mill in the 1860's, was deserted when that mill closed. In the present century, it has come back and is now a great centre of forest production (newsprint, pulp, lumber). Its population is around 20,000 (1981).

Vancouver Island boasted of two company towns which in their day had wide publicity as prime examples of town planning in rural surroundings. James Island was built to house the workers of the explosive plant of the Canadian Explosives Ltd. on that island.

148

At its peak, the island's population was over 1,000. The town, built in 1913-14, had all the urban conveniences: well-built houses in pleasant surroundings with boulevards, concrete roads and sidewalks, adequate electrical, water and sanitary services, and a community hall, general store and post office. Company employees paid low rents and could obtain the services of plumbers, carpenters, and electricians at no cost when needed.

Cassidy, some eight miles south of Nanaimo, was built by the Granby Consolidated Mining and Smelting Co. to house its work force at the Cassidy coal mine. Built 1917-18, it featured houses similar in design to those found in the better class suburbs of Vancouver or Seattle. For single men, a large hotel-like rooming house was built of 80 rooms. Downstairs were comfortable lounges, reading and billiard rooms, and a large dining hall where well-cooked, ample meals were served. The individual houses faced on well-kept lawns and tree-shaded streets.

Today, these two towns have disappeared — Cassidy a victim of the Great Depression, and James Island in the 1960's due to technological changes in the explosives industry.

Up the coast north of Prince Rupert on the west shore of Observatory Inlet, on a site now returned to a state of nature, was the copper smelting town of Anyox. Within the space of two years, 1912-14, a modern industrial town was planned, built and equipped by Granby Consolidated Mining and Smelter Co. It was no small achievement to build such a massive project 550 miles from any source of major supplies. For twenty years Anyox was known as the copper town. The residents lived almost in a mini-welfare state; all their needs were taken care of by the company. Then came the Great Depression — the company had financial difficulties. Nobody wanted to buy copper. Copper stocks climbed to unheard of records and the smelter closed down and was scrapped. The citizens left — many to go on the bread lines in Vancouver or Victoria; some to scrape a livelihood from small plots of land in the suburbs; a few to find jobs in other mining communities. No traces now remain of the town; the forest has grown over the entire site.

On the mainland, the pulp mill explosion of the fifties and sixties brought further expansion to eight of the small towns: on the coast it was Kitimat and Prince Rupert; in central and northern B.C., Kamloops, Quesnel, Prince George, and Mackenzie; in the Kootenays, Castlegar and Skookumchuck near Cranbrook. Of the 23 pulp mills operating in B.C. in 1974, 18 of these were built in the period under review. The building of these mills represented an investment of well over one billion dollars, a greater part of which went into the expansion of the small towns.

Coinciding with the forestry expansion was a mining boom. The start of copper mining in the Highland valley brought many additional dollars to Kamloops. South of Kamloops in the Highland valley the developers of Lornex mine built the new town of Logan Lake to house their workers. In north-central B.C., the copper mine at Gibraltar sparked development at Williams Lake, and Granby's Granisle mine on Babine Lake necessitated the building of a new townsite.

The achievement that got the widest publicity was the building of the new smelter town of Kitimat. Four hundred miles northwest of Vancouver, it is the only large open area between Powell River and Prince Rupert capable of supporting a town of any considerable size.

The management of the Aluminum Co. of Canada knew that electricity cannot be moved economically over long distances, therefore a smelter should be located near a source of power. The Nechako drainage system held the key to one of the greatest potential untouched areas of hydroelectric power in the province. These two factors persuaded the Aluminum Co. to build their smelter and town at Kitimat. At that time it was the largest amount of money ever invested by a private company in British Columbia. The town and smelter were built by the Aluminum Co. within a span of three or four years. It was to be the showcase of Canada — a town built to a master plan providing for all contingencies. It is 28 years now since its completion, and although it is a good example of what technology can do to convert a wilderness into an industrial city, it has not fully realized the guidelines as set out by the founders. It was built in anticipation of a population of 35,000 to 50,000. The present figure is 12,700 (1981). It was built in the hope that the work force would be stable, that people would like to live there and stay permanently. The labour turnover in the past few years has been about 45 percent per year. Bad weather, heavy rains in the spring and autumn, heavy snowfall in the winter, plus isolation from main population centres have all contributed to short stays. But it stands as a major British Columbia building and engineering achievement.

Coal, today's growth industry, has brought expansion to the towns in the Kootenays. Cranbrook now has a population of 15,700

(1981). The mines of B.C. Resources and Fording Coal provide jobs for thousands in the Fernie-Sparwood area where in the past a few hundred existed.

Tumbler Ridge, some 40 miles southwest of Dawson Creek, is the newest of the new small towns of B.C. It is being built to house the employees in the new coal mines opening up in the northeast. Population in 1983 is expected to be 3,500 rising to 5,500 in 1987. Construction of schools, municipal hall, community centre and 1,000 housing units is now underway (April 1982).

From 1951 to 1976, the population of the small cities and towns outside the two metropolitan areas of Vancouver and Victoria increased from 215,000 to 583,000 or 171 percent. In this period, the metropolitan areas increased from 732,000 to 1,385,000 or 89 percent. Thus it can be seen that expansion in the small cities and towns has been almost twice as great as in the metropolitan centres. This has had a most beneficial effect on the development of British Columbia. The great metropolitan centres have lost much of their overwhelming attraction and people are now willing to live and work in less congested areas. Industry is now finding out the advantages offered by medium-sized and small towns and that their work force is quite prepared to live and work in such places.

CHAPTER FIVE

BUILDING THE INDUSTRIAL INSTALLATIONS

Pioneer Factories

The first factories built in British Columbia were sawmills, and the first manufactured product was lumber. The first pieces of lumber produced on the mainland was that sawn over a sawpit at Fort St. James in 1806 by the fur traders to build their fort. For half a century afterwards, the only lumber sawn in B.C. was that used to build the fur traders' posts.

The influx of the gold miners from 1858 to 1865 created the first big demand for sawn timber. This was met by the setting up of small sawmills (partnerships of two or three men) powered by water in or near the mining settlements. In no sense were they "factories" as we know the term today. Gradually, in the larger settlements like Victoria and New Westminster, slightly better mills were built — some powered by steam like Joseph Homer's in New Westminster.

The first big steam-driven mill and one of the first directed to the export trade was that of Anderson's at Alberni. The mechanical equipment (the boiler, steam engine, and saws) came from England via the Horn in a sailing ship. Accompanying the machinery were twelve English mechanics who erected it on the site and then provided their mechanical skills to run it. Its appetite for logs was so great that in the next four years it ran out of timber which (in the state of logging at that time) could be taken to the mill. The mill and settlement were abandoned; the machinery sold to an American outfit across the border in Puget Sound.

During this time, two other great export mills arose on Burrard Inlet. Sewell Prescott Moody's Moodyville mill was originally run by water. In 1868 an additional building was erected to house a saw run by a steam engine. In December 1873, a disastrous fire was started, it is said, by the overturning of a lamp in the lamp room.

Rattenbury's Oak Bay Hotel, Victoria, B.C.

FROM A POSTCARD: COLLECTION G.W.T.

Victoria Harbour taken from the Parliament Buildings showing the construction of the Causeway, circa 1903.

PHOTO: VICTORIA CITY ARCHIVES

New Westminster

The C.P.R. station at New Westminster in the 1890's.

Vancouver

First C.P.R. station and wharves, circa 1890.

Hastings East at Victoria Road, circa 1900.

Where William Farrell would arrive on his visits to England to see G. P. Norton. The entrance to Huddersfield railway station.

Mt. Pleasant looking over False Creek to the town, circa 1890.

Vancouver Centennial Museum and the Vancouver Skyline.

The Growth of Small Towns

Trail and its smelter.

Kitimat, 1960, showing hospital and shopping centre.

Pioneer Industrialists

Hugh Nelson

Captain Edward Stamp

Joseph A. R. Homer

Sewell Prescott Moody

Richard Henry Alexander

John Hendry

Blast furnace, Hall Mines Smelter at Nelson in 1898. This was the first profitable smelter in B.C.

PHOTO: B.C. DEPARTMENT OF MINES

Fraser Mills in the days when it was the largest sawmill in the British Empire.

PHOTO: CANADIAN WESTERN LUMBER CO.

The mill at Powell River, 1911, during construction.

Eaton Hall, Chester, England. Seat of 2nd Duke of Westminster, promoter of the first industrial park in British Columbia.

Building the first long distance powerline in B.C. Construction crews raising a pole on the Bonnington-Rossland line, 1898.

PHOTO: COMINCO

Stave Falls Power Plant and Dam, June 4, 1938.

PHOTO: COLLECTION G.W.T.

Mica Dam.

Wanita Dam under construction.

C.P.R. wharves Vancouver, circa 1899, showing coastal boat on eve of departure and a trans-Pacific Empress.

PHOTO: CANADIAN PACIFIC RAILWAY

The C.P.R. waterfront in Vancouver at the time of its greatest expansion, showing both the trans-Pacific and Australian liners berthed at the new Pier B-C.

PHOTO: CANADIAN PACIFIC RAILWAY

A portion of the Port of New Westminster as it appeared in the 1960's. Major port activity is now on the other side of the river in Surrey.

A port up coast now abandoned. The waterfront of Anyox with the Grand Trunk Pacific Railway's coastal boat from Vancouver at the wharf waiting for passengers.

An aerial view of Roberts Bank, the great coal exporting port some 20 miles from Vancouver.

To service B.C.'s biggest industry—the lumber loading wharf in North Vancouver.

Rithet's Piers at Outer Wharf, Victoria, circa 1900.

PHOTO: VICTORIA CITY ARCHIVES

Ship loading coal at Brechin Colliery near Nanaimo, 1909.

PHOTO: B.C. DEPARTMENT OF MINES

C.P.R. Terminal, Nanaimo, in the 1960's.

Odgen Point, Victoria, 1980, showing new coastguard base.

The steam mill was completely wiped out. It was rebuilt and powered by the engine of the H.M.S. *Sparrowhawk* which had been decommissioned and scrapped at Esquimalt. This is a good example of the difficulties the mill owners and other pioneer industrialists faced in getting equipment into their factories.

The mechanical equipment of Stamp's or Hastings Mill came directly from Glasgow. Highlighting the difficulties of setting up factories in the early days was the fact that the original shipment of saws to Stamp's Mill lacked some essential parts and, for a year, Stamp was only able to cut and ship spars for ship masts.

For the next 25 years, the lumber industry in B.C. centred around the two great export mills on Burrard Inlet, and a few small ones in New Westminster and Victoria. The coming of the railway marked the real beginnings of the industry in B.C. It provided a strong local market and also for the first time access to the Northwest Territories and Manitoba. Many new mills were built — Fraser Mills on the Fraser River above New Westminster, the mill at Barnet run by North Pacific Lumber Co., Chemainus on Vancouver Island, and the British Columbia Mills, Timber and Trading Co.'s mills in Vancouver and New Westminster, which set the pace for technological advances in the industry until World War I.

In other spheres of industrial activity, factories were being built in Victoria, Vancouver, and some smaller centres in the interior. The most numerous were those connected with woodworking. There were the sash and door factories lilke Robertson and Hackett in Vancouver, and Lemon, Gonasson, and Co. of Victoria; and furniture makers with a province-wide reputation such as Victoria's Weiler Bros. Box factories sprang up for the salmon and fruit trade like the Kelowna Sawmill Co. of that town; carriage and wagon factories also developed like Ledingham's of Victoria, and the B.C. Carriage Works of Nanaimo. Wood pipes were made for irrigation projects; broom handles were also manufactured. In the field of general manufacturing, there was Storey and Campbell of Vancouver, makers of horse harnesses and saddles, and the British Columbia Chemical Works for blasting powder, and the well-known soap maker W. J. Pendray, in business since 1867. The most important of food processors was Brackman and Ker with their five-storey cereal mill at Victoria, and the B.C. Sugar Refinery in Vancouver. Later came the cement works at Tod Inlet (Vancouver Portland Cement Co.) and brickmaking at Abbotsford (the Clayburn Co.).

All these factories required power of one sort or another, the main source being the steam engine. One of the great obstacles to their operation lay in the fact that for many years there were no facilities in the province for their repair and maintenance. If a part broke and had to be replaced, it took months, sometimes years, to do so.

The problem was particularly acute at the Esquimalt naval base. As more and more warships changed from sail to steam, the mechanical difficulties of keeping them in service mounted. A good example were the trials of Chief Engineer J. R. Thomas of H.M.S. *Triumph*, flagship of the Pacific station in the years 1878-82. One of a family of five experimental iron armoured battleships built in the seventies, she early experienced mechanical troubles. In the course of duty, a cylinder on the main engine cracked and became useless. A new one had to be ordered from England. On arrival, it was found to be too large. With cutting tools devised by himself, J. R. Thomas finally shaped it to size. In the meantime, the flagship had been immobilized for months.

As more machinery was introduced into the forestry, mining, and general manufacturing industries, it became imperative to set up foundries and machine shops. The pioneer was the Albion Iron Works of Victoria. In their works at Chatham and Store streets, they made practically everything in the engineering line from tugboat engines and boilers to 30-ton coal cars for the Esquimalt & Nanaimo Railway. When H.M.S. *Amphion* on a trip from Victoria to Vancouver ran on the rocks in the Gulf Islands, tearing a large hole in her side, the Albion Iron Works was awarded the contract for repairs at a cost of $150,000. They built the 400-h.p. Corliss engine that was to generate the electricity to run the first streetcars in Victoria. The works provided one of the biggest sources of employment in the city, the work force for many years being over 230.

Vancouver started out with two engineering works — the B.C. Iron Works, and the Vancouver City Foundry and Machine Works. Both were in the business of making sawmilling, mining, and marine machinery. The B.C. Iron Works in its initial years made the boiler for Tait's shingle mill in Vancouver, machinery for a new sawmill at Port Moody, mining equipment for a Cariboo mine, cars for the logging railway of Moodyville Sawmill Co. at Grief Point and, under licence from Letson and Burpee, wiping machines for the salmon canneries. The depression of 1893-96 hit the firm hard, but on the upswing, sternwhelers were built for the Yukon trade — a package deal which included hulls, boilers, propelling machinery, and fittings.

The Vancouver City Foundry and Machine Works became a victim of the depression of 1893-96, and after many vissitudes became the Vancouver Engineering Works — a major manufacturer of machinery in Vancouver for many years.

Specialty engineering firms grew up like Letson and Burpee, who designed, patented, and made most of the early automatic machinery used in the salmon canneries on the Pacific coast. They were one of the first in B.C. to go into the making of specially designed sawmilling and woodworking machinery. Their line of machines was designed by their own staff and made in their factories in Vancouver and Bellingham. Their specially designed shingle machine was utilized in practically every shingle mill in the Pacific Northwest. When wood pipe manufacturing came into demand, many of these plants were equipped with Letson and Burpee's pipe-making machinery. They anticipated by fifty years the growing sawmilling equipment industry of B.C. by selling overseas to Australia and Japan. Today (1982), they are still in business as a unit of Kockums Group of Sweden, a worldwide distributor and manufacturer of sawmilling machinery.

Another of these specialty engineering firms was the Canadian Sumner Iron Works. It was an offshoot of the Sumner Iron Works of Everett, Washington State, which had been engaged in the making of sawmilling and logging equipment since 1898. The Canadian Sumner Iron Works started out in a small way on Pender Street in 1913, custom designing machinery for sawmills. It selected a site on East Broadway, put up a factory and under different owners — Black-Clawson at one time, and C.A.E. today (1982) — has manufactured and sold its products worldwide.

It was the mining industry that brought the first large wave of investment capital into the province. Some of this was spent in the building of smelters. The function of the smelter is to separate the ores and recover the valuable metals like silver, lead, and zinc. There have been many built in B.C. but only three have survived. In the early days, the location was along the main line of the C.P.R. at Revelstoke and Golden. Several appeared on the coast at Vancouver, Ladysmith, and Crofton. The majority constructed were for the mines in the Kootenays or the Boundary country. The Kootenays had four — Pilot Bay (1894), Nelson (1896), Trail (1896), and Marysville (1903). In the Boundary country were three — Grand Forks (1900), Greenwood (1901), and Boundary Falls (1902. The last pre-World War I smelter was at Anyox (1913-14).

The next round of building came in the 1950's when the Aluminum Co. of Canada built the smelter at Kitimat. It was the most expensive to date — the whole project costing over half a billion dollars. The latest is the one at Kamloops for Afton Mines in 1977-78.

Out of the 16 smelters built in this province to date, only three remain active (Trail, Kitimat, Kamloops). It represented a tremendous investment at well over one billion dollars. This huge outlay of money provided business not only for the equipment suppliers in England, the United States, and eastern Canada, but local business in Vancouver, Victoria, and the smelter towns. Looking back, it can be seen that far too many were built with little or no attention paid to the technologies used, high overhead cost, and the economics of smelter production. The three that have survived have made substantial contributions to the development of B.C. providing thousands of jobs and stimulating growth in the smelter towns of Trail, Kitimat, and Kamloops.

Explosives have been one of the most powerful instruments in the building of the railways, roads, and the opening up of mines. The Hamilton Powder Co., a unit in Nobel's Explosives Ltd., of Glasgow, Scotland, established a factory at Departure Bay in the early days to serve the coal mines in the vicinity of Nanaimo. This was until the opening of the factory and townsite on James Island — the principal seat of explosives manufacturing. At its peak, Departure Bay employed over 300 with a daily capacity of 75 tons of explosives. At Laurel Point, in the inner harbour of Victoria, was the B.C. Chemical Works (a subsidiary of Hamilton Powder Co.) and a source of continuous discontent with Victorians for its emissions of noxious acid fumes. The company also ran a smaller factory at Tunstall Bay, Bowen Island.

These activities were all concentrated on James Island in 1913-14 when the big explosive plant and company town were built. At the height of production, 800 were employed. This became the base of western Canada's biggest dynamite manufacturing industry. During World War I, James Island supplied immense quantities of TNT for the war effort to the British government.

In recent years, the plant has been phased out due to changing patterns in the industry, and the employees moved elsewhere. In its lifetime, the big plant on James Island has supplied most of the explosives for building the mines, railways, and roads of British Columbia.

In standards prevailing in eastern Canada and the U.S. at the turn of the century, the factories built in British Columbia were small. Here it was most unusual to employ more than 200 hands. In the east, factories employing one, two, or three thousand were common. The smallness of the factories in B.C. does not detract from the important role they played in building up the economy of the province.

The Coming of Big Factories

The start of the big factory era in British Columbia can be traced to the growing Canadian public opinion for some kind of trade reciprocity with the United States. The growth of education in the U.S. had produced a boom in the printing of newspapers and magazines. Newsprint was in tight supply. The publishers were looking with interest upon the immense resources of timber suitable for pulping that existed in Canada. Thus, the interests of the American publishers and those sections of the Canadian public which looked with favour upon reciprocity coincided. The result was that the federal government under Sir Wilfrid Laurier negotiated a reciprocity treaty with the Americans which included free entry of pulp and newsprint into the United States. The Liberals fought the Dominion election of 1911 on this issue but went down to defeat. The Canadian parliament refused to ratify the treaty. Nevertheless, the power of the American press was so great that the Taft administration had to stand by its agreement and admit pulp and paper free into the country. This started a rush by American interests and others to acquire pulp leases and to make plans to build pulp and paper mills. There were four major leases in the market in B.C. — 84,000 acres in the Swanson Bay area; 55,000 on northern Vancouver Island; 135,000 which eventually came to be the source from which the Powell River mill drew its wood; and 80,000 in the Bella Coola area which came to support the mill at Ocean Falls. All these leases finally became the sources of major supply for pulp and paper mills.

The first mill to come into commercial production was that at Swanson Bay. The Canadian Pacific Sulphite Pulp Co. was heavily underwritten by Alfred Reed of the London firm of Reed Paper, which is still a big name in the industry. Originally, most of the money and all the major equipment came from the United Kingdom. The paper machine was made in Edinburgh in the works of Bertram Ltd., an old established paper-making machinery manufacturer. The electrical equipment was made in Leith, Scotland, by Bruce Peebles Co. Ltd., an engineering firm of world-wide reputation. It was a big project but had a checkered career. The property passed into other hands and finally ended up as a component of the Whalen Pulp and Paper Mills Ltd. It closed in the 1920's and never reopened. Today (1982), hardly any traces can be found of the once flourishing mill town of Swanson Bay.

The second mill to come into production was Port Mellon on Howe Sound. Its creation had a romantic background. Captain Mellon was a retired sea captain and a Vancouver businessman. In 1907, his wife paid a social call to relations in Aberdeen, Washington. Here she met Greely Kolts who entertained the idea (thirty years ahead of his time) that pulp could be made from sawmill waste. He came to Vancouver to discuss the idea with Captain Mellon and his associates. These gentlemen agreed to form a company — the Canadian Wood Pulp and Paper Co. A mill was built at Port Mellon on Howe Sound, but it was not successful. After much reorganization, it acquired the pulp lease on northern Vancouver Island. In the boom years of the industry in World War I, it ran under Canadian and American interests. Like Swanson Bay, it was compelled to close in the 1920's.

Nineteen hundred and twelve was a big year when three pulp and paper plants went into production (Powell River, Ocean Falls, and Woodfibre). Along with two others (Swanson Bay, Port Mellon) already in commercial operation, these mills marked the emergence of a new multi-million dollar industry.

Powell River is the success story. It has expanded over the years until today it houses one of the great newsprint mills of North America. Its history goes back to 1898 when Herbert Carmichael, a pioneer of pulp and paper in B.C., surveyed the Powell River area. The reports suggested that Powell River was an ideal area for logging. When pulp leases were thrown open in 1901, Herbert Carmichael and his syndicate applied for this location. For years, the Powell River lease was offered to capitalists in the Pacific Northwest and London without success. It happened that in 1908, the Brooks-Scanlon Lumber Co., a Minneapolis-based firm, bought a small logging outfit that was working in the Powell River area. Herbert Carmichael, assisted by Charles Pretty, a Vancouver lumber broker, interested Dr. Brooks and M. J. Scanlon in the location as being a good site for a pulp and paper mill. The result was that in October 1909, the Powell River Paper Co. was born. Its job was to build a two-machine paper mill (increased to four machines in 1910), a 25,000-h.p. electrical generating station, and a townsite to house the workers. Problems arose immediately because there were no engineers in B.C. with the technical expertise required. Professionals had to be imported. George Hardy of New York, an outstanding hydro and paper mill engineer, was hired to plan and supervise construction. Construction started in the fall of 1909, and by April 1912, the first horse-drawn train of newsprint left the machine room for shipment to customers. The Vancouver *Province* was one of the first of these — an issue in April 1912 was printed on B.C. newsprint made at Powell River.

The second mill to come into production in 1912 was at Ocean Falls. This was sponsored originally by Lester W. David, a Seattle company promoter and investment dealer. In 1909, he raised $2 million in London for the Ocean Falls Co. to build a 250-ton pulp mill, a large sawmill, and a company town at Ocean Falls. James Wallace of New York, head of an engineering firm specializing in the construction of pulp and paper plants, was given the job of designing and erecting the pulp mill. The sawmill was the first unit completed and sold lumber to the contractors in 1909, who were building Prince Rupert. The promoters ran into difficulties, then the bondholders took over and finally sold to the Crown Willamette Co. of Portland, Oregon (now Crown Zellerbach). They put in a newsprint machine, and in May 1917, the first roll came off the line. Ocean Falls has been making newsprint from that day up to 1980. Its future as a town devoted to the manufacturing of newsprint is now definitely over.

The third mill was Woodfibre at Mill Creek in Howe Sound. Original equipment included a 112-inch Fourdrinier paper-making machine and two of the largest digesters on the continent. It was from the start a Whalen enterprise assisted by money raised in the north of England by the Yorkshire Guarantee and Securities Corporation.

The last mill built in this series was the one at Port Alice on Quatsino Sound where 60 acres were cleared for the mill and townsite. Equipment was supplied by American firms — the Willamette Iron and Steel Works of Portland, Oregon, supplied the digesters while Bagley and Sewall put in a 160-inch sulphite drying machine. It was completed in 1917-18 just as pulp prices slumped and remained idle for some time.

In a period of ten years from 1908 to 1918, six pulp and paper mills were built in B.C. creating an entirely new industry. This was the first pulp mill explosion. The second would occur thirty years later with the building of Bloedel, Stewart and Welch's mill at Port Alberni. Unlike previous factories built in B.C., these mills required the support of big industrial and financial corporations. In terms of size, they were some of the biggest industrial installations built in the province to that date. They required very high engineering and technical standards which could only be met by talented professionals not then living in the province. The contracts for constructing and equipping them went to the best engineering firms in the trade in the U.K. and the United States. This marked the beginning of a period of industrial and engineering consultants, which we are still in. In these years, many professional engineers, industrial architects, and consultants came to British Columbia either to establish their own practices or set up branch offices. It is a proof of the soundness of their judgments that of the six mills built, four are still operating today (1982).

Bigger factories were also appearing in the sawmilling side of the forestry industry. In 1910, the Canadian Western Lumber Company, capitalized at $10 million, took over Fraser Mills. The company immediately started to enlarge and modernize until it became not only the largest, but the most highly mechanized mill in the British Commonwealth. Its size was immense, both in the acreage covered by the buildings and also in its daily production. From a battery of 18 boilers stoked by automatic sawdust hoppers and fed by conveyors from the sawroom and planing mill, steam was raised to run engines of 3,500 h.p. These ran the three huge saws which handled logs up to eight feet in diameter and 140-feet long.

All machinery outside of the mill proper was driven electrically by power generated in a 1,300-h.p. turbine — the first of its kind in the industry. A travelling electric crane in the lumber assembly yard, with a 100-foot boom set on a tramway 1,200-feet long and operated by two men, did the work formerly done by 18 men and a horse. In 1913, the company installed the first plywood plant in B.C. At the same time, a door factory was built which has given millions of B.C. Douglas fir doors to the export market. It is interesting to recall how much this one mill has poured into the B.C. economy. For many years prior to 1939, the annual payroll exceeded $2 million. The staff employed at the mill itself ranged from 1,500 to 2,000.

Another mill which modernized and earned a world-wide reputation was Hastings Mill under the ownership of John Hendry and the British Columbia Mills, Timber and Trading Co. The company was one of the first to practice large-scale operations in the provincial forestry industry. For many years, its payroll supported over 2,000 employees.

Then there was the Canadian Pacific Lumber Co. which, prior to World War I, had mills at Port Moody, Vancouver, the Arrow Lakes, and at Port Alberni, now a unit in MacMillan-Bloedel's Alberni operations.

John Hanbury was a Brandon man who had built a successful retail lumber business in Manitoba. He came to Vancouver around 1910 and at 4th Avenue and Granville built the first large electrically operated sawmill in B.C. By this time, there were over one dozen wood manufacturing plants situated around the shores of False Creek representing the highest concentration of lumber manufacturing mills in western Canada. Local firms such as Vancouver Engineering Works, Leston and Burpee, and the Canadian Sumner Iron Works supplied most of the machinery to Hanbury's mill. Electrical installation was handled by Mather and Yuill, Vancouver electrical engineers. The mill came into production in 1911 at a cost of $225,000.

False Creek, once the main artery of western Canada's timber trade, has fallen victim to progress and now where a dozen or more great sawmills flourished, only one of medium size remains.

On the banks of the Fraser from New Westminster to the sea, the first years of the century saw many a new sawmill built. In 1923, there were 22 saw, shingle, and box mills in this area. The majority of these were on the North Arm concentrated at New Westminster or Marpole. On the eastern tip of Lulu Island in Queensborough was the plant of the B.C. Manufacturing Co. which later became the sawmilling arm of the Powell River Co. At Marpole, before the coming of the railway, was erected the factory of the B.C. Box Co. West of Marpole Bridge was built Eburne Sawmills which in 1940 came into the hands of its present owners, the Canadian Forest Products. It was and still is the largest sawmill in the Marpole district.

On the shores of the Fraser, just east of Boundary Road, lies the forestry manufacturing complex of MacMillan-Bloedel. Its growth occurred in a later period than the one under discussion. Here was situated the Canadian White Pine Co.'s mill, the first manufacturing unit purchased by H. R. MacMillan Export in the middle twenties.

Over on the North Shore at a location appropriately named Dollarton, the Canadian Robert Dollar Co. built a large sawmill in 1917 which especially catered to the Far East trade. For a decade, trade was brisk; employment in the mill running around 150. Then came the undeclared war between Japan and China followed by World War II. The markets vanished and the mill closed in the early 1940's.

Over on southern Vancouver Island, Humbird's Victoria Lumber and Manufacturing Co.'s mill at Chemainus had long been one of the great export mills. Over the years, it had been enlarged and newer machinery put in, much of it coming from eastern Canada from the factory of the William Hamilton Manufacturing Co.

The Canadian Puget Sound Lumber Co. took over J. A. Sayward's big mill in Victoria's inner harbour and made alterations to it. The Cameron Brothers bought Taylor-Pattison's small mill, enlarged it, and made it one of the big mills in Victoria. Their Genoa Bay Mill near Duncan was at one time the largest on Vancouver Island and a big factor in the export trade. Modelled after Hanbury's electric mill on False Creek, it was one of the most efficient and one of the most profitable in the industry during that time.

Outside of the forestry and mining industries, the boom years of 1905-13 saw only gradual progress in the building of a manufacturing industry. Contrary to expectation in this period, there were only two major industrial installations built in the field of general manufacturing — the American Can factory in Vancouver and the Imperial Oil refinery in Ioco. The opinion was widely held at the time that Vancouver was to be the Pittsburg of the west.

"The industrial future of Vancouver," wrote the B.C. Magazine in its November 1911 issue, "is indeed full assured for here are all the factors required for the upbuilding of a great manufacturing centre."

"Great shipbuilding yards, steel mills, car shops, and associated industries await only money and the mind," wrote another in *B.C. Magazine* during the same period.

But the fact of the matter was that the markets in B.C. were limited, the wages high, and the cost of importing the raw materials to process excessive. As James J. Hunter, writing in the same magazine August 1911 about Vancouver, put it, "There is one thing lacking — and that is more manufactories."

In Vancouver in 1910, there were 200 manufacturing plants which included sawmills and woodworking establishments. New Westminster had 70. Out of these 270 installations, only half a dozen could be called big. The rest were mostly family-owned businesses employing from five to fifty people. Some of the better known were Turner, Beeton and Co.'s clothing factory in Victoria; Leckie's shoe factory in Vancouver; and the brick factory of the Clayburn Co. at Abbotsford in the Fraser Valley.

It was in engineering that most progress was made. The Vancouver Engineering Works greatly expanded its premises, as did the Ross and Howard Iron Works, successor to the unfortunate Vancouver City Foundry. The introduction of machinery into the woods, such as the steam donkey engine and the logging locomotive, brought much business to the province's foundries and machine shops. In the words of Thomas H. Golder, provincial machinery inspector, "For many years while logs were to be had close to shore and requiring a short haulage, horses and oxen were used. Now large and powerful donkey engines are employed and as many as three or four can be found at each logging camp on the Coast."

The 350 logging camps and the 250 sawmills operating in the province in 1912 provided a much enlarged market for locally built machinery and equipment. Edward Heaps, a lumberman, established a machinery manufacturing and supply house, E. P. Heaps and Co., which grew into one of the more prominent engineering firms in the New Westminster district. The Westminster Iron Works, an old established firm situated in the city of its namesake, started to build diesel oil engines. A new firm, the Terminal City Iron Works, was set up on Powell Street, Vancouver, in 1906 to build stationary engines and waterworks equipment for municipalities and industrial plants. In 1910, there were 20 engineering plants in Vancouver. Vancouver industries employed 60 percent of all personnel engaged in manufacturing in the province, and produced 75 percent of all goods made in the province.

In 1901, the American Can Co. was founded as a merger of 90 percent of the U.S. can makers. It came into Ontario in 1904, but not into British Columbia as a manufacturing entity until 1913. Previously, the British Columbia market had been serviced at a considerable disadvantage. Tariffs were high, their factories in eastern Canada or Portland, Oregon, too far away, and there were several local manufacturers in New Westminster and Vancouver. Its decision to build in B.C. was influenced by its monopolistic position in the industry. Around 1910, it had developed automatic can-closing machinery which was a technical breakthrough in the trade. These machines were built in their own factories and could only be rented by a potential user. Furthermore, in the rental agreement, he had to stipulate that he would only buy his cans from the American Can Co. The terms of these rentals were extremely attractive, in many cases well below the cost of maintenance. This was a most effective device to corner the market. The company had no manufacturing facilities in British Columbia but wished to put their machines into the canneries here. So it was decided to build a factory at considerable expense on Alexander Street in Vancouver. It was built in 1913, enlarged in 1926, with 14 lines of production which could make 600 cans a minute. Employment ran between 250 and 300. In 1969, a $1½-million factory was built in Kelowna to service the apple juice division of B.C. Tree Fruits.

It became a custom for big league British contractors like John Laing and Son to enter the B.C. market. One of the principal companies involved in the pre-World War I construction boom in Vancouver and Victoria was the Norton-Griffiths Steel Construction Co. Ltd. of Canada. It was an offshoot of the well-known London contracting firm of Messrs Griffiths and Co. Ltd. The British directors included two members of the nobility, Lord Clinton and Lord Howard de Walden, and two members of the British House of Commons, Mr. Norton-Griffiths, M.P., and Captain Morrison, M.P. The Honourable F. Carter-Cotton, once finance minister in Sir Richard McBride's government, was the managing director in this province. On the industrial scene, they were responsible for the ten-storey addition to the B.C. Sugar Refinery and the warehouse on Beatty Street of Messrs Crane and Co. of Chicago. On the commercial side, they were the contractors for the Vancouver Block on Granville and the Belmont Building in Victoria.

One industrial installation which has had important effects on the growth of the province is the Imperial Oil Refinery at Ioco.

Construction started in a wilderness area in 1913, continued through 1914, until the plant came on stream in January 1915. It was built to refine lubricants, bunker oil, and heating fuel for the sawmills, logging camps, ships, and urban office blocks, and apartment houses which were springing up in such abundance. The crude oil came by tanker from California or Venezuela to the deep water terminal at the refinery. The refined products were then shipped by barge or company tanker up and down the coast. A townsite was developed by the company named Ioco; the first houses were built in 1921. It was not until the 1930's that it could be reached by road. All men and materials had to be shipped in by barge or boat.

In the course of years, the refinery has been expanded until it is now one of the major ones in B.C. No longer is the crude brought in by ship, but by pipe from the fields in northern B.C. and Alberta.

Industrial expansion in British Columbia seems to come in waves. From the depression years of 1913-14 to post-war 1947-48, no industrial complex of significance was built in B.C. Then came the pulp mill explosion and the mining boom of the fifties and sixties, and a resurgence of factory building.

The Post-World War II Industrial Explosion

The first and most compelling factor in British Columbia's post-war industrial expansion since 1946 has been a world-wide demand for forest and mine products. It first showed up in the fantastic demands for wood pulp. From the laboratories of the chemical companies came wood-based textiles such as rayon. As a raw material, plastic was being put to many commercial tasks. Food processors were learning the handling ease and other advantages of packaged goods. All were potential large users of pulp. Today there are over 25,000 industrial processes which depend on wood pulp as a supply. It was the dawn of cellulose forestry.

The existing pulp mills were all thirty or more years old and could not meet the demand. Prior to World War II, Bloedel, Stewart and Welch had made some feasibility studies with the idea of establishing a pulp mill at Port Alberni. The war intervened and the plans were not activated until 1946. Construction took a year and it was not until 1947 that the mill became operative. Local manufacturers supplied most of the heavy machinery. Canadian Sumner Iron built the four chippers and the Vancouver Iron Works was responsible for the 80-ton digester. H. A. Simons of Seattle (whose Vancouver firm today is a world leader in the design of industrial installations) was the consulting engineer. The mill was unique in the fact that it used sawmill waste as its raw material and was the first integrated forest operation in B.C.

The use of sawmill waste in making pulp was a major factor in influencing other forestry companies in B.C. The building of Harmac south of Nanaimo by H. R. MacMillan Co. in 1950 was largely the result of their desire to utilize the waste from their sawmill operations. H. R. MacMillan and Bloedel, Stewart and Welch merged in the early fifties and achieved in the Alberni district one of the highest concentrations of wood manufacturing facilities in North America.

In the meantime, the Columbia Cellulose Co., a subsidiary of the Celanese Corporation of America, was building a pulp mill on Watson Island a few miles south of Prince Rupert at an original cost of $15 million. Almost in the planning stages, capacity was increased 90 percent to 300 tons per day. Even this was not sufficient as president Harold Blanke pointed out in June of 1951: "World markets for this new mill's product are already larger than the company can supply with present facilities." The main market was within the organization — pulp being shipped to Canadian Chemical's Edmonton plant where it was processed into acetate yarn. From there it went to the great textile mills of Celanese in the U.S.

Problems of utilizing sawmill waste were also being experienced by the Canadian Western Lumber Co. at its huge Fraser Mills plant. A somewhat similar situation existed at Crown Zellerbach's mill at Ocean Falls. These two giants combined to build a pulp and newsprint plant at Duncan Bay just outside of Campbell River at a cost of $21.5 million. Its production debut was in June 1952.

The B.C. Forest Products Ltd. is a collection of logging, sawmilling, and timber holding companies gathered under one umbrella by the Toronto industrial tycoon E. P. Taylor. With sawmill waste coming from their big mills at Youbou and Victoria, the new uses which it could be put to encouraged them to build a pulp and paper mill at Crofton in 1956, a few miles north of Victoria.

At Powell River and in the lesser mills at Woodfibre, Port Mellon, and at Alice Arm on northern Vancouver Island, expansion and modernization were progressing at a modest rate. At Powell

River, a new paper machine was put in and a hydraulic barker, the first of its kind in western Canada. Up to that time, the B.C. Pulp and Paper Co. owned the smaller mills, but when control was acquired by Koerner and Abitibi interests, $15 million in improvements was spent. Modest expansion was also registered by the Westminster Paper Co. Between 1947 and 1953, it erected two more paper machines in its New Westminster mill. It also had an interest in the Pacific Coast Paper Mills of Bellingham, Washington, the largest industrial complex in that town and now a unit of the Georgia Pacific, a forestry giant in the United States.

The second phase of the pulp mill explosion ended with the building of four new mills. This also marked a trend in the industry towards a pulp economy instead of a sawmilling one. It saw the building of a dozen or more highly automated sawmills replacing scores of smaller, less efficient ones. There was a growing demand for sawmill waste, and wood chips, and a higher value placed on small logs.

The decade of the sixties witnessed the third phase of the pulp mill explosion. By this time, the multinationals in the southern coastal districts had become fully integrated. The sawmill slipped from its dominant position as the main producing unit in the industry to one of equality with several others in a highly integrated structure. In nine years from 1962 to 1971, the number of active sawmills in the province dropped from over 1,600 to 627 — a decrease of 161½ percent. The older mills were being replaced by newer, larger and more automated ones.

In 1960, there were ten major pulp and paper mills in B.C. By 1973, the number had increased to 22 — a rise of 120 percent. This was a remarkable achievement within that short period. One contribution was the effort of the provincial government in developing hydroelectric power. No manufacturing enterprise of any lasting significance (outside of the smelter at Trail) had up to this time been built in the interior. When W. A. C. Bennett placed all the resources of the government behind Peace River power, it thus became possible to build a succession of pulp mills in the north-central interior.

The first of these was the Prince George Pulp and Paper, originally owned jointly by the Canadian Forest Products Ltd. and the Reed Paper Co. Reed, it is to be remembered, was the large British pulp, paper, and publishing enterprise whose head in pre-World War I days sponsored the pulp mill at Swanson Bay. The Prince

167

George project for its time was huge ($84 million) and came on stream in 1966. It is now 100 percent owned by Canadian Forest Products Ltd. Also in Prince George is the second mill, Intercontinental Pulp, originally a consortium of Canadian Forests Products, Reed Paper, and West German paper maker Feldmuehie A.G. Reed Paper has now sold out to Canadian Forest Products.

One of W. A. C. Bennett's dreams was to open up that great area of north-central British Columbia known as the Rocky Mountain Trench to industrial development. This has been partially fulfilled by the B.C. Forest Products Ltd. at a site where Alexander Mackenzie camped in 1793 on his historic journey to the Pacific; there the company has built a modern forestry complex equipped with the most up-to-date machinery to chip, saw, and pulp. It incorporated the best in North American and European technology. It also meets the level "A" standards of the B.C. Pollution Control Branch of the provincial government. Electronics plays a great part in controlling the production processes. The town named Mackenzie has all the modern urban conveniences. Also located here is another pulp mill, a joint venture of a local forest company and two Japanese firms. The design of the mill, purchase of equipment, and construction were carried out under the direction of the Japanese engineering staff of the Jujo Paper Manufacturing Co., a somewhat unusual arrangement in British Columbia, where most of the expertise comes from the United States or Europe.

Southward from Prince George at Quesnel is the last mill built in the series — Cariboo Pulp owned jointly by Weldwood of Canada, the Daishowa Paper Manufacturing Co., and the Marubeni Corp. of Japan. It operates on wood chips procured from the surrounding sawmills.

At Kamloops, Weyerhaeuser has built the largest market-oriented pulp mill in B.C. Wood chips, sawdust, and shavings come from dozens of independent and company-owned sawmills within a radius of 150 miles. Weyerhaeuser of Tacoma, the largest U.S. forestry company, has contributed much to make the Kamloops mill the biggest producer of pulp in B.C. for the open market.

In the East Kootenays near Cranbrook is the pulp mill of the Crestbrook Forest Industries, a joint Canadian-American-Japanese venture. Previous to World War I, many sawmills existed in this region catering to the prairie trade. The area is experiencing a forestry comeback. Like the Intercontinental at Prince George, Japanese engineers drew up many of the construction plans. Much attention has been paid to prevent pollution of the Kootenay River. Its importance in the eyes of the Japanese was emphasized by the attendance of the Japanese ambassador to Canada, Shinichi Kondo, at the opening on October 3, 1969.

Also in the Kootenays at Castlegar is a pulp mill originally built by the Canadian Cellulose Co. and now owned by B.C. Resources Corporation. It was one of the earlier mills built in the third phase of the pulp mill explosion and came into full production in January or February 1961. At the time, it was a big operation for the southern interior and has over the years provided hundreds of jobs in the Castlegar-Arrow Lakes district.

Possibly the biggest technical advance in this period was made in the construction and equipping of new sawmills. Outside of a few examples like Hanbury's electric mill on False Creek, the engineer and the architect had never been employed in the building of sawmills. This was to change dramatically in the sixties.

One classic example was Bulkley Valley Forest Industries sawmill at Houston. In an all-enclosed work space, something with great appeal to the workers in the cold winter months, it housed batteries of machines designed to incorporate a high degree of automation. An electronically controlled saw automatically sized up logs as they came up the greenchain, and then cut them up to the best advantage. The computer-controlled conveyor lines guided the sawn lumber to its proper destination. Trimming, sorting, drying, and packaging equipment was all electronically directed. Such a tight computer-controlled factory was a far cry from the erratic stop-and-start operations of the older manually operated mills. On top of the common mechanical failures, were the problems encountered in the familiarization of personnel with the new conceptions. Lumber workers in Houston and surrounding districts were not used to assembly line methods in sawmilling. Production was unsteady and unreliable, ranging from 10 to 90 percent. The owners, Bowater Canadian Corp. and Consolidated Bathurst Ltd. (eastern Canadian forestry giants), lost heavily and finally sold to Northwood Mills. Northwood scrapped the heavy machinery and put in types which would handle smaller logs.

The most recent example of the art of modern sawmill construction is the modernization and re-equipping of Rayonier's Silvertree mill on the banks of the Fraser River east of Marpole. It is the first large mill to be completely remachined on the coast in the last 35 years. It is built for the large logs but, if necessary, is flexible enough to handle small ones, a characteristic not evident in the majority of the mills built in the seventies. The trend so evident in the Houston mills of automation, tight controls, enhanced safety standards, and regard for employees' comfort in the work place has been extended to the point that the employees are housed in air-conditioned soundproof booths whenever possible. A new departure in sawmill construction was the employment of a colour designer to develop attractive colour schemes on the walls and ceilings of the work places. The operation of the mill is controlled by nine computers which give precision sawing, electronic production, sorting, and inventory controls, and a memory bank which holds specific information as to species, grade size, etc., of every piece of lumber sawn. High technology has come to the sawmill. A new generation of sawmill workers is arising as programmers and computer technicians. The whole project costs $23 million, took 15 months to complete, and came into production in October 1980.

One of the success stories of the seventies was the emergence of the mill built to handle the small log. Smaller logs are easier to handle in all situations, and in the past were in very little demand. With the pulp mills demanding more and more chips, the small log has become a source of considerable revenue. One of the most successful firms in this field is Doman Industries Ltd. of Duncan. They now (1982) have four mills on Vancouver Island (Cowichan Bay, Chemainus, Ladysmith, and Nanaimo). Sales have climbed tenfold from $14 million in 1969 to $113 million in 1979.

It was the American demand for pulp and paper which set off the pulp mill explosion of the fifties and sixties, but it was the Japanese intentions that triggered the mining boom of the period. It sparked the great mining development in the Highland Valley, Bethlehem, Craigmont, Alvin, and at a more recent date, Lornex with its company town, Logan Lake. At Princeton, it was Similkameen Copper; in the Okanagan, Brenda. Up in the Cariboo near Williams Lake, it was Gibraltar, and further north on Babine Lake, Granisle with its townsite. In the coal-bearing regions of the East Kootenays, it was Kaiser Resources and Fording Coal. These new mines developed new methods and used heavier and more complicated equipment. The evolution of 200- to 300-ton off-highway trucks and powered shovels of high capacity made open-pit mining possible at fantastic production rates of 40,000 or 45,000 tons per day.

This factor along with the ever-increasing number of machines used in the forest industry, created a demand for repair and maintenance shops. The machine shops of B.C., 220 in number, are located in practically every town and village. Many are housed in substantial buildings. Many have branched out into full-scale manufacturing concerns.

A case in point is the Finning Tractor and Equipment Co., a major distributor of industrial equipment in B.C. In 1979, they did a business of $375 million and gave employment to over 2,000. The company now has most branches in B.C. housed in modern facilities. In the five-year period (1974-79), it spent nearly $41 million in property acquisitions, the expansion of older buildings, and the construction of new shops.

On the manufacturing side, Canadian Car, a division of the British multinational Hawker Siddeley, built a factory on 32 acres in Surrey, B.C., in 1975. The prime reason was to make a highly proficient automatic machine known as the Chip-N-Saw. It turned the suitable parts of the log into lumber and automatically processed the remainder into chips. Four hundred and fifty of these units have been sold (1980), principally in Canada and the United States but also to the U.S.S.R., Sweden, and South Africa. They have now branched out into the making of other sawmilling equipment and employ betwen 500 and 700 people.

Heavy off-highway trucks are used both by the mining and the logging industries. These are usually custom-made — many in British Columbia. Hayes Trucks Ltd. until recently made over 50 of these trucks per year in their factory in Burnaby exporting many to Africa and the Far East. There are still two firms in B.C. engaged in this business. Canadian Kenworth Co. of Burnaby, exporting mainly to Southeast Asia, and Pacific Truck & Trailer Ltd. of North Vancouver does business world wide. Each in normal times employ over 300.

B.C. machine shops have initiated many specially designed machines to work in the forest industry. Special machines have been made to meet special needs such as mobile steel spars, log loaders, tree-cutters, etc. S. Madill and Co. of Nanaimo, Q.M. Industries, and Muirhead Machine Co. Ltd. of Prince George, and C.A.E. Machinery Ltd. of Vancouver are leaders in this field. All have built substantial manufacturing facilities. Producers of forestry equipment are found in many other areas of the province.

171

The seventies was a period of relative calm in the building of big industrial plants in B.C.; there were no new pulp or paper mills built. The building of factories in other fields were either additions to existing ones or of a minor nature.

The 1980's are seeing an addition to the existing pulp mill at Elk Falls by Crown Zellerbach to supply pulp to the third newsprint machine, in operation since February 1982. Adding to manufacturing capacity in Nanaimo is a new sawmill built by Doman Industries Ltd. at Duke Point within the new harbour facilities which came on stream in 1981. Up the coast at Kitimat is a small petrochemical plant built by Ocelot Industries Ltd. of Calgary, which produces methanol for export to Japan. There is much talk of putting in a larger complex there using B.C. natural gas as its raw material.

CHAPTER SIX

ELECTRICAL POWER

Its Birth and Growth

The first demonstration of electric power for illumination in British Columbia was staged by the Royal Navy. At the command of the Rear-Admiral in charge at Esquimalt, the ironclad H.M.S. *Triumph* turned on its searchlight the evening of May 15, 1871. It was such a novel event that close to 1,200 people crowded into four excursion steamers which sailed into Esquimalt Harbour to witness "the wonder."

Another such demonstration was organized by the principal owner of the Moodyville Sawmill Co. and later Lieutenant-Governor of British Columbia, Hugh Nelson, who arranged a special boat excursion from Victoria in the spring of 1882 to view the electric lights which had recently been placed on the loading wharf at Moodyville for night work.

Electric lighting in the west in the eighties was a rare phenomenon, but in the cities of the eastern and central states it was not unusual to find some streets lighted by bright carbon arc lamps. In the cities on the B.C. coast, it was the need for better street lighting that prompted enterprising entrepreneurs to establish small steam-driven generating plants. In the interior, it was the need to supply cheaper power to the mines.

Victoria had a small plant driven by a steam engine in 1883, but it was only in 1887 with the introduction of Edison's incandescent lamps that electric lighting came into the stores and homes.

Electric lighting arrived in Vancouver in 1887 when the Vancouver Electric Illuminating Co. Ltd. built a steam-fired generating plant at the corner of Pender and Abbott.

The first industrial use found for electric power was driving streetcars. Soon it was found that street lighting and running the street railways could be done more economically under the banner of one company, and there were many mergers. The prime source of power for the whole economy had been the steam engine and it is not surprising that in Victoria up to 1898, and in Vancouver and New Westminster up to 1903, that all electric power was being generated in steam-driven plants.

The idea of driving electric generators by water rather than steam dated back to the earliest days of the industry, but it had not been developed. British Columbia was particularly fortunate in having many potential hydro power sites, and this fact was evident to a group of Kootenay mine owners under the leadership of Sir Charles Ross. He was one of the Scottish landed aristocracy and owner of vast estates in Ross-shire and Larnarkshire, Scotland. He arrived in the Kootenays in 1895 and quickly became heavily involved in the mines. It was said (*B.C. Mining Record*, September 1896) that he was "better posted on Kootenay mines than any other foreign capitalist."

Along with his associates Patrick A. Largey and Oliver Durant, president and manager respectively of the Centre Star Mining and Smelting Co., and C. R. Hosmer, Montreal capitalist and manager of the C.P.R. Telegraph Service, he was interested in the Kootenay River as a potential source of hydroelectric power.

The operators of the Centre Star Mine at Rossland, including Sir Charles Ross, were plagued by the high cost of running their mining machinery. Most of the mine machinery was run by compressed air. Air was compressed in a compressor above ground, run by a steam engine, and then piped to the drills in the underground workings. The running of the steam compressor was very expensive and the Centre Star management decided that electricity could do the job more cheaply. This was the reason for the founding of the West Kootenay Power and Light Co., the company which built the first major hydroelectric installation in B.C.

Two problems presented themselves, the first of which was to find a suitable site, and the second, how to transmit the power thus generated to Rossland and the Centre Star. The first was quickly solved. Surveys were made in the spring of 1897 which pointed out that the falls in the Kootenay River west of Nelson could be utilized. The water fell some fifty feet over a granite cliff. In 1897-98, a dam was built and a brick powerhouse erected which was equipped with a Canadian General Electric generator built in Peterborough, Ontario. The waterwheel came from the Stillwell, Bierce, and Smith Vaile Co. of Dayton, Ohio. The site was named Bonnington Falls, after one of Sir Charles Ross' ancestral estates in Larnarkshire. The second problem proved more difficult. The distance from the power-house to Rossland was 30 miles and, at that time, electricity hadn't been transmitted such a distance. In the previous year, a project had been completed at Manitou, Colorado, which transmitted its power eight miles to work drills driving a tunnel in the Pike's Peak Range, which was to bring water to the town of Colorado Springs; and at Niagara Falls six months previously, power had been transmitted at 10,000 volts to Buffalo, 26 miles away. The West Kootenay people were proposing an installation that would step up the power to 20,000 volts and carry it 30 miles. This was a risky venture as the promoters were not in the electrical business but were hard-rock miners. Construction of the line commenced in 1898 and it was finished by November of that year. Cedar poles 30 to 40 feet in length, 50 to a mile, were used to carry the transmission lines. The insulators had to be imported from Germany as no North American manufacturer was in the business of providing products for a line of such high voltage. Small cedar roofs protected them from the weather, giving the appearance of a row of birdhouses sprouting in the forest. Below the cross arms, was strung the telephone wire — the first long distance telephone line in the interior of B.C.

The venture was a success from the start. Costs of running the air compressors in the Rossland mines dropped from $5.15 per h.p. per month to $3.87 per h.p. per month. The mines put in heavier electrically driven equipment like the electric hoist ordered by the War Eagle Mine. Made in Montreal, it was the largest electric hoist made to that date in the world. It could lift 60 tons in the War Eagle's 700-foot shaft with an ease and speed not seen before in Rossland.

The lighting of homes, stores, and city streets, was a secondary consideration. However, the advantages of cheaper electricity induced the city of Rossland to contract for West Kootenay Power in 1899. From that date, the company has promoted sales to most of the cities and towns in the Kootenays, the Boundary country, and the Okanagan.

There was a continuous curve upwards in the use of electrical power in the smelter at Trail and the surrounding mines. Plant No. 2 was started at Upper Bonnington Falls in 1905 and completed in 1907. It was designed by Ross and Holgate of Montreal, and in place of a waterwheel, the new technology utilized turbines (I. P.

175

Morris) to drive four generators developing 34,000 h.p. West Kootenay Power was now available in the Boundary country via an 89-mile transmission line to Greenwood constructed in 1906. It was a very profitable venture: net profits in some years climbed as high as 24 percent of gross revenue (1912-13). Two additional units were installed in Plant No. 2, one in 1914, and the other in 1916. In the middle of World War I, Sir Charles Ross encountered financial difficulties and was forced to sell out to the Consolidated Mining and Smelting Co. That company or its successor, Cominco, has remained in control to the present day.

West Kootenay Power could not have made the contributions that it has to the economic and social life of southern British Columbia without the resourcefulness and skill of Lorne Campbell, its general manager. He was one of those strong personalities that the economic climate of the late nineteenth and early twentieth centuries seemed so prone to encourage. Born and educated in Perth, Scotland, he came out to Canada as a young man. He got a job in the Edison General Electric Co. of Toronto in 1889, was sent to the west to supervise the company's installation at Bonnington Falls, and stayed on as a general manager of West Kootenay Power.

Many and varied were the improvements that he initiated in the early days of the electrical business in the Kootenays. He became an autocrat in the affairs of the company and many a story is told of his inflexible will and desire to have his own way. This was a major asset to a small company doing pioneering work in a new field.

West Kootenay Power has not only made possible the carrying on of big business in the region which it serves, but has helped in many ways to bring a better standard of living to its customers. It pioneered the use of electrical home appliances in southern B.C. and made possible more comfortable surroundings in restaurants, saloons, and business establishments. It introduced to the Kootenays and the Boundary country many of the conveniences of modern life.

The mine owners of Rossland were not alone in anticipating the benefits of hydroelectric power. In the later years of the nineties, substantial amounts of low-grade copper ore were found in the Boundary country. The London and British Columbia Goldfields Co. Ltd. was a London-based company interested in acquiring mining and other property in B.C. In 1897-98, there was mining activity around Phoenix, Greenwood, and Grand Forks. In a few

176

years time, power would be in great demand. At Cascade, 12 miles east of Grand Forks on the Kettle River, there was a site suitable for the generation of hydroelectric power. In 1897, the company directors authorized the building of a plant to develop 3,900 h.p. at this site. A company was incorporated, The Cascade Water Power and Light Co. Construction started in 1898 and, after long delays, the plant began producing electricity in 1902. Equipment consisted of three turbines built by S. Morgan Smith of York, Pa., connected to three Westinghouse generators. Power was supplied to the Granby Consolidated mine at Phoenix and to the town for lighting. It also supplied part of the power required for the smelter at Grand Forks. The venture ran into difficulties due to the variability of the flow of water in the Kettle River which gave peaks and declines in the amount of electricity that could be generated. The parent company, London and British Columbia Goldfields Co. Ltd., ran into financial troubles. Granby Consolidated had built their own hydroelectric plant at Grand Forks and West Kootenay Power had invaded the territory by putting in a line to Greenwood. This was not the first time West Kootenay Power had appeared in the district as a competitor. In 1900, West Kootenay had offered to deliver power to Granby at Grand Forks for $75 per h.p. per annum. All of these factors induced Cascade Power to sell out to the West Kootenay Co. By 1919, logging in the area had so shortened the runoff period that operation of the plant was no longer practical and it was closed down.

At the same time, another interesting experiment in generating hydroelectric power was occurring at Ashcroft, B.C. In 1898, the Ashcroft Water, Electric, and Improvement Co. secured water rights on the Bonaparte River four miles outside of Ashcroft. They erected a 200-foot dam built of heavy timbers and filled in with rocks and gravel. Power was generated by two waterwheels geared to two turbines, made by the William Hamilton Co. of Peterborough, Ontario, which ran a generator to deliver power to Ashcroft. The waterwheels served a secondary purpose and operated a pump which forced river water to a height of 250 feet onto the Boston Flats where it was used for irrigation. The steel pipe used in the irrigation had been made by the Albion Iron Works of Victoria. All farms on the irrigated land were lighted by electricity and had telephone connections with Ashcroft.

Even in those early days, Kamloops had a city-owned power station. It was a steam generating plant which had begun operation

177

in the spring of 1896. The engine was built in Amherst, Nova Scotia, and the generator was made by the United Electric Improvement Co. in Philadelphia. It eventually proved unsatisfactory and a new plant was constructed in 1902.

The first hydroelectric plant on the coast was located at Goldstream, some 13 miles away from Victoria. The city of Victoria had for many years run on its own a steam-driven generating plant located within the city. The function of the Goldstream plant which was built by the B.C. Electric Railway Co. was to supply power to the streetcars, homes, and commercial establishments. It was planned in 1897 and began operation in 1898. The generators supplied by the Canadian General Electric Co. were run by two Pelton waterwheels which produced power stepped up to 17,500 volts. The line, 13 miles in length, came down the Esquimalt & Nanaimo Railway right-of-way into Victoria.

Almost from its formation in 1897, the directors of the B.C. Electric Railway Co. were searching for possible hydroelectric generating sites. Approximately fifteen miles east and north of Vancouver lies Lake Coquitlam. The waters in this lake were viewed by Vancouver businessmen as being a natural resource with great potential for hydroelectric power. In 1886, a company called The Coquitlam Waterworks Co. was formed to build the necessary works to bring the water to the city of Vancouver. In spite of having Mayor David Oppenheimer as one of its sponsors, the contract to supply Vancouver with water went to its competitor and the North Shore. For ten years, the company tried to sell the water rights on Lake Coquitlam and its watershed. Finally, the management of the B.C. Electric became interested and bought the company through its subsidiary, The Vancouver Power Co., to develop the most ambitious hydroelectric power project yet launched in British Columbia. It became known as the Buntzen Power Project, and entailed the diversion of the waters of Lake Coquitlam through a tunnel 12,750 feet in length to Lake Beautiful, or as it was renamed, Lake Buntzen. The name was in honour of the general manager of the B.C. Electric Co. The powerhouse was to be built at tidewater so that the waters of Lake Buntzen would be delivered through the pipes to the turbines with great force.

Work started in 1902 and, as the project engineer reported to general manager J. Buntzen in September of that year, "the bunkhouse and the boarding house for the tunnel work have been completed." There were problems both with the weather and the work force. "As the rain has been almost continuous," he wrote in November 1902, "and as men could not be had that would furnish their own waterproof clothing, we were obliged to supply the clothing in order to get the work done. This seemed to be the only solution for outside winter work with the class of men obtainable."

There was also difficulty in getting men at all as the report for July 1903 points out. "Some difficulty has been experienced in getting sufficient help and this applies to all the work, the reason being that the salmon fishing is on and for a few weeks men can make more money in that way."

"On the 13th of August 1903, stone masons commenced laying up the walls of the powerhouse," the engineer reported, "more rapid work should be done but it seems impossible to get masons. Stone masons are receiving 55 cents per hour and are hard to get at that price."

Then in September 1903, "Owing to the rain and delay caused by it, advantage was taken during the last week to reduce the force and at the same time get rid of some undesirable workmen."

One of the problems was how to span the inlet by the transmission line. The crossing was the longest ever attempted to that date in the field of electric transmission. It was decided to erect two steel towers 135 feet high and 270 feet above tidewater and make the crossing of 2,750 feet at Barnet. The contract was awarded to Messrs C. F. Jackson & Co. of Liverpool, England. Another problem was that the Pelton Water Wheel Co. of Quebec did not have the tools large enough to cast the main bed plate for the waterwheel and generator and had to subcontract the job, making the delivery 2½ months late. It arrived in Vancouver, November 16, 1903, one month before the plant was to go into operation.

The first Lake Buntzen power was delivered in Vancouver December 17, 1903, the initial equipment being one generator of 3,000 h.p. The foresight displayed by the planners was shown over the years by the addition of three more 3,000-h.p. units and two giant units of 10,500 h.p. each, raising the capacity of Plant No. 1 to 33,000 h.p. For eight years Lake Buntzen No. 1 was the main producer for the B.C. Electric on the lower mainland. In 1910-1911 the tunnel connecting Lake Coquitlam and Lake Buntzen was enlarged and a second plant was built, bringing another 60,000 h.p. to meet Vancouver's growing electrical needs.

The succeeding period, up to the outbreak of World War I, saw the completion of two more major hydroelectric developments and several minor ones, such as Powell River, Ocean Falls, Swanson Bay, Anyox.

Jordan River was built not so much in anticipation of future needs in the Victoria area, but to meet a commitment given to the city of Victoria. It was not an industrialized area and the population in 1911 was only ⅓ of that in the lower mainland. The big power users had their own plants, like the cement works at Tod Inlet and the Empress Hotel. It appeared there was little need for such a large hydroelectric project at Jordan River. The real reason seems to lie in the fact that the directors in London were sensitive to the monopolistic position held by the company in the fields of urban transportation and electric power. In England these fields had come under constant attack as belonging to the public and not the private sector. The corporations of the great cities of Leeds, Bradford, Liverpool, and Manchester had either initiated or taken over the tramways from private enterprise. Their actions were familiar to G. P. Norton and the investors which he represented as they lived in the north and there was a great deal of apprehension that the same thing might happen in British Columbia. The company, in the areas in which it operated, did all in its power to obtain franchises prohibiting the municipalities from setting up their own electrical systems. There had been trouble with city council in Victoria on this point and to win them over the company agreed to institute a large investment program. This came to include the Jordan River hydroelectric project and the building of the Saanich inter-urban. Jordan River flows into the Strait of Juan de Fuca some 37 miles west of Victoria. The powerhouse was to be built at the mouth of the river and fed by a flume of wood and steel pipe which took the water from the Jordan River, six miles further up, and dropped it down to tidewater. Originally it was planned to have only one generator of 5,500 h.p. but in time more were added, bringing capacity in 1922 to 21,500 h.p. In time it became the chief source of electrical energy for southern Vancouver Island and the Goldstream plant was dismantled. Up island, in 1913, Canadian Collieries put in a hydroelectric plant on the Puntledge River some six miles above Courtenay, which served the company mines and the towns of Comox and Courtenay. It was taken over by the B.C. Power Commission in 1953.

Other developments were occurring on the mainland. A group of Vancouver businessmen, including John Hendry of the B.C. Mills, Timber & Trading Co., one of the most influential industrialists in B.C., had acquired the water rights on the Stave River with the objective of developing Stave Falls and selling cheap power in Vancouver. The Stave Lake Power Co., incorporated in 1901, had a stormy career. Control soon passed into the hands of C. H. MacIntosh and the British American Mining Corporation, a London-based company controlled by Whittaker Wright. He was considered one of the financial wizards of the London stock market, a company promoter of international reputation whose financial empire collapsed amid a wave of frauds and scandals a few years later. The Bank of Montreal, in an effort to recover loans advanced to some of his Canadian ventures, acquired the shares of the Stave Lake Power Co. The bank restructured the company, replacing it by a new entity: the Western Canada Power Co. which was ⅓ owned by the bank, ⅓ by the Royal Securities Co., the Canadian fund-raising arm of Lord Beaverbrook, and ⅓ by several shareholders including Lord Shaughnessy and C. R. Hosmer of the Canadian Pacific Railway. This was the heart of the Canadian financial establishment. Eastern money then began to flow westward and in 1910 the necessary steps were taken to build a hydroelectric station with two generators at Stave Falls to produce approximately 21,000 h.p. Further, a 60,000-volt transmission line was authorized to be built to Vancouver and an aggressive sales campaign was mounted to sell the power to industrial users. This was a direct threat to the B.C. Electric Co. and was met in two ways.

The first was the outright purchase of the Burrard Power Co., owners of the water rights in Alouette Lake. "To checkmate Stave Lake and prevent their expanding into a really large proposition," explained George Kidd, secretary of the company in the London office, to H. Sperling, general manager in Vancouver. The significance lies in the fact that Alouette Lake is west of Stave Lake and no further electrical expansion was possible on the Stave River without additional water from that source.

The second was the purchase of bulk power from the Western Canada Power Co. The newer company, however, was still selling power independently to industrial users in Vancouver. For a number of years that market was practically lost to the B.C. Electric Co.

Industrial sales declined after the Armistice in 1918. Western Canada Power got into difficulties resulting in its takeover by B.C. Electric in February of 1921. Over the next few years the company spent $7 million to fully utilize the water resources of the Stave

River. The two lakes were connected by tunnel, and a new dam and generating plant were built at Ruskin.

The twenties was a period of growth in British Columbia's industries. The population of the province increased 77 percent from 392,000 in 1911 to 694,000 in 1931. Electrical generating capacity had almost doubled, mainly by means of additions to existing plants. In 1910 only 38 B.C. communities had electric service, supplied by 23 generating stations. By 1930, the number had jumped to 118 communities served by 58 generating stations. All signs pointed to a need for further generating capacity. The managements of the B.C. Electric and the West Kootenay Power Co. were aware of this and were investigating possibilities further north and on the Kootenay River. In 1924 preliminary surveys were made by the B.C. Electric on the Bridge River, and on the Kootenay River by West Kootenay Power for building No. 3 plant at South Slocan and water storage for No. 4 at Corra Linn, which only became operative in 1932. Next year the Bridge River Power Co., which had held the water rights since 1912, were bought out by the B.C. Electric. The 1926 plans called for a diversion dam across the Bridge River, a storage dam at Gun Lake and a 14,000-foot tunnel to divert the waters of the Bridge River into Seton Lake. The tunnel was started that year and completed in 1930. In 1930 the Great Depression struck and all work on the project was suspended for 15 years. In the West Kootenays, the South Slocan and Corra Linn stations were built, for a total of four plants on the Kootenay River between Castlegar and Nelson, making it the most productive stretch of water in southern British Columbia.

The thirties witnessed no new hydroelectric development. It was not until the end of World War II that the momentum was regained and British Columbia entered into its maturity as the home of world-renowned dams and hydroelectric generating stations.

Maturity

The early post-war years saw much of the province in need of additional power. Instead of the expected decline in demand there was a marked increase. The three major suppliers, B.C. Electric, Cominco, and the B.C. Power Commission, each expanded capacity in its own territory. The B.C. Electric Co. commenced construction on its Bridge River project at the point where it left off 15 years previously. The tunnel, which allowed water from Bridge River to flow into Seton Lake, had been completed but the turbines and generators and the transmission lines to bring the power to the markets of the lower mainland remained to be completed. Work on powerhouse No. 1 was started in an atmosphere of some urgency with the first generator coming into service in 1948. Three more were added at intervals until 1954, the total output being 180,000 kilowatts, the largest individual source of power in the province at the time. The final completion of the project came in 1960. With 10 generating units it was the largest in the B.C. Electric system until it was dwarfed by the Peace and Mica dams. Cominco's solution was the building of the Waneta station on the Pen-d'Oreille River, a few hundred yards north of the international boundary. The company installed turbines of 120,000 h.p., second only in size to those at the Grand Coulee Dam in Washington State. The B.C. Power Commission's response was the John Hart development, a much smaller endeavour near Campbell River on northern Vancouver Island. With these new plants British Columbia enjoyed a surplus of power from 1947 to 1955.

The problems which have faced the promoters of hydroelectric power in B.C. have been many. First and foremost has been the problem of the distances involved. In B.C., the best sites for power generating are situated far from the markets which they would have to serve. Unlike most of the sites in Ontario and Quebec, the flow of water in B.C. rivers varies according to the season. In the spring, with the melting of the snow on the mountains, the volume is tremendous, rising at times to flood levels. In late summer and the autumn it decreases, drying up in some rivers to a mere trickle. The flow of water has been controlled and regulated by the building of dams, and in recent years the trend has been to build larger and higher dams capable of impounding greater quantities of water so that an assured supply would be available the year round. This greater flow of water has enabled the engineers to install larger turbines, giving the generators more power to produce greater quantities of electricity. The electrical pressure (the voltage) in the transmission lines has also been increased so that power can now be sent greater distances with less loss. The greater quantity of electricity produced by all the improvements in the technology of generating and transmission, has made it possible to sell the product in the market place at or under competitive prices.

In the late forties and early fifties many western industrial leaders saw in British Columbia one of the last of the great unexploited areas of North America. Some of the schemes presented to the provincial government were fantastic. In 1947 the Aluminum Co. of America proposed a plan to dam Lake Bennett, Lake Atlin, and Lake Taslin and carry the waters through a tunnel to a power site north of Skagway. It was a one-half billion dollar project and the provincial government turned it down because exporting Canadian water to build up industry in a foreign country was not in the interests of B.C. and was not a proposition which they wished to endorse. The Frobisher plan of 1953 proposed using the waters of the Yukon River and Lake Atlin to drive generators in a power-house situated at the lower end of Lake Atlin and sending the power to the head of Taku Inlet where an industrial city could be built. No suitable site was found and in a location so lacking in population there was no market for power. The scheme survived on paper until 1959 when the government returned the deposit to the company.

Increasing demands for aluminum in the 1950's encouraged the Aluminum Co. of Canada, through its subsidiary Alcan, to build a smelter in British Columbia. The spot chosen was Kitimat, at the head of the Douglas Channel some 70 miles southeast of Prince Rupert. Electric power was to be obtained from the waters of the Nechako River drainage basin, a system of interconnecting rivers and lakes in central B.C. The project involved the damming of the Nechako River at a point some miles south of Fraser Lake, and the creation of a storage area to the west. The water would cross the coast range in a tunnel ten miles in length and drop 2,600 feet to the powerhouse situated inside a mountain at Kemano in the Gardner Canal. High voltage lines would then transmit the power to the smelter site at Kitimat 50 miles away. It was an ambitious scheme which could only be undertaken by a strong multinational company.

The location had been known as a potential hydroelectric site for many years. The first survey had been authorized by the provincial government's Water Rights Branch in 1928, when Frederick W. Knewstubb led a party into the Nechako River drainage basin. His suggestions for hydroelectric development were to be closely followed by Alcan's engineers.

The decision to locate in the Kitimat-Kemano area was only arrived at by the Aluminum Co. of Canada after much investigation and study. Sites on the Gold Coast, North Borneo, New Zealand, Venezuela, and Guiana had all been looked at and turned down. Even a site at Churchill Falls, Labrador, had been under discussion. On December 30, 1950, the company finally signed an agreement with the provincial government to develop a large power project in the Nechako-Kemano area, consisting of a dam on the Nechako River which could impound the waters in a storage area, a 10-mile tunnel under the coast range of mountains which would bring the water to tidewater, and an underground powerhouse at Kemano where the generated power would be transmitted over a high voltage line 50 miles to Kitimat. The Kemano project ranks with the one at Shipshaw, Quebec, and are Alcan's biggest hydroelectric plants. Although Alcan is one of the largest privately-owned producers of electricity in Canada, and Kemano is the second largest project in this system, its capacity has been exceeded by several of the newer installations in B.C. The Peace River or Mica projects have, in their own stations, twice the capacity of the Kemano project. The Revelstoke project, when completed, will have three times the generating capacity.

The Rocky Mountain Trench stretches 1,000 miles from the U.S. boundary to the Northwest Territories. In the south section its most important river is the Columbia; in the north, the Peace. In the 1950's it possessed the greatest concentration of potential hydroelectric power generating sites in the world.

The Columbia River, being nearer to the settled communities, received the first attention. The focus, at first, had been directed to the river as it flowed through Washington State. Hydroelectric development at Grand Coulee had first been proposed in the Depression days of the thirties. The program was completed in 1942 and was one of the world's largest dams and hydroelectric installations. It came on line just in time to provide power to the newly-erected atomic plant at Hanford in Washington State. The U.S. authorities foresaw the coming need for more power, and in 1944 the American and Canadian governments initiated a study of the Columbia River. This was the start of the series of studies and controversies which were to result years later in the Columbia River Treaty and the building of the Columbia River dams in British Columbia.

At a ceremony at the Peace Arch on the international boundary at Blaine on September 16, 1964, President Lyndon Johnson of the United States, Prime Minister Lester Pearson of Canada, and Premier W. A. C. Bennett of British Columbia signed the Columbia River Treaty. This marked the end of years of controversy between American and Canadian officials and the federal and provincial governments. This international controversy centred around the value of Canadian water to American industry. The sale across the border of electricity generated in B.C. did not seem to be a question of discussion. It had been federal policy since 1907, incorporated in "An Act to regulate the Exportation of Electric Power," to restrict the sale of electricity across the border. Conversely, the export of Canadian water has never enjoyed federal protection. Water was one item that the Americans were most anxious to obtain. They had 10 hydroelectric plants on the Columbia, all subject to fluctuations in the flow of water from upstream. If the water could be regulated and the flow stabilized year round the plants would always be able to operate at capacity. This is what the Columbia Treaty set out to accomplish.

The treaty called for the building of three dams in southern British Columbia: Duncan, at the upper end of Kootenay Lake; Hugh Keenleyside, at the lower end of the Arrow Lakes; and Mica, 85 miles north of Revelstoke near the bend of the Columbia River. In return for building these dams and providing the land for the water storage areas, the Americans gave a cash payment of approximately $274 million. Owing to the unexpected inflation this lump sum payment did not entirely cover the cost of building the dams and British Columbia had to raise the difference. Two other benefits were to accrue. The first was flood control. In the past, flooding had been a serious problem on the farm lands adjacent to the river and in some towns on its bank. For example, in the great floods of 1948, the business section of Trail suffered serious damage. These problems are now completely solved, as the flow of water is controlled at the storage dams. Under the treaty British Columbia received cash payments for the protection now conferred upon the American communities on the lower Columbia.

Second, the treaty recognized that there were potential power sites at the dams which could be utilized to great profit. The date of their development was left open to British Columbia. The development of the Mica power station is a case in point. The dam today rises 650 feet above the riverbed, creating a reservoir stretching 135 miles north to Valemount which impounds enough water to run six huge generators at Mica and a similar number of higher capacity at Revelstoke. The largest contract ever awarded to a single contractor to date (1980) was given to the Mannix Co. Ltd. to build the powerhouse at Mica. It is situated underground on the west bank of the river and hewn out of solid rock. It is 145 feet high, 80 feet wide, and 773 feet long and houses at the present four Canadian General Electric generators. The additional two will be installed when demand requires. The turbines for the project were imported from the U.S.S.R. and Japan. Work is now progressing on the site some three miles from Revelstoke, and two generators are expected to be in operation in 1983-84. The power from Mica and Revelstoke will be among the cheapest in North America, as the Americans (under the Columbia Treaty) paid for the building of the dam and the impounding of the water.

In the three decades since the end of World War II the wealth and power of the multinational companies has increased tremendously. In many respects they have become the equals of governments. It became the fashion for governments, in the interests of security or industrial progress, to court such companies, and it was not surprising that British Columbia, with its undeveloped resources, would attract their attention.

It has been mentioned how the Aluminum Co. of America, and Frobisher, the international mining corporation, had negotiated with the provincial government for concessions in northwestern B.C. In the south it was the Kaiser Aluminum & Chemical Corporation. In total disregard of the studies that had been undertaken by the International Joint Commission, they approached the provincial government with a scheme to build a storage dam near Castlegar and use the waters for generating power in Washington State. The power would be used to refine aluminum at a price far below any of their competitors. Surprisingly enough, the British Columbia government agreed, but the federal cabinet turned it down as the matter was before the International Joint Commission.

It appeared that the southern portion of the Rocky Mountain Trench was under reserve but not the northern. Then Axel Wenner-Gren, a controversial international financier, appeared on the scene. He was born in Sweden and educated in Germany. His first appearance on the international business scene was to do with the supplying of the electric lights which illuminated the Panama Canal at its opening in 1914. We then find him as owner of the Electrolux

Co., a highly successful manufacturer of vacuum cleaners. He became interested in pulp and paper, and, with German munitions manufacturer Krupp, was majority shareholder in the Bofors Munitions Co., maker of the famous Bofors anti-aircraft gun. He sold to both sides during World War II and was blacklisted by the Allies. In the fifties he became interested in northern British Columbia and signed an agreement with the provincial government in October 1957 to make a survey of the northern portion of the Rocky Mountain Trench. It was not electrical power that he was after, but timber and mineral wealth. As the survey continued, sites were discovered that could produce immense amounts of electricity. Up to that time little had been known of the power potential of the Peace River. G. R. S. Conway, in his pamphlet *Water Powers of Canada* published by the Department of Interior, Ottawa, in 1915, had written of the Peace River country: "Between the junctions of the Findlay and Parsnip — and the eastern boundary of the Province there are no water powers." But it was not too far from the point where the Findlay and the Parsnip rivers join the Peace in the Peace River canyon that the greatest potential was found. In the early fifties a scheme had been brought forward to dam the Peace River to make a lake some 240 miles long in a southward direction and divert the water into the Fraser somewhere near Prince George. It was Wenner-Gren's engineers who showed it would be practical to dam the Peace River near Hudson Hope and transmit the power via a 500,000-volt line to Vancouver at competitive prices.

A company, the Peace River Power Development Co., was set up to make engineering studies of the project. Its chairman was Sir Andrew MacTaggart, a British civil engineer of international reputation. He represented Balfour Beatty & Co. of London, engineers and contractors with world-wide interests in developing and building hydroelectric power installations and other utilities. Associated with them was the Thomson Houston Co. of Rugby, one of the oldest established electrical equipment manufacturers in England. A fellow director was Lord Chandos, head of the Associated Electrical Industries and spokesman for more than one half of the British electrical manufacturing industry. His company subscribed for a 25 percent interest in this new venture. Representatives of John Laing and Son, and Taylor Woodrow, two of Britain's leading contractors, sat on the board. Holding a small but important position was the Western Development Co., a subsidiary of the B.C. Electric Co.

The big question was whether or not they could sell the power once it was produced. In spite of the fact that Premier W. A. C. Bennett and A. E. Grauer, president of the B.C. Electric Co., were both in favour of the project, no industrial buyers could be found prepared to take big blocks of power. Neither pulp and paper companies nor mining corporations were at that time interested. The B.C. Electric Co. had its own sources of supply and was not prepared to make a commitment for large blocks of power which it would be unable to sell. The whole scheme of northern development was in jeopardy.

Premier W. A. C. Bennett, in a flash of intuition, decided to gamble. In a surprise move on August 1, 1961, it was announced in the provincial legislature that the government would take over the B.C. Electric Co. This was done under Bill No. 5, "The Power Development Act of 1961."

Within a year it was merged along with the B.C. Power Commission into a new public entity, the British Columbia Hydro and Power Authority. The new corporation was given the task of developing Peace River power.

Two gigantic construction projects have significantly influenced the British Columbia economy: the Panama Canal, and the Peace River hydroelectric project. Both have been huge earth-moving jobs. To complete the canal, 413,000,000 cubic yards of earth were removed by the Americans with an additional 30,000,000 handled by the original French contractors. For the Peace Portage dam, engineers handled 57.2 million cubic yards of fill. At the canal it meant cutting a way through a mountain (the Culebra Cut); at the Peace it meant moving a mountain from one site to another.

The W. A. C. Bennett Dam at Portage Mountain is one of the largest man-made earth-filled structures in the world. Six hundred feet high, it extends for 1¼ miles across the Peace River. It was built by moving specially selected material from a hill some four miles away from the damsite. The fill was carried by a system of conveyors (the longest high capacity conveyor belt in the world, built at a cost of $10 million) to a central distribution point where it was mixed to rigid specifications and then hauled by 100-ton dump trucks to its proper location. Work on the dam was started in the spring of 1964 and completed three years later in September 1967.

The powerhouse is second only to that at the Mica Dam in size. It is 500 feet underground, carved out of solid rock, and 890 feet long, 67 feet wide and 150 feet high. The contract for $77 million was given in June 1965 to a consortium headed by the Northern Construction Co., and J. W. Stewart Ltd. It was designed for ten generators, the first five becoming operative in 1968. The tenth and final unit was installed in February 1980. The generators were supplied by Canadian General Electric of Peterborough, Ontario, and the turbines by Mitsubishi of Japan.

Another dam has been built 14 miles downstream from the W. A. C. Bennett Dam at the eastern outlet of the Peace River canyon. It reuses the water that comes through the turbines at the W. A. C. Bennett Dam to drive four turbines manufactured at the Leningrad Metal Works in the U.S.S.R. It is a medium-sized generating station which emphasizes the fact that water, a renewable resource, can be used many times.

The Peace River Dam and its hydroelectric development compares very favourably with the major American installations south of the border. The Grand Coulee project, built in the Depression years of the thirties, took about nine years to finish and generates 1,920,000 kilowatts. At its peak, it gave employment to some 6,000 workers. The Peace River project, built in the boom years of the sixties, has taken about 16 years to bring into full production and generates some 2,470,000 kilowatts. At its peak, it employed a work force of 4,850 men.

There are several other sites on the Peace River suitable for the generation of suitable amounts of electricity. One of these is known as Site C and is about four miles southwest of Fort St. John. Here (1982) B.C. Hydro contemplates building a station housing six generating units with about the same capacity as Alcan's Kemano project.

"The significance of these dams is not to be found alone in the magnitude of their dimensions nor in the workmanship that has gone into construction. It lies rather in the ends which are to be served," said Harold L. Ickes, U.S. Secretary of the Interior, some forty years ago when speaking of the Columbia Basin Project.

The significance of the Peace, Mica, and Revelstoke projects is to be found in the greater productivity made possible to B.C. industry by the abundant supply of low cost electricity.

The great developments occurring on the Columbia and the Peace rivers have overshadowed the additions to electric power generation which have occurred in other parts of the province. The main events have taken place in the area which was once the domain of West Kootenay Power & Light. An arrangement has been made between B.C. Hydro, West Kootenay Power, and Cominco that B.C. Hydro guarantees to meet all West Kootenay and Cominco new power needs. This places upon the public utility the responsibility of making arrangements for new power when required. B.C. Hydro has now gone into the power generating business in the area which West Kootenay Power was previously supreme. It has meant building a dam and a new plant seven miles upstream from Cominco's Waneta Dam and powerhouse on the Pen d'Oreille River. Construction was started in 1976 and the dam and generating station are now completed. It is a three-generator station and there is room for a fourth when required. Its capacity is in the medium range, all four generators providing 810,000 kilowatts.

In the heart of Cominco's domain, a fifth plant has been built between Castlegar and Nelson. By present-day standards it is of minor capacity, 529,000 kilowatts.

Ironically in British Columbia, the land of water power, the B.C. Electric Co. and its successor, B.C. Hydro, have placed great emphasis on the building of gas and thermal power plants. These plants, of which B.C. Hydro has 83 at the present time, run on natural gas or bunker C oil. A major one is the Burrard thermal plant situated on the north side of Burrard Inlet, adjacent to Imperial's Ioco refinery. It houses six turbo-generating units manufactured and supplied by the Associated Electrical Industries, the giant British firm that was to supply the electrical equipment for the Peace River project. The plant is capable of running either on bunker C oil or natural gas. The oil comes directly from the refinery next door via a pipeline. The plant's capacity is 912,500 kilowatts, making it a major unit in B.C. Hydro's battery of 124 generating stations.

Another turbo-generating station, having four units of smaller size (100,000 kw), is located at Port Mann. Across on Vancouver Island is the plant at Chemainus with turbo-generators supplied by the General Electric Co. of U.S.A. One of its novel features is the deep-water dock adjacent to the station where large oil tankers can dock. To the north, in the pulp city of Prince Rupert, is the fourth large gas turbine plant which provides the electricity for that city and surrounding areas.

In the field of hydroelectric power British Columbia has come to maturity. Its dams and generating stations (Peace, Mica, Revelstoke) are among the largest in the world. In technology, both in the production of power and its transmission, B.C. is far advanced. B.C. Hydro and its predecessor, the B.C. Electric Co., have long been leaders in high voltage transmission. The lines bringing Bridge River power to the lower mainland at 380,000 volts were, for a number of years, using the highest voltage of any lines in North America. When Peace River power was first brought to southern B.C., lines using 500,000 volts were the exception and not the rule. Today, B.C. Hydro operates a province-wide grid, automatically controlled by a microwave system that co-ordinates power generation and transmission, overseen from a control building on Burnaby Mountain.

CHAPTER SEVEN

HARBOUR FACILITIES

Vancouver Island

For a hundred years after the arrival of the first white men to what is now British Columbia, most of the trade was carried on by ships. In the earlier years, this dependence upon the sea as a means of transportation placed great importance upon the harbours and harbour facilities. Among the most important was Esquimalt. Not only did all ocean-going commercial craft call there, it was also the base of Britain's Pacific naval squadron. It was therefore important that there be facilities for the maintenance and repair of ships. In 1865, a Shore Establishment for the naval base was authorized by an Imperial Order-in-Council. The matter of repairing and maintaining the ships stationed there was causing concern to the British officials in Whitehall. If repairs were necessary to their machinery, the nearest British naval dockyard was six months' travel and 7,000 miles away. The nearest drydock was the U.S. Navy's maintenance base on Mare Island in San Francisco Bay. These facilities were often used by Her Majesty's ships on the Pacific Station, a condition unacceptable to the dominant naval power of the time. A drydock was needed at Esquimalt. It is not known who first suggested the idea of building one. It must have been in the minds of many people — Admiralty officials in Whitehall, colonial administrators at Government House in Victoria, capitalists in the city of London, bankers, merchants, and newspapermen in the colony, and even perhaps unemployed miners looking for work to keep them from starvation. The hundreds of merchant ships which called at Esquimalt and the Puget Sound ports in the gold rush days, and the warships which the British, the Russians, and the French were sending into North Pacific waters, all seemed to suggest that there existed a market for ship repair facilities. There was enough support for Governor Sir Anthony Musgrave to include in the terms which he had prepared with the help of the Executive Council for British Columbia's entry into the Dominion of Canada, a request for financial assistance for building a drydock at Esquimalt.

One of the greatest stumbling blocks in the negotiations was not the railway (immense as this responsibility came to be) nor taking over the colonial debt, but assuming some financial responsibility for the contemplated drydock:

With regard to the Dry Dock they did not wish to grant it because it was a purely local work. If they granted it to B.C., every other province would require the same thing. It was not the amount they (the Canadian cabinet) dreaded so much as facing parliament with so unusual a demand

wrote Dr. John Sebastian Helmcken in his private diary.

But the British Columbia delegation stood firm and the Canadian government "had to give in, which they gracefully did but considered that it was the hardest thing they had to swallow as it would open so many questions in the House."

In the end, parliament agreed to guarantee the interest on a loan not to exceed £100,000 for ten years. The issue became bound up with the railway question and "better terms" for British Columbia and became a source of endless bickering between federal and provincial governments.

The consulting engineering firm of Messrs Knipple and Morris of London and Greenock was engaged to draw up the plans and make estimates. Eventually the Admiralty in Whitehall gave a grant of £50,000, conditional on the dock being designed to accommodate the latest class of cruisers now on the shipyard stocks.

A site was purchased from Messrs Finlayson and Tolmie at Thetis Cove in Esquimalt harbour. With the assistance of Gilbert Sproat, contracts were signed for the building of the cofferdam by Reed Bros. & Co. of London, and for pumping machinery by Watt & Co. of Birmingham.

It became a political football in the provincial legislature. The contractor abandoned the job and walked away because the government would not advance any more money. A change in government occurred in Ottawa and Sir John A. Macdonald consented to make an outright gift of $250,000 towards its completion. Tenders were advertised in British Columbian and English papers for the construction of the dock itself. Several were received from the United Kingdom and seven from firms in North America, but the British tenders were all considered too high. Of the seven North American offers, one came from San Francisco, another from a firm in Tacoma with interests in Victoria, one from New Brunswick, two from Montreal, and two from Victoria. The Montreal firm of F. B. McNamee & Co. was the lowest at $350,997 and was the one eventually chosen.

On being awarded the contract, F. B. McNamee paid a visit to Victoria, and on reappraising the situation, he decided that F. B. McNamee & Co. should have as little to do with this particular contract as possible. He persuaded three local residents, J. J. Robertson, John Huntington, and John Nicholson, to come in as partners with full responsibility for the drydock contract. Two of them were local contractors while the third had a small blacksmith and wagon-making shop. Naturally they had neither the technical ability nor the equipment to do the job. Under these conditions the project did not progress satisfactorily and within 20 months they had ceased work. The new provincial premier, William Smithe, took office in 1882, and made a settlement with the federal government of all outstanding issues including the drydock. Ottawa agreed to take over, complete, and operate the drydock as a public works project.

The Dominion government then signed a contract with Larkin, Connolly & Co. of St. Catharines as general contractor for the dock's completion. Several major contracts were given to eastern Canadian firms, including one for $50,000 to the Dominion Bridge Co. of Lachine, Quebec, for the dock gate. It was officially opened in the presence of Lieutenant-Governor Hugh Nelson and Rear Admiral Sir M. Culme-Seymour, Commander-in-Chief Pacific Station, July 20, 1887, 16 years after the initial agreement between the federal and provincial governments and 22 years after the establishment of a shore base by the British Admiralty. For a short time it ranked as the best and most modern drydock on the Pacific coast. Its major contribution to the development of port facilities in B.C. was that in the 16 years it took to build, it was the second largest construction project undertaken in B.C. to that time.

Gradually, as more and better equipped machine shops became established, major repair work on ships could be handled in Esquimalt. As explained in Chapter 5, when H.M.S. *Amphion* sustained extensive damage to her hull in November 1889 travelling to Burrard Inlet with Governor General Lord Stanley, she was drydocked and repaired at Esquimalt. Mention has been made in Chapter 2 of the establishment of Bullen's yard in Esquimalt and its purchase by Sir Alfred Yarrow. Much of the work done there was for the British Admiralty. Prior to World War I, major repairs were undertaken on the British warships *Warspite, Flora,* and *Amphion.* In the war years, major repairs were made to H.M.S. *Kent* on damage sustained at the Battle of Falkland Islands, on the cruisers *Newcastle* and *Lancaster,* and in the conversion of passenger liners to auxiliary cruisers. This was all made possible because these vessels could be drydocked adjacent to the repair facilities. Peak employment during this time was over 800.

The second drydock at Esquimalt was actually planned in pre-World War I days, the conservative government of Sir Robert Borden purchasing the site at Skinner Cove in 1913. It was held in abeyance during the war years and construction started in 1922. One of the sponsors (as had been the case with the earlier drydock) was the British Admiralty. It was to be one of a world-wide chain erected in the interests of the defence of the British Empire. Southampton, Cape Town, and Singapore were all supplied with the largest of drydocks, each capable of berthing the biggest British battleships. The dimensions in Esquimalt were staggering: length 1,173 feet, beam 125 feet, and depth 49 feet.

The general contractor was Peter Lyall & Sons of Montreal. Local subcontractors were such firms as Hobson, King & Marble for pumphouse erection, and the Pacific Construction Co. of Vancouver for excavating, dredging, concreting, and stone-setting. The fittings were massive, the outer gates weighing 1,500 tons and the inner ones 1,800. Cost was approximately $6,000,000. Some of the world's largest vessels have docked here — the *Queen Elizabeth,* with a beam of 118 feet filling nearly the total length of the dock, and tankers such as the 110,000-ton *George Champlain.* Its usefulness was amply demonstrated in October 1929. Coming into Victoria on her first voyage after being re-engined in Scotland, the *Empress of Canada* ran hard ashore near the William Head quarantine station. Her hull was damaged over a length of 145 feet and some twenty plates had to be replaced. This work was done by Yarrows Ltd. while she rested in the new drydock, giving employment to 275 men. The dock is still in extensive use for the maintenance and repair of large ships.

The inner harbour of Victoria has always been a haven for the coasting trade. It was there that the Hudson's Bay Company had its wharf and warehouses. From that point the port facilities spread southward towards James Bay and the Parliament Buildings. On the south side of the harbour the coastal services of the Canadian Pacific Railway had their wharves and headquarters. Across the harbour, below the post office in the early days of this century, the Grand Trunk Pacific built their wharves. The Admiral Line, running from Puget Sound to San Francisco, called in the inner harbour as well. In the heyday of the coastal traffic, there was a constant movement of ships in and out. However, the inner harbour was not suitable for the larger ocean-going liners.

When the C.P.R. inaugurated its trans-Pacific service, the merchants of Victoria made strong representation to have the city made a port-of-call. R. P. Rithet, the largest importer of groceries and exporter of B.C. products, saw the opportunity and organized a company, the Victoria Wharf & Warehouse Co. Ltd., to build wharves in the outer harbour. Jutting out into the water from 16 acres of company-owned land, the Outer Wharves served for a generation as the first inward and last outward stopping place for the C.P.R.'s trans-Pacific Empresses and the Royal Mail boats to the Antipodes.

The Panama Canal held the same fascination for the people of Edwardian British Columbia as Peace River power projects did for their descendants sixty years later. It was expected, by shortening the distances and reducing transportation charges, to open new and rich markets for British Columbia products. This expected increase in water-borne trade sparked much port construction in B.C. To provide Victoria with harbour works to handle this expected trade, the federal government in 1911 commissioned Mr. Louis Coste, M.I.C.E., to report on new requirements.

"The inner harbour is a very valuable asset to the city of Victoria and the Province," he reported. "Coasting trade is very large but it is not possible to accommodate large ocean liners within its limits."

He advocated creation of a man-made harbour at Ogden Point consisting of a breakwater, five concrete piers, and a railway ferry slip. A proposed railway bridge at the entrance to the inner harbour would connect the new docks with the Esquimalt & Nanaimo railway yards.

A careful study of existing conditions was made by Consulting Engineer Mr. Louis Coste and as a result of his report plans were prepared and tenders invited for the construction of a breakwater from Ogden Point wrote the Minister of Public Works on March 31, 1912. The contract for $1,797,000 was awarded December 20, 1912, to Sir John Jackson Ltd. of London, England, for the construction. All the material was procured within easy reach of Victoria, a quarry being opened at Albert Head for the rubble and stone. It was not until April 9, 1913, that any rock was dumped at the site. Much equipment had to be set up at the quarry at Albert Head, and wharves and scows built. Huge granite blocks weighing up to 700 tons were laid on the seaward side of the breakwater. Over one million tons of stone were transported from Albert Head to be used on the site. The concrete came from the new factory at Bamberton and Tod Inlet. The docks were completed late in 1916.

A contract for $2,244,000 was given to Messrs Grant, Smith & McDonnell of Toronto for two concrete piers within the breakwater. Angus McDonnell, a Toronto lawyer, was a conservative member in the House of Commons for South Toronto, 1904-12, who had much influence in the government circles of the day. Financial help and technical know-how was furnished by Willard Eugene Hauser, a New York contractor. The foundations of the piers consisted of cribs built in Esquimalt harbour, towed to the site and sunk. In the building of the cribs, 4,600 tons of steel and thousands of cubic yards of concrete were used. It gave employment to over 200 men for a period of several years. Speaking of these projects, the *B.C. Magazine* of December 1913 wrote:

When this outer harbour (Victoria) is completed it will be second to no harbour on the coast as to modern and ample facilities for handling freight and passenger traffic.

Today practically all the shipping business once enjoyed by Victoria has moved away or disappeared. The coastal trade is now handled by barge or government ferry. The trans-Pacific and Australian passenger liners are no more, the victims of air travel. Outside of the summer cruise ships, very little use is now made of the facilities at Ogden Point.

When the coal deposits on Vancouver Island began to assume importance in the 1860's, Nanaimo, Departure Bay, Union Bay, and Ladysmith became noted as coal-exporting ports, coal having been shipped from Nanaimo harbour as far back as 1854. Commander R. C. Mayne, R.N., speaking of Nanaimo in 1862, had this to say in regard to harbour facilities for loading coal: "The appliances for delivering coal for instance were so faulty that a ship had to lie there often for three or four weeks before she could take on a load." As the coal trade with San Francisco developed, better means of loading the boats were installed. The Vancouver Coal Co. built railway lines from the pit head to the loading wharves where "the cars containing over 5 tons each are placed over a chute leading to the vessel's hatch, the door in the bottom of the car is opened and the coal deposited in the hold." The company, at that time (1882), had facilities for loading and shipping 1,000 tons per day.

At Departure Bay, Dunsmuir, Diggle & Co. had a narrow-gauge railway 4½ miles in length from its mine at Wellington to the loading wharves. These wharves, three in number, had a capacity of 1,000 tons in a ten-hour day. The company regularly employed and owned two colliers which made weekly trips to San Francisco.

At Union Bay there was a wharf over 550 feet in length to which coal from Dunsmuir's Comox mines was brought by rail. This was one of the main ports for ship bunkering, a mainstay of the industry in the nineteenth century.

A wharf and coal bunkers holding 8,000 tons were built by James Dunsmuir at Oyster Bay in 1898 to service his newly-opened Extension Mine, two years before the company town of Ladysmith was planned and built at this location. In 1899 the port handled 40,000 tons of coal, in 1901 405,000 tons, and varying amounts according to the fluctuations of the industry until the Extension Mine closed permanently in 1931. Ladysmith became a transfer point on the Esquimalt & Nanaimo Railway, the terminal for barging all freight cars to and from the mainland.

Today the coal ports of Departure Bay, Union Bay, and Ladysmith no longer exist. When the coal mines closed, their function disappeared. Ladysmith and Union Bay are no longer ports, and Departure Bay has become the upper island ferry terminal for the B.C. Ferries. Nanaimo, once the greatest of the coal ports, has now turned to the export of forest products.

The assembly wharf is a comparatively new innovation, now very popular with forestry management in British Columbia. Forest products such as lumber, pulp, chips, and sawmill waste are brought to a central wharf from the scattered mills up and down the island. There it is loaded onto specially designed bulk carriers. No longer do deep-sea ships go from mill to mill picking up their cargoes and spending days in transit and tied up to mill wharves. They now berth at the centralized assembly wharves where a full load is picked up in as many hours as it took days twenty years ago. Nanaimo, now, is the most active port on Vancouver Island. It has an assembly wharf with three berths and a depth of 35 feet which can accommodate vessels up to 27,000 tons.

A major program to improve Nanaimo port facilities has been launched by the federal and provincial governments at Duke Point, a few miles southeast of the city. The Nanaimo Harbour Commission is building a new forest products shipping terminal, consisting initially of two shipping berths, a warehouse, and 40 acres for the storage of lumber products. Adjacent to this will be an industrial park occupied by two major sawmills and secondary industry. It is anticipated that 1,800 new permanent jobs will be created. The project, in the words of Mayor Ney, "will establish Nanaimo as one of the major industrial ports of the Pacific Northwest."

There are several smaller ports on Vancouver Island situated in great centres of lumbering activity such as Port Alberni and Chemainus. Both of these ports have long and interesting histories. Anderson's mill at Alberni, in the 1860's, shipped lumber to many parts of the Pacific such as Australia, China, and Honolulu. In 1864, for months on end, there were no less than five vessels in port loading either spars or lumber. When the mill closed, port activity ceased and was not revived until the 1920's. Today the port is host to between 130 and 150 deep-sea vessels annually, picking up forestry products from MacMillan-Bloedel's group of mills. The sheltered waters of the Alberni Canal offered ideal conditions for the anchorage of oil drilling rigs undergoing refits or repairs.

The port of Chemainus goes back to the founding of the Victoria Lumber & Manufacturing Co. in the 1880's. From that time it has shipped millions of board feet of lumber to all parts of the world. In World War II it was the embarkation point for the Canadian troops who went in brigade strength to help the Americans drive the Japanese from the Aleutian Islands.

Vancouver Island's ports have had a very colourful and interesting history. In the gold rush days they saw thousands of gold seekers. In later years they provided the only connection that this part of the world had with the outside. In more recent times they have provided the facilities by which British Columbia products reached world markets. They have contributed much to growth on Vancouver Island and the province as a whole.

The Mainland

For thirty years, from 1858 to 1888, the gateway to the interior of British Columbia was the port of New Westminster. It was a river port, catering to the needs of the upper country and the Cariboo gold mines. At New Westminster were located the offices of the riverboat companies that ran up to Yale and intermediate points. It was also the port for the passenger ships to Victoria and the sailing vessels which picked up lumber at the mills of Joseph Homer and Debeck of Sapperton. In the early days the port of New Westminster also had jurisdiction over the ships loading at Moodyville on Burrard Inlet. With the emergence of Vancouver, New Westminster lost more of its trade. In the first decade of this century and subsequent years, the sawmilling and manufacturing complex of the Canadian Western Lumber Co. at Fraser Mills attracted many lumber carriers to its wharves. A partial revival came in the 1920's, when the Consolidated Mining & Smelting Co. decided to build a terminal to handle the export of their metal shipments from the smelter at Trail. The idea of the unit train had its first practical use in connection with the operation of this terminal. Special boxcars were earmarked for this traffic to run exclusively between Trail and the wharf at New Westminster. Pacific Coast Terminals also built a cold storage warehouse on the dock to cater to the Okanagan fruit trade. Hundreds of thousands of boxes of Okanagan apples were loaded into Royal Mail, Holland-American, or French Line ships for markets in Europe. Pacific Coast Terminals were, for many years, the principal wharf owners in New Westminster. Today the port facilities have moved across the river to the Surrey side. The Fraser Surrey dock, managed by Johnston Terminals Ltd. of Vancouver, handles general cargo and the container trade to and from Australia. Steel from Japan is another one of the important commodities unloaded there.

Since the coming of the white man, Burrard Inlet has been a centre of lumbering activity. The lumber from Moodyville and Hastings Mill was world famous. Until the coming of the railway, port activities were all connected with the transportation of logs to the mills and the shipping of sawn lumber from them. For many years the potential of Vancouver as a great port has been much publicized. Mayor David Oppenheimer, in his inaugural address, said: "Through Vancouver will pass the immense trade of the Dominion with Asia and Australia." As early as 1885, Lord Mount Stephen had stated that the C.P.R. would only be completed after it had "an ocean connection with Japan and China." The opportunities for trade with China and the Japanese had excited not only James J. Hill and the management of the Northern Pacific Railway, but thousands of others.

Land-locked, sheltered from storms, and with ample anchorage and plenty of deep water, Vancouver was an ideal location for the building of a seaport. It is not surprising that one of the first projects built by the C.P.R. in Vancouver was a wharf 500 feet long. It was built in 1886-87, parellel to the water but some yards offshore and connected by a wooden bridge to the station. The further growth of the C.P.R. port facilities depended upon the company's entry into the trans-Pacific trade.

This, however, was not an easy thing to do. There were strong competitors in the field and some of the biggest transportation corporations in the States were waiting to enter. The Pacific Mail Steamship Co. had been running a trans-Pacific service out of San Francisco since the 1870's. It had on order from British shipyards the S.S. *China*, a vessel which could provide stiff competition to any that the C.P.R. could procure or charter at that time. The Pacific Mail Co. had the backing of the Southern Pacific Railway, one of the giants in the transportation industry.

Running into Tacoma was the Northern Pacific Railway, whose management was as eager as the C.P.R. to enter the trade. Tacoma had all the advantages possessed by Vancouver and an enthusiastic citizenry who entertained great hopes, as expressed by an editorial in the *Tacoma Ledger* dated January 1, 1891. "Its (Tacoma's) rise to metropolitan greatness and worldwide fame within a space of a few short years has been one of the romances of the nineteenth century. . . . Like a new Venice Tacoma looks forth over glassy waters and prepares to handle the commerce of the world."

Slowly working his way to the coast was James J. Hill and his Great Northern Railway. He had his eyes on the Oriental trade which, in a few years, would result in the creation of the Great Northern Steamship Co. and the building of the largest ships ever to enter the Oriental trade at that time.

The policy of the C.P.R. was to enter into this field as quickly as possible. In 1886, they signed an arrangement with Frazar & Co., an exporting firm in the Orient, to charter and find cargoes for seven sailing vessels which would bring tea and other commodities from China and Japan. The first to arrive was the American barque *W. B. Flint*. There were no facilities in Vancouver at the time to discharge her cargo of tea so she had to proceed to Port Moody. The tea was immediately placed on a special train and rushed to Montreal, breaking all previous transcontinental freight records.

Sailing vessels, though, were not the best answer. George B. Dodwell, a partner in the firm of Adamson Bell & Co., far eastern merchants and internationally known in the silk, tea, and shipping trades, in co-operation with Sir William Pearce, head of the famous Fairfield Shipbuilding and Engineering Co., made a proposal to Sir William Van Horne who was by this time president of C.P.R.

Sir William Pearce had three vessels, ex-Cunard line ships, on his hands for charter or sale. It was proposed to the C.P.R. management that they could be used in the trans-Pacific service by way of charter, Adamson Bell & Co. taking full responsibility for securing cargoes and managing them. Such a timely, well-organized, and well-equipped proposal met with instant approval by Sir William Van Horne and a contract was signed. The first of these vessels to come into service was the *Abyssinia*, which left Hong Kong with a cargo of silk in May 1887 and tied up at the new C.P.R. wharf in Vancouver some time in the early morning of June 14. The second voyage of the *Parthia* brought Sir Francis Plunkett, the British minister to Japan, and his wife to Vancouver, the first of many distinguished persons to travel on the C.P.R. trans-Pacific service. The service proved so popular with the far-eastern merchants that six extra sailings in 1888 had to be arranged by Adamson Bell & Co. in specially chartered ships. The old Cunarders found it difficult to compete with the newer vessels put into service by the Pacific Mail, especially the S.S. *China* built by the Fairfield Co. of Scotland which went into service in November 1889. She was the finest trans-Pacific liner of her day. The chartered C.P.R. boats had limited accommodation and mechanical problems which interfered with their schedules. It was therefore with a sigh of relief that Vancouverites heard that the company was to build three new, faster liners. It was fully expected that the order would be given to the Fairfield Shipbuilding & Engineering Co. but, to the surprise of many, it went to the Naval Construction & Armament Co. of Barrow-in-Furness. The Fairfield people were much put out, and when the charter and management contract expired in 1891 they were not renewed. The chartered ships were gradually withdrawn and replaced by the "Empresses." Adamson Bell & Co. (now Dodwell,

Carlill & Co.) lost their position as managing agents for the trans-Pacific service. It is interesting to note that the original ships, still owned by the Fairfield interests, continued to run out of Tacoma in the far-eastern service in co-operation with the Northern Pacific Railroad and in direct competition with the C.P.R.

In spite of the coming of the "Empress" liners and the inauguration of an Australian service, the C.P.R. built no new harbour facilities in Vancouver for the next 16 years. Then came Pier A, resting on piles of Australian gumwood, the first of the C.P.R. wharves that was built out into the harbour. Growth in deep-sea facilities in the earlier years was slow and erratic with spells of heavy construction interspersed with long periods of stagnation.

It was in providing facilities for the coastal shipping that the greatest development occurred. Coal Harbour became the haven of the "mosquito fleet," the tugs and barges and small craft used mainly in forestry work. East of the C.P.R., the two main docks were that of the Union Steamship Co., and Evans, Coleman & Evans. The Grand Trunk Pacific entered the coastal trade in 1910 and built a substantial dock at the foot of Westminster Avenue (now Main Street) which still stands today. Further east was the dock of the Great Northern Railway Co., completed in 1914.

The Panama Canal had a tremendous impact on West Coast businessmen. Markets which heretofore could not be reached because of the great distances involved, could now be served economically (for example, the distance from Vancouver to Liverpool would be halved). This sparked a great deal of port development. The first major pier completed with government funds, and the first one of any size built east of Hastings Mill, was Lapointe, finished in 1914. Adjacent to Lapointe Pier, and completed about the same time, was Vancouver's first government grain elevator. Both these projects were completed due to the efforts of Harry H. Stevens, who had been federal member of parliament for Vancouver since 1911. He had long advocated the building of new facilities in the port of Vancouver, much against the wishes of the C.P.R. and the other waterfront owners. "At the present" (July 1913), he wrote, "it may be safely said the port is not well equipped with those devices necessary for its expanding business." His greatest contribution to port development was his assistance given in passing through the House of Commons at Ottawa the bill establishing the Vancouver Harbour Commission. This body was empowered to administer the port and raise funds for the construction of harbour works by a levy on cargo rates and tonnage dues. Under its authority, the ship channel in the First Narrows was deepened and dangerous shoals removed, the Ballantyne Pier was built, and two new government grain elevators constructed.

The temper of the times was illustrated in the fantastic scheme brought forward by the Vancouver Docks & Extension Co. to turn the whole of the western shoreline of Lulu Island into a great complex of docks, warehouses, trackage, and manufacturing plants, as explained by the promoters Messrs Wooley & Dauphinee to a meeting of the Richmond Progressive Association on May 18, 1912. Briefly, the development contemplated the reclaiming of the tidal flats from Steveston to the South Channel of the North Arm of the Fraser River, making 8.4 miles of harbour. There would also be 4.9 square miles of reclaimed land on the piers to be devoted to working dock space, warehouses and storage sheds, industrial sites, and terminal trackage. In addition, 36 miles of tidal and ship channels were to be dredged to a depth of 30 to 36 feet. The whole magnificent scheme included 33 warehouses, 44 industrial buildings, 57 miles of railway track, three draw bridges, and one double-tracked tunnel.

The tunnel was one of the more interesting aspects. Bridges were to be thrown across the North and South Channels of the North Arm of the Fraser, striking the highland of Point Grey somewhere in the neighbourhood of Highbury Street. Then, a tunnel was to be drilled some four or five miles northeast to False Creek between the Granville and Cambie bridges, thus providing quick and easy access to and from the heart of Vancouver.

Sea frontage on the western boundaries of Lulu Island was bought by the company in 1911 and a year later plans had been drawn up by the engineering firm of J. G. White & Co. of London and New York. No construction seems to have been started.

What happened is one of the unsolved mysteries in the industrial development of the lower mainland. Whether the C.P.R. bought them out or World War I diverted the attention of the promoters to more pressing problems, is not known. It was a scheme well thought out, excellently planned, and apparently supported by big money in the east. Today it has been partially realized, although in a slightly different location, by the building of the superport at Roberts Bank.

To cater to the growing number of ships run by the B.C. Coast Service of the C.P.R., Pier D was built at the foot of Granville

Street. The west side was reserved for coastal shipping while on the east were berthed the 16,000-ton *Empress of Asia* and the *Empress of Russia*. The pier burned down in a spectacular blaze July 27, 1938, after 21 years of useful service and was never rebuilt. For many years the showpiece of the port was Pier B-C. A concrete pier 1,140 feet long and 331 feet wide, it was built by the Sydney E. Junkins Co. Ltd. in a space of four years, after four years (1919-23) had been spent in laying the foundations. It was dedicated to the cause of Empire Trade July 4, 1927. This period was possibly the longest time ever spent on one construction job in the history of Vancouver. For 35 years it served as the Vancouver terminal for the Australian and trans-Pacific passenger liners. The sheds and terminal buildings have now been demolished to make room for a proposed convention centre.

Shipping prairie grain through Vancouver to overseas markets has for a century attracted the attention and utilized the activities of many organizations and people. Dr. J. M. Lefevre, C.P.R. surgeon and Vancouver entrepreneur, speaking before the mayor and city council of Vancouver June 18, 1887, said, "The C.P.R. should work up a new industry in bringing the wheat of the great North West to Vancouver where mills could be erected to grind it and from thence distribute to our Eastern Hemisphere."

Small shipments of wheat and oats (sacked) have been shipped through the port of Vancouver since the first years of the century. An experimental shipment of wheat in bulk was sent via Panama to Liverpool in 1916. To feed a starving Europe, five vessels carrying 800,000 bushels sailed from Vancouver during the period 1918-19, followed by a pilot shipment of 2,000 tons on a commercial basis in 1921. It was not until the Board of Railway Commissioners ruled that the Crow's Nest Pass rates applied to grain shipped to the Pacific coast ports (if it was for export) as well as the Lakehead, that shipments through Vancouver began to grow. This boom in grain initiated the building of several more elevators, the largest being the Alberta Wheat Pool built in 1927-29. This marked the high point in grain elevator construction until the 1960's when the Saskatchewan Wheat Pool elevator was built on the North Shore adjacent to the site where, one hundred years before, Sewell P. Moody had run his sawmill. The latest one to be built is the Pioneer Grain Terminal, which became operative in October 1979. It incorporates the latest in grain-handling techniques. Computerized controls ensure that the grain is automatically sorted, cleaned, and distributed to the right bins. The loading onto the bulk carriers is done by two Peco shiploaders, an innovative type of loading equipment unique in Canada. The dust control system is the most effective that current technology can provide. The dust is collected, pressed into pellets, and then sold as animal feed. The elevator is owned by the Pioneer Grain Co., a subsidiary of James Richardson & Sons Ltd. which has over 400 country elevators on the prairies. Wheat is now the second largest commodity shipped through the port of Vancouver. There are five elevators with a capacity of over 24,000,000 bushels, which in the peak season process from 500 to 600 railway cars per day.

The past two decades have witnessed a revolution in deep-sea transportation. Not only have the types of ships changed but also the commodities carried. The general purpose ship, which used to go from port to port on what was virtually a liner schedule, has disappeared. In its place have come vessels built to carry specialized products such as automobiles, packaged lumber, containers, wood chips, etc., running on a shuttle service from one designated port to another perhaps half the world away. This has called for the building of special kinds of harbour facilities and wharves. The first was the Pacific Coast Bulk Terminals, a subsidiary of Cominco Ltd., at Port Moody, which was opened for operations in March 1960. The commodities handled there are coal, potash, and sulphur. The loading is done by two huge mechanical shiploaders. Each has the capacity to load thousands of tons per hour. For example, No. 1 can load 3,000 tons of potash or sulphur, or 2,250 tons of coal per hour. The terminal also has acreage capable of storing half a million tons of these materials in covered and open sheds.

Vancouver Wharves Ltd., owned by the Williams-Hudson Group of London, England, started in May 1960 on land leased from the Squamish Indian band on the North Shore in the First Narrows opposite Stanley Park. It was primarily built for the storage and loading of potash, but has since branched out to handle sulphur, copper concentrates, and packaged lumber.

Neptune Terminals, which is owned by a consortium of its customers — the McIntyre Mine at Grande Cache, Alberta, the Consolidation Coal Co., and the government of Saskatchewan and its potash mines — is situated on 70 acres of land leased from the National Harbours Board in North Vancouver, west of the Second Narrows Bridge. It is mainly a coal loading terminal, which gets its coal from Alberta mines and ships it to Japan and to the east coast of North America. The terminal has two loading berths which can accommodate vessels of up to 120,000 tons.

Seaboard Terminal, near the mouth of Lynn Creek in North Vancouver, effected a radical change in shipping methods for lumber when it was opened in August 1971. It functions as an assembly point for lumber sold overseas and produced in the mills on the lower mainland associated with Seaboard Lumber Sales Ltd., the selling arm of a group of British Columbia lumber manufacturers. One innovation was the central scowing system operated by the Gulf of Georgia Towing Co. Scows would call at the different mills, pick up what was required, and take it to the terminal. Lumber comes by scow, train, or truck to the assembly wharf, saving many days of travelling time previously spent by the deep-sea carriers in going from mill to mill. The idea has now been accepted by the industry and several more assembly wharves are in operation in different localities on the coast.

An integral part of the port of Vancouver is Roberts Bank, purely a coal loading terminal. The idea that the metallurgical coal of the East Kootenays could be sold at competitive prices overseas had attracted the attention of many people over the years. In the sixties the industry was in a decline and something had to be done. One remedy for the decline was the creation of the B.C. Harbours Board by the provincial government. They were empowered to provide, if possible, the necessary links, engineering studies, land access roads, rail transportation, etc., to ports or potential ports which could move B.C. products to overseas markets. They, with other agencies, were responsible for the building of Roberts Bank plus the eagerness of the Japanese in persuading the Kaiser Corporation to develop their mines in the East Kootenays. The port is a man-made island some three miles offshore, just south of the South Channel of the Fraser where it empties into the Strait of Georgia. Here, vessels up to 160,000 tons can dock with ease, load, and turn around within a matter of days. The terminal was originally built for Kaiser Resources, to deliver 75 million tons of coal over a 15-year period to a consortium of Japanese steel makers. Today, it is also used by Fording Coal, the coal mining arm of Cominco, and the Canadian Pacific Railway interests.

New developments are taking place at Roberts Bank. It includes three new extensions to the man-made island. Technically called pads, they will be built in the 1981-82 dredging season by the National Harbours Board. The first is now ready and will be in opera-

208

tion in the fall of 1982. The construction of these three pads will bring the coal storage capacity of the port to 27 million metric tons. Another ship's berth will be built by Westshore Terminals Ltd. to accommodate vessels up to 250,000 tons with the necessary coal stacking and delivery equipment. To provide for the rapid flow-through of the increased tonnage, the causeway will be widened to accommodate two railway tracks.

The additional tonnage will come from new mines of the B.C. Resources Corporation at Sparwood and increase output from the Byron Creek Collieries, Fording Coal, and the Crow's Nest Industries. It is anticipated that some coal will also be shipped from southwestern Alberta. By 1984, from 25 to 27 million tons per year will flow through Roberts Bank.

The most significant innovation in the handling of general cargo has been the emergence of the container. In ease of handling, in the economics of space, in protection from theft, there is no better method than the container. This is now recognized world-wide and every port of importance has made provision for handling containers and container ships. The port of Vancouver was slow to recognize this need and up to the middle of the seventies had only one berth on the old Hastings Mill site to handle this kind of traffic. In 1975, Vanterm Terminal on the south side of the harbour just west of Lapointe Pier, became the first modern container terminal in the port. It comprises 76 acres, with two container berths, one roll-on/roll-off slip and 1,400 feet of berthing for general cargo.

The disposal of sawmill waste has always presented problems for the industry. Up to about 35 years ago the usual method was to burn it in wigwam burners, long a prominent feature of every sawmill. With the advent of cellulose forestry it was found that sawmill waste could be recycled into pulp and paper. Instead of being a liability to the industry it was now an asset with a certain marketable value. Up until a few years ago the provincial government would not allow the export of sawmill waste and the surplus eventually became so great in the interior mills that something had to be done. After much lobbying by the sawmill operators the government reversed its policy and issued permits for the export of wood chips to overseas markets. Hugh W. Cooper, a business consultant, with the help of the Department of Economic Development, found markets in Japan and Europe. He then created Fibreco Export Inc., a consortium of some 45 independent interior sawmill owners. A site was chosen on 23 acres of waterfront property east of the

Vancouver Wharves for a bulk terminal to export wood chips. This is the first terminal in British Columbia to engage in this type of business. It was completed in 1979 at a cost of $16 million, and will generate $50 million annually in new export business. The operation is geared for speed and efficiency, as vessels up to 30,000 tons can be loaded in one day. It has created 28 new full-time jobs and a new commodity on the list of Vancouver's exports.

In the past decade the volume of goods moving annually through the port of Vancouver has increased tremendously. In point of tonnage, coal now is the principal commodity handled, followed by grain, sulphur, and potash. Bulk commodities now form 85 percent of all volume handled. Vancouver is therefore first and foremost a bulk handling port, the largest on the Pacific coast of the Americas and the second largest export port in North America. Its bulk loading terminals and their material handling equipment are comparable to any of the other great ports of the world. As more and more of the natural resources of the province become developed, their outlet to various markets will be through British Columbia ports. A major part of this expansion will flow through the port of Vancouver.

The pattern of shipping from the pulp and paper ports on the mainland has changed drastically. In the past, Powell River, Ocean Falls, and Swanson Bay were the stopping places for the coastal ships on regular schedules. Coasters and deep-sea freighters would pick up their consignments of pulp or newsprint and there was thus considerable port activity. The port of Swanson Bay was permanently closed in the thirties, the coastal ships have disappeared and the newsprint or pulp is now shipped out by barge. From Powell River, newsprint is now barged to California and Washington State, or loaded in boxcars and taken via barge to Vancouver, and then by Burlington Great Northern Railway to its destinations.

At the head of Howe Sound are the Squamish Terminals, constructed in 1972 for Norwegian interests to handle pulp from the mills in the Prince George area. Surprisingly, they also look after pulp originating at the mill of the Prince Albert Pulp & Paper at Prince Albert, Saskatchewan. Half a million tons are shipped yearly to Europe on some 80 ships, providing employment to 75 local people.

The destinies of the northern British Columbia ports of Prince Rupert and Kitimat have been closely linked. When the choice of a western terminal to the second Canadian transcontinental railway had to be made, it lay between a site at the mouth of the Skeena River (Prince Rupert) or at the head of the Douglas Channel (Kitimat). President Charles Hays of the Grand Trunk Railway chose Prince Rupert because his surveyors had told him that it had one of the finest harbours on the Pacific coast. It is entirely land-locked, and offers good anchorage with adequate entrances both from the north and the south. At Kitimat, on the other hand, the port is at the head of the Douglas Channel, 35 miles from open water with no proper anchorage for deep-sea vessels.

The promoters of Prince Rupert, like in an earlier day the pro-moters of Vancouver, envisaged a glamourous future. President Charles Hays dreamed of it as a mighty seaport funnelling a cease-less flow of North American goods to a hungry Orient. It was his claim that the Grand Trunk Railway could deliver wheat in Liver-pool via Prince Rupert and the Panama Canal at the same cost as from the Lakehead. The best of town planners, Messrs Brett & Hall of Boston, was commissioned to lay out the terminals and townsite. F. M. Rattenbury, the famous B.C. architect, was to design the magnificent 450-room railway hotel. The terminal would include a 20,000-ton floating drydock, a shipyard, grain elevators, warehouses, and fish plants. The plans were grandiose, made to be a serious threat to Vancouver. The reality, however, was that a certain amount of building was done but not nearly as much as had been planned.

The drydock, started in 1912, was completed in 1916 but, along with the shipyard, remained idle until September 1919. A few freighters were built and launched at this time but the stagnation experienced by the shipbuilding industry on the west coast pre-vented any further work. Both the shipyard and the drydock re-mained virtually unused until World War II. The plans of the Grand Trunk Railway to make Prince Rupert a major city and seaport disappeared as its position deteriorated. Burdened with debt, it finally ended up in the hands of the Canadian government. For the next twenty pears Prince Rupert was a quiet, isolated commu-nity, depending upon fishing, logging, and coastal shipping for its livelihood.

The Japanese attack at Pearl Harbor on December 7, 1941, brought Prince Rupert to the attention of the Pentagon in Wash-ington, D.C. The port became a supply base, servicing the Aleutian and Alaskan theatres of war. It was made a sub-port of Seattle's Army Port of Embarkation for the trans-shipment of military supplies to Alaska, and the equipment for the capture of the islands of Attu and Kiska passed through Prince Rupert. To help in the building of the Alaska Highway, supplies were routed via Prince Rupert to Skagway and then on the White Pass & Yukon Railway to Whitehorse. Foremen, winch operators, freight checkers, and storekeepers of the American Army Transportation Corps were stationed at Prince Rupert for periods of over two years. A large dock was built at Port Edward by U.S. Army engineers to service a U.S. Army camp and ammunition dump. Here it was not unusual to see six ocean-going freighters docked at one time. The town became a staging area for troops and supplies destined for points in the North Pacific. The drydock, empty for so many years, was now filled with ships awaiting repairs. In the shipyards, 10,000-ton freighters were under construction. The population of Prince Rupert increased fourfold.

After the war, things returned to normal. The hopes that Prince Rupert would become Canada's second port on the Pacific seemed to be as small as ever. In 1954 the drydock was dismantled and sold. The coastal shipping, which had played so large a part in the maritime life of the town, was gradually phased out. Partial relief was given by the coming of the Alaskan Ferry System in February 1963 and the B.C. Ferries May 30, 1966, but from a coastal shipping standpoint Prince Rupert had become more isolated than ever.

Hopes have again been raised that it might become a major port. Within recent years the Fairview terminal, a $26 million installation to handle lumber and sulphur, has been built. Plans are now well advanced to build a bulk commodity shipping terminal on Ridley Island, a few miles south of the town. Here, a modern grain elevator will be built by private enterprise and two provincial governments. It is planned that through this terminal will come much of the coal from the newly developed mines in north-central B.C.

In the past few years, Kitimat has handled more deep-sea traffic than Prince Rupert. Its two industries, aluminum smelting and forestry, have each accounted for over 1½ million tons per year. Geographically, it is ideally situated to handle the bulk export commodity trade from north-central B.C., but it has lost out to Prince Rupert because its position as a port is hampered by being at the head of a long narrow channel with little space for anchorage. It appears very unlikely that it will ever become one of the major export ports on the Pacific coast.

The development of the ports on the mainland has depended largely on what the overseas countries want to buy from Canada. Most of these goods have to be brought to the coast, so that the main thrust of port development has always been at the points where the railways reach tidewater, such as Vancouver or Prince Rupert. A secondary phenomenon which has sprung up is that of small ports devoted to the export of one commodity which is either found or manufactured nearby. In pulp and paper it is Chemainus, Powell River, and Port Alberni; in mining it was Anyox and Britannia Beach for copper; and Texada Island, Zeballos, or Tasu on the Queen Charlottes, for iron ore. Overall, however, it is the port of Vancouver where the most development has taken place.

ADDENDUM: GENERAL SOURCES

Sources for the industrial history of British Columbia embrace a wide variety of material from the standard histories of Howay & Scholefield and Dr. Margaret Ormsby through technical journals like the *Canadian Engineer* and the trade press as in the *B.C. Lumberman* to news items in the local papers. Locally published general magazines such as *The B.C. Magazine* are helpful. Books on British Columbia which were written for promotional or status purposes, popular prior to World War I, such as Henry J. Boam's *British Columbia — Its History, People, Commerce, Industries and Resources* are mines of information. Likewise books written on the British Columbian scene by visitors such as Commander R. C. Mayne's *Four Years in British Columbia* or C. J. Galloway's *The Call of the West* contain sketches of sawmills, coal mines, etc. Then there are the histories of individual industries such as G. W. Taylor's *Timber — A History of the Forest Industry in B.C.* Last, but not without considerable merit, are the company histories like the *B.C. Sugar Refining Co.* by M. J. Rogers, or the one published by the Burrard Drydock Co. called *Progress*. Company house magazines such as *Telephone Talks* by the B.C. Telephone Co. or *Crown Zellerbach News* of Crown Zellerbach Canada Ltd. contain much of interest.

In the field of government publications the list is almost unlimited, from the Sessional Papers (provincial and federal) through statutes, royal commissions, yearbooks, to what the Department of Economic Development, Victoria, has and still is printing.

Of great importance are company documents, minutes of directors' meetings, auditors' reports, annual statements, letters sent or received by company executives. Correspondence of entrepreneurs who set up businesses in B.C., sent to business associates or to friends and members of their family, often contain matters of great interest; in short, any material that can throw light on company activities of the time. Such papers might be found anywhere: in provincial or civic archives, in company files, in accountants' or lawyers' offices, or in private hands.

In the academic field over the years many excellent theses have been written on industry in B.C., such as Patricia Roy's "The B.C. Electric Railway Co. 1897-1928" or Joseph C. Lawrence's "Markets and Capital — A History of the Lumber Industry in British Columbia 1778 to 1952." These are obtainable in the university libraries.

For more recent events the companies involved possess much information. In the majority of cases the building of new pulp mills, sawmills and other factories are documented and kept in company offices.

In the following pages appear a list of sources covering the more important events, statements, and opinions expressed in this book under their chapter headings.

CHAPTER I

Primary sources for the early trails and roads are in the colonial correspondence in the Provincial Archives, Victoria. These include Governor Douglas' dispatches, letters of the colonial administrators, ordinances passed by the executive councils, etc. Two other important sources are Walter Moberley's report on the roads in B.C. in 1863, reprinted in the January 1945 issue of the *B.C. Historical Quarterly*, and Sir Joseph Trutch's report of 1868 on *The Overland Coaching Road*. The Cariboo Road has been described by many travellers, which includes a book, *The Great North Road*, by W. M. Futcher. Description of its use in later days is contained in "The BX and the Rush to Fort George" by Willis J. West, *B.C. Historical Quarterly*, July-October 1949. The story of the camels is told in the *Okanagan Historical Society*'s Vol. 1-5. This is a different version than that narrated in Howay & Scholefield but I believe more authentic.

Information on steam traction comes from five sources:

1. Colonial ordinances and petitions in the B.C. Provincial Archives.

2. The files of John Fowler & Co. in Reading University, Reading, England.

3. Documents relating to **R.** W. Thomson and Tennant & Co. in the Scottish Public Record Office, Edinburgh, Scotland.

4. There are a number of books on road traction engines. *Steam on Common Roads* by William Fletcher, 1891, reprinted by David & Charles, Newton Abbot, Devon, in 1972, gives a good technical account of the Thomson Road Steamers but nothing on B.C. *The Industries of Scotland* by David Bremner, 1869, reprinted by David & Charles, 1969, gives an account of Tennant & Co.

5. Letter files of Hayfield & Archibald in the author's possession.

The importance of roads in the confederation negotiations comes from Dr. J. S. Helmcken's diary as outlined in the *B.C. Historical Quarterly*, April 1940.

Information on recent road building has been supplied by the Ministry of Transportation and Highways, Victoria.

The source material on railways is very extensive. The granting of the original contracts for building in B.C. can be found in the Dominion Sessional papers, 1879-82. Intimate glimpses of construction days are in Reverend H. H. Gowen's book *Bishop Sillitoe* or in *Forty Years in Canada* by Colonel Sam Steele. A glimpse of operating conditions in the Rockies is in an article, "The Passing of the Big Hill," by C. F. Carter in the magazine *World's Work* of June 1910. The collapse of the tunnel comes from page 647, the *Canadian Engineer*, 1920. The building of the Grand Trunk Pacific is very adequately covered by J. A. Lower in "The Construction of the Grand Trunk Pacific Railway in British Columbia" in Vol. 4, 1940, of the *B.C. Historical Quarterly*. Concessions granted to the Canadian Northern Railway are found in the B.C. Sessional papers of 1910.

CHAPTER 2

Norman Hacking, an authority on B.C. marine history, has contributed several articles to the *B.C. Historical Quarterly* on early steamboating January 1946, April 1947, and April 1952. One of the best books on lake and river steamers is *Paddlewheels on the Frontier* by Art Downs, published in 1972. There are some interesting letters and documents on the Canadian Pacific Navigation Co. in the Provincial Archives, Victoria, especially on the building of the *Islander*. The best account of the B.C. Coast Service of the

C.P.R. is found in the *Princess Story* by Norman Hacking and W. Kaye Lamb. There is a typewritten history of the Union Steamship Co. of B.C. 1889-1943 by Jessie M. Vander Burg, of which the author has a copy. The story of Wallace's is told in the publication by the Burrard Drydock Co. called *Progress*. Something on Yarrows can be gleaned from *Sir Alfred Yarrow*, a book by Lady E. C. Yarrow, London, 1928, where mention is made of Norman Yarrow, his son, who was put in charge at Victoria. Shipbuilding activities in the war years are described in *Down Our Ways*, the house magazine of the West Coast Shipbuilders Ltd.

A good summary of the background of the early street railway industry can be found in a chapter on Frank Julian Sprague by Harold C. Passer of Princeton University in *Men in Business*, a Harper & Row book of 1952. Proposals for electric tramways in the smaller B.C. communities are contained in private bills passed by the Legislature in Victoria. Information on British Electric Traction and the interest shown by British investors is in a book, *The Golden Age of Tramways*, by Charles Klapper, published by Routledge & Kegan Paul, London, 1961. The story of the Nelson tramway is written up in *Bulletin* No. 3 of the B.C. Railway Historical Association, 1961. Subsequent proposals for a tramway in Nanaimo in 1910 is in the Premier's correspondence (Sir Richard McBride), Provincial Archives, Victoria. Much information about the early days of the B.C. Electric is in a *Lighted Journey* by Cecil Maiden. Additional information has been found in the offices of Messrs Armitage & Norton, chartered accountants, of Huddersfield, Yorkshire, England. G. P. Norton was the senior partner in this firm for many years. He was instrumental in the founding of the Yorkshire Guarantee & Securities Corporation and was directly involved for forty years in the street railways of Vancouver and Victoria. For thirty years he served as a director of the B.C. Electric, second only in influence to R. M. Horne-Payne. The Vancouver executives of the Yorkshire Guarantee or its subsidiaires, William Sully and William Farrell, were directly involved in the reorganization schemes which culminated in the B.C. Electric. Many of the business papers and much correspondence of these two men are still held in the offices of Armitage & Norton. Much of the information in this section has come from this source.

Much material on the background of pioneer air flights in B.C. is contained in the *B.C. Historical Quarterly*, October 1939 issue "Pioneer Flying in B.C., 1910-14" by Frank H. Ellis. Also very helpful is a series of two articles in the *Richmond Review* of January 8 and 15, 1964. The Zeppelin episode is mentioned in a news item in the Vancouver *Province*, June 30, 1910. The background material on the effectiveness of commercial airships comes from *Giants in the Sky* by Douglas H. Robinson. The gradual development of air services in B.C. comes from various sources: newspapers, trade magazines, philatelic journals, etc. In the *Hiballer* magazine of July 1966 appeared an article on "Aerial Forestry Reconnaissance" describing the establishment of the air squadron at Jericho. The story of Yukon Airways is told in *Stamp Collecting* magazine of August 4 and 11, 1977. Pioneer northern and continental airmail flights are found in news items in the Vancouver *Province* or *Sun*, or documented by letters actually carried on the inaugural flights, many in the possession of the author. The drama of the Canadian Pacific Airlines can be read in the *Richmond Review* of September 26, 1966, in an article entitled "C.P.A. History — A Growth Miracle." Much of the information on the use of private planes by commercial companies has been furnished by the companies themselves.

Information on the pipelines (oil and gas) mostly comes from the companies involved. The building of the Trans Mountain pipeline is described in a book written by Neill C. Wilson and Frank J. Taylor entitled *The Building of the Trans-Mountain*. Oil and gas activities in B.C. are mentioned in *The Great Canadian Oil Patch* by Earle Grey and also in the *Peace River Chronicles* edited by Gordon E. Bowes. Much information can be obtained from newspaper clippings and the annual reports of the companies.

CHAPTER 3

Good material on Collins Overland Telegraph is found in an article by Corday Mackay in the *B.C. Historical Quarterly* of July 1946. The reactions of the colonial administrations both in New Westminster and Victoria are documented in the colonial correspondence in the Provincial Archives, Victoria. The extension of the telegraph in B.C. can be traced in the annual reports submitted by the Superintendent of the Dominion Government Telegraphs to the Minister of Public Works and published in the Dominion Sessional papers. Intimate details of the working of the system in B.C. is found in R. McMicking's diary in the B.C. Provincial Archives.

Early telephone developments are so closely linked with the telegraph that R. McMicking's diary is a mine of information. Another diary, that of Edgar Crow Baker, traces the history of the first commercial telephone company in B.C. Both diaries are housed in the Provincial Archives, Victoria. This industry, like the telegraphs, came under the Minister of Public Works and, in his annual reports, information and statistics concerning it can be found. Documents in the Scottish Public Record Office, Edinburgh, suggest that in the nineties there was a group in Edinburgh led by Bruce Peebles & Co. which was interested in investing in new electrical enterprises in Canada. Bruce Peebles & Co. were long established manufacturers of gas meters and equipment for the gas industry, and were at this stage turning to the designing and making machinery for the newly established electrical industry. It is highly probable that this was the group which tried to buy the Nelson & Vernon Telephone Co. in the early nineties. It was also this group which was in competition with Horne-Payne and G. P. Norton in the reorganization of the Vancouver tramways.

Much of the information of G. P. Norton's involvement in the telephone industry comes from the papers in the office of Armitage & Norton, Huddersfield. The B.C. Telephone Co. employs an archivist, who is well informed about the company's story. A treasury of information is also contained in the house magazine *Telephone Talks*.

Material on the postal history of British Columbia is not very extensive. For the colonial period a book of great value is A. S. Deaville's *The Colonial Postal Systems and Postage Stamps of Vancouver Island and British Columbia*, published in 1928. Gerald E. Wellburn, in collaboration with Henry C. Hitt, has written an article on the express companies in the colony of British Columbia with emphasis on their role as mail carriers in the *Stamp Specialist* of 1945. The difficulties of postal communications in the Pacific Northwest is well brought out in a book published by the Portland bankers, Ladd & Tilton, *Sixty Milestones of Progress 1859-1919*. The attitudes of British postal officials are documented in *Britain's Post Office* by Howard Robinson, Oxford University Press, 1953. From Confederation onwards, the annual reports of the Postmaster General detail the growth of the postal services. For recent events the public relations department of the post office is helpful. The growth of the airmail is recorded in news items in the *Province* or the *Sun* and in the "first day covers" letters which were sent on the first flight of each airmail route. These are carefully stamped at point of departure and destination and thus supply a documented record of that historical incident. Much airmail information has been obtained from the author's collection of these items.

CHAPTER 4

Extensive information is available concerning the growth of the metropolitan cities. Both Vancouver and Victoria support civic archives which house original material. An important source on nineteenth-century Victoria is a small booklet published by the city council entitled *Victoria Illustrated*, in 1891. Victoria cannot be discussed without mentioning the architect, F. M. Rattenbury. His life is ably told in the book *Rattenbury* by Terry Reksten.

Much information about New Westminster and its citizens can be gleaned from early directories such as T. N. Hibben's of 1877 and R. T. Williams' *B.C. Directory* of 1882. Newspapers have been published in the city since the 1860's which contain much detail of local interest. The museum attached to Irving House on Royal Avenue and the city librarian, Allan Woodland, have much to offer.

Along with the routine sources (newspapers, books, magazines), a great deal of use has been made in describing the growth of Vancouver from the Yorkshire Guarantee and Securities Corporation papers in the office of Armitage & Norton, Huddersfield. In the early days, many of the major real estate transactions, the reorganization of the utilities, and the setting up of early commercial enterprises, were all handled in one form or another by this company. The boom years of 1905-13 have been extensively written up. One of the best sources for this period is the locally published *B.C. Magazine*. Post-World War II years, especially the important part played by John Laing & Son, come from information made available to the author at the Carlisle office of the firm and the Carlisle Public Library, which has copies of their house magazine. For early land transactions on Burrard Inlet, the Surveys and Land Records Branch of the Ministry of Lands, Parks and Housing in Victoria has many of the details. They have, it is thought, the only plan now in existence of the city of Liverpool.

In the realm of small towns, local histories are a valuable source. The smelter stories are taken from an article by the author in the *Hiballer Miner* magazine, spring 1971, entitled "Many Smelters

Built in B.C." Trade magazines and local newspapers are additional sources.

Material on early factories in B.C. is very limited. Details are mostly hidden in small news items in the local Victoria, New Westminster, and Vancouver newspapers. The growth of sawmills and newsprint plants is well told in *Timber* by G. W. Taylor. The introduction of machinery into mining can be traced in the annual reports of the B.C. Department of Mines.

Starting in the 1890's, trade magazines like the *B.C. Commercial Journal, B.C. Mining Record* and *Western Lumberman* cover their respective industries.

Much information for the middle period can be gleaned from such promotional books as Henry J. Boam's *British Columbia*.

CHAPTER 5

The second and third phases of the pulp mill explosion is recorded in the trade magazines like the *B.C. Lumberman* or the *Hiballer*. News items in the newspapers are also helpful. A chapter on the subject is contained in the book *Timber* by G. W. Taylor. The companies themselves are a fund of knowledge on their own mills and current developments in the industry. Company house magazines like *Crown Zellerbach News* or B.C. Forest Products *Timberline* are full of current happenings. Much information can be obtained from the annual reports of the companies.

Information on sawmilling is also included in the above-mentioned sources. An article on the Houston sawmilling venture appeared in the *Hiballer* magazine of March 1972 under the title of "A Tale of Three Companies." Details of the remodelled Rayonier's Silverton mill came from the company.

Information on the scope of manufacturing in B.C. and its many factories is obtained in many ways. Newspaper clippings, trade and house magazines, and the companies themselves are some of the best sources. Mention also should be made of the provincial Department of Economic Development, either in Victoria or Vancouver.

CHAPTER 6

Much of the material on hydroelectric development in the East Kootenays appears in the trade magazine *B.C. Mining Record*. The writeup on Sir Charles Ross is found in the September 1896 issue of that magazine; the power plant at Ashcroft is described in the July

1900 issue; the Manitou project is written up in the November 1896 edition. Figures on the reduction in cost in running the air compressors are quoted in the *B.C. Mining Record* of 1903, page 491. Profits accruing to West Kootenay Power come from their annual statements. A character appreciation of Lorne Campbell appears in *A History of Mining in B.C.* by G. W. Taylor.

Early power projects of the B.C. Electric Railway Co. (Goldstream, Lake Buntzen) are described in *Lighted Journey* by Cecil Maiden. A closer look is in letters written to J. Buntzen in the Norton papers in the office of Armitage & Norton, Huddersfield. A partial explanation of the big expenditures on Vancouver Island (Jordan River and the Saanich inter-urban) is found in the Norton papers in Huddersfield.

The troubled history of Stave Lake Power Co. is recorded in the business connections of the principals and letters between the head office in London and the Vancouver office of the B.C. Electric Railway Co. Further expansion of West Kootenay Power can be found in the Cominco magazine of March 1964, which features the story of that company. The book *Lighted Journey* and the annual reports of the company continue the story of the B.C. Electric Railway Co.

In post-World War II British Columbia, the power situation was always dominated by the potentials of the Columbia and Peace. There have been so many controversial news items, articles and reports published on the subject that it entails considerable effort to pick out the essentials. The annual reports of the B.C. Electric Railway Co. and its successor, B.C. Hydro and Power Authority, furnish a good background to what was actually built. Primary sources, the legislative acts like the Power Development Act of 1961 of B.C., and agreements signed by the federal government like the Columbia River Treaty, create the legal background of the projects. Technical details for construction and equipment can be found in the trade magazines. Some aspects of the political ramifications and the role of the British Columbia government is in Paddy Sherman's *W. A. C. Bennett*. Information on recent developments in the electrical generating field is obtainable from the head office of B.C. Hydro.

CHAPTER 7

The Esquimalt drydock was a matter of public discussion for over fifteen years. One primary source for its involvement in the Confederation negotiation is Dr. J. S. Helmcken's diary in the Provincial Archives, Victoria. For the next twelve years numerous mention of it can be found in the B.C. Sessional Papers. The naval base at Esquimalt is ably dealt with in F. V. Longstaff's book *Esquimalt*. Newspaper clippings on the 1922 drydock can be found in the Victoria Public Library. The accident to the *Empress of Canada* is mentioned in W. Kaye Lamb's "Empress Odyssey" in the *B.C. Historical Quarterly*, June 1948. Improvements to Victoria harbour, 1911 onward, is documented in the annual reports of the federal Minister of Public Works. Coal docking facilities at Nanaimo, Departure Bay, etc., come from R. T. Williams' *B.C. Directory* of 1882. Ladysmith's port facilities are described in *A History of Mining in B.C.* by G. W. Taylor. Recent developments at Nanaimo come from news items, Nanaimo Harbour Commission, and the Department of Economic Development, Victoria.

In the early days, the future of Vancouver as a port depended upon the trans-Pacific trade. This is well brought out in *The House of Dodwell*, a company history published in London, 1958. None of the standard works on the Canadian Pacific Railway (John Murray Gibbon or Harold A. Innes) does justice to the part played by George Dodwell in this regard. This is an invaluable source for this particular aspect and has been used by the author in preparation of this section.

The material for the story of the Vancouver Docks & Extension Co. is found in an article in the *Richmond Review* of January 22, 1964, entitled "A Fantastic Plan for Port Steveston." There was a special issue of the *Journal of Commerce* published in July 1927 for the construction and opening of Pier B-C.

The grain trade through Vancouver is documented in various publications. Dr. J. M. Lefevre's statement on the importance of looking into the matter appears in the *Vancouver News-Advertiser* of June 18, 1887. There is a short summary in a pamphlet written by Norman Hacking and published by the National Harbours Board entitled "History of the Port of Vancouver." E. Nichol's book *Vancouver*, published by Doubleday, 1978, mentions "Steven's Folly" and early grain shipments through Vancouver. Information on the new Pioneer Grain Terminal has been supplied by the company.

Several articles on shipping and the port of Vancouver have appeared in the *B.C. Magazine*, one of the most valuable being "Vancouver's Harbour and Shipping" by Ronald Kenvyn in the June 1911 issue.

Data on present facilities and trends in ocean transportation has come from the National Harbours Board, the companies concerned, or trade magazines such as an article on "The Transport Revolution" in the *Hiballer* magazine, December 1971.

The importance of Kitimat as a port and the coming of age of Prince Rupert are outlined in *The Story of the Port of Kitimat* by the B.C. Harbours Board, 1977, and, in the case of Prince Rupert, information was released by the provincial and federal governments.

INDEX

225

Vancouver   16, 20, 61, 65-69, 79,
    122, 124, 133-43, 155, 173,
    201-02, 204, 206-10, 213
  outstanding buildings   139-41
Vancouver City Foundry and Machine
    Works   135-36, 154-55
Vancouver Docks and Extension Co.
    205
Vancouver Engineering Works   155,
    163
Vancouver Harbour Commission
    204-05
Vancouver Improvement Co.   66,
    135-36, 138
Vancouver International Airport
    79-81, 83, 124-25
Vancouver Loan & Securities Corp.
    66-67, 138
Vancouver & Lulu Island Railway
    Co.   64, 69-70
Vancouver Post Office   122, 124
Vancouver Power Co.   178-79
Vancouver Wharves Ltd.   207
Vanterm Terminal   209
Van Horne, Sir William   17-18, 37,
    40-42, 121, 203
Vaughan, Walter   17
Vernon   63, 107, 146
Vernon & Nelson Telephone Co.
    107, 109-10
Victoria   16, 20-21, 62, 73, 103,
    120-21, 126-31, 152, 173, 180,
    196-98
  early luxury hotels   130
  outstanding buildings   126-27, 130
Victoria-Cape Beale Telegraph line
    103-04
Victoria & Esquimalt Telephone Co.
    105-07
Victoria Lumber & Manufacturing
    Co.   153, 162, 200

Victoria Machinery Depot   128
Victoria's Outer Wharves   197
Victoria Post Office   120-21
Victoria and Sidney Railway   122
Victoria Wharf & Warehouse Co.
    197

Walbran, Captain John T.   56
Warspite, H.M.S.   196
Webb, Dr. William Seward   18
Wenner-Gren, Axel   87, 187
Westcoast Transmission Co. Ltd.
    86-89
West Kootenay Light & Power Co.
    12, 16, 64, 174-77, 182-83, 191
Western Canada Power Co. (formerly
    Stave Lake Power Co.)   181
Western Development Co.   188
Western Union Telegraph Co.
    92-94, 100-02
Westminster & Vancouver Tramway
    Co.   63, 67-70, 132
Weyerhaeuser of Canada   144, 168
Whistler (skiing resort)   19
Whymper, Frederick   17
Williams Lake   150
Wright, Gustavus Blin   24, 27, 29, 51
Wulffsohn & Bewicke   63, 106-07
Wulffsohn, John   63, 106-07

Yale   23, 25, 38, 51, 143, 201
Yarrow, Sir Alfred   57-58, 196
Yorkshire Guarantee Securities Corp.
    66-68, 70, 74-75, 107-108, 128,
    136-38, 159
Yukon Airways & Exploration Co.
    78, 123

Zeppelin venture, Ashcroft-Prince
    George   76-77

231